Running Wild

Running Wild

JOHN ANNERINO

PHOTOGRAPHS BY CHRISTINE KEITH

THUNDER'S MOUTH PRESS
NEW YORK

Published by
Thunder's Mouth Press
632 Broadway, Seventh Floor
New York NY 10012

Library of Congress Cataloging-in-Publication Data
Annerino, John.
      Running wild /
John Annerino; photographs by Christine Keith; foreword by Charles
Bowden.
      p.   cm.
      Includes bibliographical references.
      ISBN 1-56025-175-1
      1. Running—Arizona—Grand Canyon.   2. Grand Canyon
(Ariz.)—Description and travel.   3. Indian trails—Arizona.
      I.Title.
GV1061.22.A6A56   1997
796.42'09791'32—dc20   92-25214

Manufactured in the United States of America

Book Design by Pauline Neuwirth, Neuwirth & Associates, Inc.

Among the Mountains, with these he ran.
In Flashes of Lightning, with these he ran.
In the Body of the Black wind, with these he ran.
In the midst of Thunders, with these he ran.
With the Sons of Long-life Happiness One, with these he ran.
With these he ran, with these he ran.
With these he ran, with these he ran . . .

The Coyote-Way
of the Navajo

CONTENTS

ACKNOWLEDGMENTS

I would like to thank support crew members Chris May, Dick Yetman, Ginny Taylor, Brian Gardner, Margie Erhart, and Bob Farrell; canyon climbers Dave Ganci and George Bain; boatman Wesley Smith; photo-journalist Chris Keith; author Charles Bowden, and map designer Michael Taylor; Mel Scott; Phoenix media people Bill Heywood, Ann Johnson, and John Schroeder; and Tony Ebarb, Dennis Casebier, Michael Thomas, Kimmy Johnson, Rich Nebeker, Jack Cartier, Gary Dysmala, Daniel O'Connor, Pauline Neuwirth and Ed Hedeman. I also would like to thank the Native Americans whose ancestral lands I crossed: the Pápago, Sand Pápago, Pima, Maricopa, Apache, Navajo, Hopi, Kaibab Paiute, Yavapai, Hualapai, Havasupai, Mojave, and Chemehuevi. I am indebted to Tony Mangine for his "Hail Mary" catch—and for first introducing me to long-distance running—and to Neil Ortenberg for reading the future in the past. Thank you!

Drawn by Michael Taylor

Foreword

OFF THE RIM AND INTO THE HEART OF STONE

HE IS RUNNING DOWN A TRAIL IN THE MOUNTAINS, AND THERE IS NO ONE THERE. He is running across a desert flat in the heat of midday, and there is no one there. Once it is the Sierra Estrellas, a hard-rock spine under burning desert sun near Phoenix. He leaps from rock to rock, the water is never enough, his body hurts, and still he runs on. Or it is the Grand Canyon, the Chiricahuas, the San Francisco Peaks, always running. A man of average stature, the smile flashing easily, the body trained to do what it is told, and inside his head ideas of adventures, adventures to be made by foot, a world that demands running.

John Annerino was raised in Phoenix and fled to Prescott to recover from this fact. I first met him when he began popping into the office where I worked for a small magazine, and he had these ideas about places he should run. He would cross the terrain, take photographs of what he saw, and then write a story. He talked with great animation of these plans, his voice rising and falling.

To certain lucky souls in the Southwest, the point of life is less to plot a career than to get into the country, to hustle and cajole the wherewithal for that next trek, probe, adventure. They will not leave the place; they refuse to advance up career ladders that threaten them with plush jobs in distant cities. Money cannot sway them. Instead, they plot elaborate scenarios that will enable them to remain here and do what they want to do. Which is always the same: go into the country, deeper and deeper. The late Edward Abbey was a model of this type, but they are everywhere, skulking about and wearing various disguises. In order to live this life, one must have soul and an absolute lust for this dry ground that others look at with fear and apprehension. I must be ruthless on this point because I am absolutely certain about this type—I have to look at one of the beasts every morning when I shave.

Once Annerino came into my office and discussed an ambitious adventure with me. He had a simple idea: he was going to run on trails across Arizona, south to north from Mexico to Utah. He wanted to see and photograph this wild ground the way the Indians and pioneers once saw it. I knew what he wanted, what we all want. What really glinted in his eyes was the idea of floating down trails day after day, crossing mountains, dropping in and out of canyons, eating up all the country alone. He did the run, and it all splashed across the page with words and pictures.

Like all such people in this part of the country, Annerino keeps returning to the Grand Canyon. If you wonder why, then you must never have been there. And if you have not been there, put down this book and go right now. No doubt you've read somewhere about how long it is and how deep it is and how old the rocks are. I am sure these are important matters. But what really counts is that the Canyon is a huge hole and when one goes into it, the world falls away. The ears start listening to the rocks, and thoughts flood out that before were not permitted. When this happens often enough, after years and years of dropping off the rim and going into the heart of stone, well, then the change begins to happen, one that no one is ever quite prepared for.

Running, running across the rock plateaus, the trail undulating, the body warmed up, the mind . . . well, the mind seems to be doing nothing but existing. The huge walls of the Canyon encircle; there is silence everywhere except for the pounding of the feet, but even this sound seems to vanish and the body glides as if by magic across the ground. Pain? It is always a possibility, but it seems hardly to matter. Destinations also fade away because the very goal of the run turns out to be this exact instant. At these moments the only time that exists is ticking on that watch on the wrist, and this time, though accurate, has ceased to tell one anything. Now the dead begin to appear, the Indians whose language no one knows, the Spaniards wearing those awkward leather vests, the early prospectors, the strange beasts that vanished ten thousand or twenty thousand years ago. Scientists tell us that such experiences occur because the mind under the stress of running is being bathed in a kind of natural morphine produced by the body. Could be, but who cares? No one who has had these experiences ever desires a tidy explanation any more than one craves a scientific dissection of the emotion we all call love.

This is a book about such experiences in such places. It is about going into the country the only way that seems to work—on foot. For us, it is a fantasy. Our legs are light, our feet are flying, and we glide, truly glide, over the roll of the land. The sun is up, the air is fresh, the stone is old, and we are free and at peace and the clocks have stopped because another kind of time has taken over, one where the dead can speak and nothing ever really dies. The Canyon, well, they tell us the Canyon is called Grand, but we have moved past such words. Our feet are taking us right into the stone.

CHARLES BOWDEN

For true friends,
my family's love,
and Tim and Craig.
Without them, this odyssey
would not have been possible.

Natural Selection has designed us . . .
for a career of seasonal journeys
on foot through a blistering land
of Thornscrub . . . desert.

Bruce Chatwin, *The Songlines*

1

"You'll Never Run Again"

The closer you get to death,

The clearer the image of life.

Roger Marshall,
Himalayan climber

I AM FALLING UNCONTROLLABLY. I'M NOT SURE HOW FAR, BUT WHEN I HIT I KNOW I'm going to die. At any moment I'll bounce on the end of my rope, the fragile anchors will rip out of the rotten crack, and I'll slam brutally against the jagged rocks below—my helmet crushed, my back broken, my lungs punctured with splintered bones and gorged with blood. It'd happened to better climbers than myself, and now it was happening to me. And there is nothing I can do about it except scream as I plunge backward, still clutching the broken handhold in my left hand.

"*Aagggghhhhhhhh!!!*"

The day hadn't started out that way. It was a spring-warm winter morning in the Valley of the Sun when Tony Mangine and I decided to postpone a long-awaited climbing trip to Granite Mountain a hundred miles north. Camelback Mountain was only minutes away in the heart of metropolitan Phoenix, and we hoped it would offer us a challenging new climbing route as well as a much needed break from teaching and traveling. As an outdoor instructor at a local community college, I'd been in the boonies virtually every weekend for the previous seven months teaching climbing and wilderness survival, and I was starting to burn out. So I looked forward to a day alone, climbing with a friend.

It was a leisurely Saturday morning. The balmy Sonoran Desert air was still heavy with the musty scent of orange blossoms, and coveys of Gambel quail ran back and forth across the trail in front of us as Tony and I trudged up the steep climbers' route through Echo Canyon. We had made this same jaunt many times before, leading students up a spectacular finger of rock called the Monk. But today we'd eyed a stiff crack climb ominously called Suicide Direct. We'd heard it wasn't a particularly difficult route overall, but the crux move out of a small overhang was committing and needed to be protected by placing "bombproof anchors" just below the crux.

I felt confident as we roped up and didn't pay much attention to three members of a local rescue team practicing rope maneuvers on another route nearby.

"On belay?" I asked Tony, as I buckled on my helmet.

"On belay," he said, carefully holding the nylon rope tied to me.

"Climb," I said, double-checking his belay.

"Climb!" he said.

I scrambled up a short apron of dark conglomerate rock that ended atop an awkward ledge at the base of the small alcove or overhang. I put in a nut, clipped a carabiner to it, and fed the rope through it. "I'm in," I yelled down to Tony. In the parlance of rock climbers, this is a way to let your belayer know that you have your first anchor in, so that if you fall he'll be able to catch you before you take a "grounder," or hit the ground.

Doing a difficult move on glacier-polished Yosemite granite was one thing, but doing a hard move on grungy desert rock was more uncertain.

I looked up. The dark crack arched out of the overhang to the crux move thirty feet above me. Before continuing, I needed a solid place to put my next anchor in, somewhere between the crux and the prow of rock I was standing on.

"Watch me, Tone," I yelled down. "I want to get some good protection in before doing it."

"I gotcha."

I climbed up a few feet and slotted a small nut alongside a chockstone wedged into a V-shaped crack. Tenuously perched, I tugged at the aluminum nut to see whether it was secure; from the shallow crack it was wedged in, I realized that if I fell off the crux the force of the fall could pull it out—and I'd take a grounder. So I quickly slotted in another nut on the opposite side of the chockstone to counterbalance the first one. I tugged at it to set it in place. Once I did, I was confident the two nuts would hold a short fall—if the chockstone itself didn't pull out. I carefully down-climbed back to the alcove and then rehearsed in my mind the sequence of moves I'd need to make in order to reach the safety of the anchor bolt just above the crux.

"Ready, Tone?" I yelled. I took a deep breath.

"I gotcha."

I started up again, promising myself not to go for the crux above my anchors unless I could safely reverse the moves if I didn't make it on the first try. A few quick moves brought me back to my high point, and I realized my palms were sweaty. I continued up, my feet jammed in the crack below, my left arm stretched out as far as I could reach, my right hand groping for another hold. Just inch up a little more, I goaded myself. But suddenly I was struck by how rotten the rock felt as it crumbled beneath my feet; a small cascade of pebbles rained down on Tony. Doing a difficult move on glacier-polished Yosemite granite was one thing, but doing a hard move on grungy desert rock was more uncertain. You couldn't blindly trust that a hand- or foothold wouldn't break off mid-move.

A sickening feeling came over me when I realized just how exposed I'd be if I continued the last few feet to the crux. I'd nervously climbed too high too quickly to safely reverse my moves, and I no longer trusted my life to the two shaky anchors below. My only hope was to gracefully negotiate the crux and clip into the eye of the bolt hanger dangling above me. If the rest of the climb looked this rotten, I'd rappel off, call it a day, and head for Granite Mountain and some real rock.

As I stretched for the crux, my right leg started trembling; rock climbers call it "sewing machine leg." I was gripped with fear, and I couldn't stop my leg from shaking. I was about to peel off when I made a desperate reach for the hold with my left hand. I fingered it and felt the coarse grains of sand behind it. I had it, and I breathed a sigh of relief as I pulled down with all my strength in order to mantle on top of it. As I did, it broke off.

And suddenly I am falling backward, still clutching the rotten hold in my left hand. I am going to die, and I scream with terror, hoping to warn Tony to brace himself for the tremendous impact of the fall: "Aagggghhhhhhhh!!!"

The grisly details of how I'm going to die, not the image of family and friends, flash before me as I hit a small protrusion of rock with the force of a body being thrown off the roof of a three-story building. I scream again when I hit, long mournful wails, then spin around, hanging in midair at the end of my rope. One nut slides down the rope and smacks me in the face; it has ripped out. So I know the other nut will pull out at any moment, and I'll plummet the rest of the way to the ground.

Swinging back and forth at the end of my rope, I look down to see how much farther I have to fall before I die. But I'm more horrified to see the grotesque shape of my left ankle. The sole of my black climbing boot is facing me; worse, the tibia is about to tear through the wafer-white skin. I start whimpering, waiting for the life-saving nut to rip—and to end the excruciating pain. Instead, I keep swaying at the end of the rope, overcome with nausea and pain.

"John! Are you all right?" Tony knows I'm not; even from his stance I know he can see my mangled left foot.

"Tone! You got me?" I shriek. My breathing is shallow and frantic.

"I got you! What do you want me to do?"

Tony is holding all my weight with his bare hands, and I know he won't drop me if he can help it. But I'm terrified that, if the tiny metal nut miraculously holds my weight while he lowers me, the slightest jarring will cause my ankle bone to puncture my leg like a stone knife from the inside out and I'll bleed to death before I reach the ground.

"Tone! You've got to lower me! . . . carefully! . . . or the nut will rip!"

"Tell me when you're ready!"

"Okay, easy!" On the verge of panic, whimpering from pain, I tuck my left leg behind me in hopes of protecting it during the descent. I spread my two hands above me and my right hip against the wall; by using the friction of my body against the coarse rock surface, I hope to relieve some of the tension on the nut.

"Easy, Tone! I don't think I'm going to make it."

"You'll make it!"

Tears are running down my cheeks and snot is dribbling out of my nose, as my friend begins slowly lowering me toward safety. I know my weight on the rope is oppressive for Tony to hold, but if anybody can lower me through the overhang without dropping me like a stone it's Tony.

The abrasive rock tears the palms of my hands and scrapes viciously at my bruised right hip, but the ground slowly, painfully gets closer and closer until Tony sets me down as though he's lowering me on eggshells.

Still sniveling and moaning from the pain, I look up at my bearded friend and at the rescue team now gathered around me. I can tell by their worried expressions I'm in dire straits; it looks like a horn of bone will poke through the taut film of skin and a deadly geyser of blood will come spurting out. Without thinking about it, I roll over on my back and start telling people what to do. If I'm going to die, it's not going to be without a fight.

"You," I point to one young climber, "call an ambulance. Tell them we need a litter and men to carry it." I collapse in agony, crying as I bite down on a piece of nylon sling to alleviate the pain. "Tone, make sure someone calls my mom and Anna."

The wait is interminable. The pain is greater than anything I'd ever experienced before, a torturous throbbing as though my ankle were being beaten by a rubber mallet. Tony stands by my side, reassuring me over and over: "You're going to make it, John. Hold on. You're going to make it."

I want to believe him. Tony never lies.

II.

THE CRUNCH OF FOOTSTEPS AND THE MUFFLED CLANG OF CLIMBING GEAR PRECEDE the men who struggle through the underbrush to reach me. "He's over here," someone yells, and soon the men huddle around me, snorting like horses from the steep climb. I knew that although my leg bone hadn't ruptured the delicate membrane of skin while Tony lowered me it could never endure the rugged carry down to the ambulance, which now seemed so impossibly far away.

I drift in and out of consciousness from the throbbing pain but rear up and watch in terror as the EMT cuts into my boot. I don't want to scream in front of these strangers, so I bite down on the nylon sling until it feels like my teeth are going to crack. But as soon as the medic tries to slide the black boot off my mangled left foot, I wail. When he touches my foot, I take the fall all over again, screaming as I hurl backward through space. But when he wraps the plastic air splint around my leg and inflates it like a blood pressure cuff, it feels like my foot is going to explode. I howl with pain and black out.

When I come to, I hear a voice overhead quietly repeating, "You've got to breathe evenly, or you'll go into shock . . . you've got to breathe evenly, or you'll go into shock . . . you've got to breathe evenly, or you'll go into shock . . . " Obediently, I try to take deep, even breaths, but when I realize I'm being carried down off this ancient desert landmark, man-handled over boulders, barrel cactus, and brush, I claw at the metal railings in terror that someone will slip, I'll be dropped, and a horn of bloody bone will gnash through my splinted leg.

I black out again and come to when I hear the ear-piercing scream of the siren as the ambulance careens through traffic. The medic keeps asking me the same monotonous question until it finally registers, "What hospital do you want to go to? What hospital do you want to go to? What hospital do you want to go to?"

"County . . . I don't have insurance."

I try to make peace with the throbbing pain by closing my eyes, but as soon as I do I fall backward through black space into the nightmare of my first emergency room visit. Years earlier, I accidently butted heads with another kid playing freeze tag on our grade school's asphalt playground. Fortunately, school was already dismissed for the day, so my mother was there to peel me off the pavement. She then ran into the middle of a Chicago intersection and held up rush-hour traffic until a truck driver saw the blood streaming down my face and white shirt. "Get in, lady," he said, swinging open the door. My mom pushed me over her head, and the truck driver dragged us both into the cab before thundering to Cooke County Hospital in an eighteen-wheel tractor-trailer rig, just like the one my dad drove.

A ritual often repeated throughout my teens, that was my first trip through the revolving doors of ERs spread across the country: the Christmas in Kentucky when my knife-wielding cousin—and childhood nemesis—Johnny mistook my hand for a ham hock; the back flip off the diving board gone awry; the Friday night cruisers beating me with wrenches. . . . Each time I'd bled like a pig, but each time I was pronounced fit enough to wait the two to three hours it took the intern or trauma specialist to triage me before stitching me up.

But when I'm rolled through the swinging metal doors of Maricopa County Hospital's emergency room, I know this time is far more serious. The attending physician takes one look at my foot flopped out at the end of the air splint and says, "We've got to reduce this—now."

I'm rushed into an adjoining room, where the doctor, an orthopedic specialist, begins poking my foot with an index finger that feels like a blunt metal spear.

"Does this hurt?" he says, jabbing me.

"*Agghhhh!*"

"How about this?" he says, jabbing me again.

"*Agghhhh!*"

"And this?" he says, jabbing me yet again.

"*Agghhhh!*"

He leaves the room and returns with two assistants; I have no idea why they are needed until he instructs them to hold me down. They each grab one of my arms. Then I look up at the doctor; he is the size of an NFL full-back, and he is about to do the unimaginable. He grabs my foot in his vicelike hands and pulls back on it.

"*Aagggghhhhhhhh!!!*"

He tries again, this time leaning all the way back on his three-hundred-pound frame. But his assistants are no match for this brutal round of tug-of-war, and I slide halfway across the table screaming.

"*Aagggghhhhhhhh!!!*"

"It's not going back in," the doctor says, without giving me a second look. I lay there crying and groaning.

"Please," I beg him, "please give me something for the pain." But the doctor and his assistants leave the room without saying a word.

I lie there alone, moaning, "Oh, God, help me! Please!" A sterile dome of light beams down on me, and I wonder how much longer the pain will continue. But I have no idea this nightmare is only beginning. Minutes later, four people file into the room ahead of the doctor. The first two are dressed in green scrubs, but when I notice the other two men are wearing brown khakis, I realize the doctor has enlisted the help of the maintenance department. The janitors grip my arms, a third assistant pins my shoulders down, and the fourth holds my left leg at the hip.

"Please," I beg him again, looking for an inkling of mercy. "Please give me something for the pain. Please!"

"Just relax," he says, before he and his tag team commence another round of tug-of-war.

"*Aagghhhh!!!*"

"I can't believe it's not going back in," he says, shaking his head. "Prep him for surgery."

I had no idea at the time, but the orthopod headed back into the waiting room to get permission from my mother to cut off my foot.

Writhing in pain and drenched in a nervous, foul-smelling sweat, I'm wheeled into an elevator and rushed upstairs to another room, where two nurses begin cutting off my pants. I plead with them, "Please give me something for the pain. Please."

"Soon," one of the nurses assures me; her soft, gentle black hand brushes the matted hair off my damp forehead. "Soon."

I'm relieved when it happens so quickly. The anesthesiologist gives me an injection, a plastic mask is cupped over my nose and mouth, and I'm told to count backward.

"Ten, nine, eigh . . . "

When I come to, I'm groggy. The thobbing pain has not diminished, and my left leg is encased in heavy, white plaster from hip to toe. My mother is at my side, whispering, "I wouldn't let them take it off, son." My mother, thank God! She'd nursed her diabetic mother's gangrenous right foot and watched in horror as doctors amputated first the foot, then the rest of the leg, bit by suppurating bit, all the way to her hip; and when gangrene set in in the other foot, their stainless steel saws took away Grandma's life piece by piece. "Sonny-la," Grandma used to call to me in her thick German accent, "you go hunting with Grandpa and the men today."

> The doctor . . . the size of an NFL fullback . . . grabs my foot in his vice-like hands and pulls back on it.

I look at my mother, and I can plainly see she is reliving the horror of her mother's torturous amputations; she'd never left her side. I try to thank my mom, but my tongue is too thick from the morphine, and I pass out in spite of the throbbing pain.

When I come to again, my mother has disappeared, and I watch the big hand on the wall clock slowly spin around, chasing the small hand past 10, 11, 12, 1. I am drifting in and out, but my ankle still feels like it's being beaten with a mallet. At first I see the shadow of a man lifting a sledge over his head then beating my ankle as though he were spiking a railroad tie: *KA-WHAM! KA-WHAM! KA-WHAM!* But the beating is suddenly interrupted when a dark, masked man opens the door and stalks dreamlike across the room to the bed next to me. Dressed in black, he raises a knife over his head and is about to plunge it into a cloud of white sheets when a nurse the size of a small black bear comes out of nowhere, wrestles away the knife, and throws the man to the floor. I remember hearing the double concussion of her fist hitting his face and his head slamming against the cold tile floor before she yelled for help. "Security!" Two armed rent-a-cops storm into the room, handcuff the masked man, and drag him into the hallway.

"It'd be better if we amputated it," he says, holding an X ray overhead. "With an injury like this, the pain will be unbearable. You'll never run or climb on that ankle again."

"I told you he was going to come back and off me!" I hear someone scream. For the first time, I realize there is someone else in the bed next to me. The nurse turns on the fluorescent lights. A young black man is lying in the bed, with tubes dangling from his nose and arm. But that's all that registers before my heavy eyelids droop closed and I see the shadow of what appears to be the Arm and Hammer man beating my ankle: *KA-WHAM! KA-WHAM! KA-WHAM!*

The next morning I practically jump out of bed when I feel somebody roll me over and rub my ass with a cold swab of alcohol. I look up and see that I'm about to be stabbed with a knife; but when I blink my eyes and focus, I see the glimmer of a thick stainless steel needle. "No, no more!" I yell, rolling back over to cover my ass. "It doesn't help."

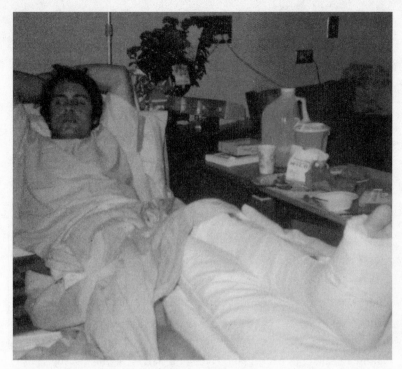

Annerino in the hospital after the climbing accident. He just received the prognosis: "You'll never run or climb on that ankle again." *Annerino collection*

"Are you sure, honey?"

"Just aspirin. Please. That's all I want."

The morphine, or Demerol—whatever they've given me—has done little to alleviate the throbbing pain; worse, it's given me terrible nightmares about masked men with knives and sledges. Somewhere on the periphery of those bad dreams, there was also the chilling vision of what would happen to me once I got out of the County: if I needed hard drugs to endure the pain of lying in a hospital bed, what kind of daily fix would I need once I tried walking again?

But I needn't have worried about that. Later that same morning, the orthopod tells me I'll never use my ankle again.

"It'd be better if we amputated it," he says, holding an X ray overhead. "With an injury like this, the pain will be unbearable. You'll never run or climb on that ankle again."

The throbbing pain has not diminished; he knows it. And he's obviously ready to wheel me back into surgery and fire up his bone saw. But the finality of an amputation is too depressing for me to consider, and I'm not about to let anyone cut off my left foot without seeing for myself just how bad it really is.

"I'll see what I can do with it," I tell him, trying to hold back the tears as he plods out of the room with his clipboard and X ray.

The prognosis devastates me, but the day goes from bad to worse when I realize the young man next to me is a gunshot victim. A dark red hole in his left thigh oozes yellow pus, and he assures me I wasn't having a nightmare about a masked man trying to murder him in his sleep. . . . But before he can finish telling me the details of a nickel drug deal gone sour, my fiancée, Anna, strides into the room pushing an empty wheelchair. Saying little more than hello, she wheels me down the hallway into an empty waiting room, where we can have some privacy. But just when I expect her to maul me with love and tell me there's a rainbow at the end of this nightmare, she does a Jekyll and Hyde and starts screaming at me.

"Look what you've done to us! How are you going to make a living now? You're in the county hospital, and you can't even pay the bill! How are you going to take care of us? What am I going to tell my parents about the wedding? Huh?!"

When Anna wheels me back to my room, I feel like a broken man being sealed in a tomb. She storms out, her voluptuous Italian breasts bouncing to her schizoid march. I lie there crying and try to take my mind off the throbbing pain, and the sorrow in my heart, by talking to the guy next to me. But all he wants from me now, thank you very much, are the pain pills the nurses have been trying to force-feed me. Life, as I've known it for the last three and a half years, has ended. I didn't plan it that way, and I have no idea how I'm going to crawl out of the black hole I've fallen into.

III.

WHEN MY MOTHER WHEELS ME OUT OF THE HOSPITAL A WEEK LATER, I FEEL LIKE someone has slid open the lid on my crypt. I squint my eyes, then blink nervously, trying to adjust to the glaring Arizona sunshine again. But the sun is too bright, so I shade my eyes with one hand as she rolls me toward the car. I take a deep breath; the faint whiff of orange blossoms is still in the air, and a chorus of sparrows and mourning doves is heralding the arrival of spring. I am alive again—wobbly, but alive. And I have only one thing on my mind: to climb Squaw Peak.* It was the sole vision that kept me from plunging into the depths of despair the long hours of torment I lay trapped in the county hospital.

But Anna wants nothing to do with my climbing Squaw Peak. "Not with your leg still in a cast," she tells me later that day. "You're only going to hurt yourself worse!" she says. She slams the door to my apartment and barrels down the driveway in her red convertible, kicking up a rooster tail of dirt and gravel.

I lie there alone on the sofa wondering why I'd confided my deepest fears in her, my fear of being forced to relinquish the one thing I loved most—the wilderness. If I can't use my foot, I wondered, how am I going

---

* The 2,608-foot summit of the Phoenix Mountains has been called Squaw Peak since Dr. O.A. Turney named it in 1910. Native American activists are making a justifiable effort to change the derogatory name, which was first anglicized by English colonists from words used by many different Northeastern indigenous groups. In Plains Cree, for example, *iskwe 'wiwin* translates to "vagina"; in Powhatan *usqwausum* translates to "bitch." In Arizona alone, this insensitive term appears on twenty-four other landmarks.

to climb mountains? How am I going to explore canyons? How am I going to cross deserts?

Maybe the doctor was right. The throbbing pain has been my curse since the fall. It's with me under the sheets when I try to sleep; it's with me when I crawl to the bathroom in the middle of the night; it's with me when I try losing myself with long hours of reading. But no matter what I do, I can't shake it without using painkillers—and those I've vowed *not* to take. Most of the time, it's a throbbing pain; at other times, it feels as though the teeth of a pit bull are buried in my ankle, and I'm forced to drag it around my small apartment as I lurch from couch to bed, to bathroom, to cupboard, to stove, and back again. So how much more painful could climbing Squaw Peak be, I wonder? At least I'd be outside, in the sunshine, trying to do something about my predicament. And what was there to hurt anyway? They already want to amputate my foot.

I have only one thing on my mind: to climb Squaw Peak.

Still racked by interminable pain weeks later, I realized my entire life hinged on climbing the mountain, because the future never looked bleaker: I was broke. I was about to be evicted from my apartment. And I had no way to earn a living unless I could somehow teach the backpacking and wilderness survival course that had been postponed while I was in the hospital. But if I could somehow climb the mountain, I knew in my heart I'd be able to teach again. Without my foot, I couldn't teach. And without teaching, I'd have to take handouts, but pride and Sicilian blood ran too deep for me to accept that as an option. As the walls of my apartment slowly closed in on me and as the pain continued to chew away at my emotional resolve, I realized teaching had become my life and livelihood.

What had started out as a modest proposal—that a local community college offer a few outdoor courses—had, without my planning it, caught the crest of the backpacking wave. And after one marginally successful test course, and a flurry of press releases, I found that I had unknowingly stumbled into a full-time profession. At the time, however, I was already a full-time drama student at the college, living hand to mouth, taking any low-end job that offered an evening meal and a weekly paycheck. So the opportunity to earn enough money as a teacher to move my sleeping bag out of a photographer friend's claustrophobic, dektol-drenched darkroom was too good to pass up.

But I quickly learned I had taken on more than I could handle by myself. To my surprise, more people stood in line to take the courses I was offering than to see the plays I acted in. So I was faced with the dilemma of squeezing more and more students into each course or offering another course the following month to accommodate the overflow, until the whole thing snowballed.

That's when Tony Mangine and Gary Drysmala entered my life. Like me, they were drama and art majors, and they both had a passion for the wilderness. They'd also proved themselves two of my best students and field assistants during the first courses I taught, and I came to trust and rely on them. The core backpacking and wilderness survival course I was offering wasn't exactly a walk in the park; as modest as my paychecks were, I didn't feel anybody needed to pay me good money to show them how to feed the ducks at the local pond. Spun out over four consecutive weekends, interspersed with exhausting midweek

> I realized my entire life hinged on climbing the mountain, because the future never looked bleaker: I was broke. I was about to be evicted from my apartment. And I had no way to earn a living unless . . .

lectures shoehorned between play rehearsals, each course was designed to build confidence in my students so that by the time they finished they'd have a solid background in wilderness travel and survival. The best way to do that, I discovered, was to let Arizona's magnificent terrain and wild ground impart its own indelible lessons: first by leading them on trekking and survival expeditions into rugged and remote desert ranges like the Eagletail Mountains; then by scaling Arizona's highest mountains, the 12,633-foot San Francisco Mountains; and finally by descending into the depths of the Grand Canyon along one of its historic, seldom-used miner trails. Together Tony and Gary provided the safety net for my students to explore some of the most challenging and awe-inspiring country in the Southwest.

But even with soul mates like them to rely on, the strain of constantly making sure a student never got injured was taking its toll on me—especially with the winter mountaineering and rock climbing courses. The more I taught, the less I climbed for myself. After a successful three-and-a-half-year run of back-to-back courses, I became increasingly aware that, if I were ever to fulfill my burning ambition to climb eight-thousand-meter peaks in the Himalayas and the Karakorum, I would have to test myself outside the arena of a climbing instructor who'd long since memorized every move on every rock climb he'd ever led a student up. That, then, is what led to my fall.

Held hostage by pain in my apartment, there was little to distract me from my plight other than analyzing the events leading up to my fall. It wasn't the difficulty of the route; on Granite Mountain the same move would have been protected, and the same handhold would have held the weight of a pickup truck. It was simply fatigue and rotten rock. Stretched out on the sofa, tossing and turning from pain, I knew I couldn't change the past. But somehow I had to come to grips with the present and how I was going to survive the future. I was convinced I had to climb the mountain to see whether the journey itself would provide any solutions.

Fortunately, Tony understood, and when I was ready to punch holes in the walls of my apartment, he gave me a ride to Squaw Peak.

"When do you want me to come back and get you?" he asked.

"Late this afternoon," I said.

"Sure you don't want me to go with?"

"This is something I've got to do alone, Tone."

"I know."

Squaw Peak stands as the bold, pyramidal high point of the Phoenix Mountains. At one time, it was roamed by members of the ancient Hohokam culture, and they undoubtedly first climbed the 2,608-foot peak to harvest saguaro fruit, hunt desert bighorn sheep, and make sacred offerings. From circa A.D. 700 to 1450, the Salt River Valley surrounding Squaw Peak was the hub of this great desert civilization that may have numbered a hundred thousand people. That's because the Hohokam irrigated the Sonoran Desert on a scale unparalleled in this hemisphere. Using stone hoes and crude wooden digging sticks, they etched three hundred miles of canals in the burning, snake-infested black *malpais,* "badlands," and stone-hard caliche. As a result, silver rivulets of cool water ran where no water had run before— under the flaming yellow sun. Pioneer Phoenician O. A. Turney wrote that the Hohokam had "450,000 acres under ancient cultivation . . . while up on the mountains [including Camelback] are found sacrificial caves and pueblos of stone." But after seven centuries, the Hohokam disappeared, and the Salt River Valley once again became the desert it always threatened to be.

> As I crutch up the first switchback, I gasp for breath and realize the craggy summit of this ancient Hohokam refuge is far beyond my feeble reach. . .

Some historians speculate the Hohokam fled to the high ground, where visions of fertility could be realized closer to the sources of the life-giving Salt and Gila Rivers. Others said they'd gone south, as they had been doing for centuries on ritual quests to the Gulf of California for shells, a blistering two-hundred mile desert journey few could survive today. Yet others said they perished from the "Aztec Plague," epidemic diseases carried north from Mesoamerica by ancient traders.

Whatever happened to the *Hohokam*, "those who have gone," they left behind clan castles, sun temples, and ball courts. "When they forsook their last cities," wrote Turney, "all remained untouched; ollas and axes, bracelets and beads, votive and funerary offerings . . . dedications to the ruling forces of nature. All suffered and all became fugitives alike; the barren mountains and drought-stricken valley again became a long silent wilderness."

One barren mountain that reared up out of this silent wilderness was Squaw Peak, and the indefatigable Spanish missionary, explorer, and cartographer Padre Eusebio Francisco Kino may have been the first non-Indian to see it when he viewed the Salt and Verde Rivers from the south on March 2, 1699. Several centuries later, a rough miner's trail was chiseled into the side of the mountain to reach a "glory hole" dynamited into a small notch below the summit. But long after those slim pickin's went bust, valley residents began making daily pilgrimages up the mountain, both for their health and as a way of fleeing the stranglehold of development that gnaws at the flanks of this jagged desert peak.

For my students, Squaw Peak was both a testing place and a training ground en route to more sublime and rugged adventures like the Grand Canyon. Yet, for many, including the thousand Phoenicians who climb their black pyramid of rock and rubble each day, it remained an enthralling destination in itself. Seen from the distance, Squaw Peak could be mistaken for a mountain of daunting proportions. It is dark, angular, and brooding, yet it is always captivating, beckoning most who approach it.

As I crutch up the first switchback, I gasp for breath and realize the craggy summit of this ancient Hohokam refuge is far beyond my feeble reach, so I resign myself to seeing how far I can get before turning back. I plant both crutches on the rocky trail in front of me, swing my right leg out front, and plant it squarely on the ground like the third leg of a tripod; then, I swing my heavy plaster cast beside my right leg and hold it in midair as I swing my crutches out front again. I plant my right foot again and swing my heavy cast. Each time I do, blood rushes to the bottom of my left foot and my ankle throbs with pain. But the pain is tolerable, as long as I don't put any weight on the foot. And as long as the trail remains smooth and flat, it's like crutching up a sidewalk.

Gouged into the steep, rugged flanks of this desert peak, the trail climbs twelve hundred vertical feet through sparse stands of towering saguaro, barrel cactus, and paloverde trees in a little over a mile; to ascend that abruptly, the trail angles steeply, frequently zigzagging back and forth on itself. As soon as I hit the first steep switchbacks, my rhythmic crutching ends and my progress slows to a crawl. I stop, hold my crutches to one side, ease into a sitting position, and stick my left leg out in front of me across the trail. I lean back against the warm black rock and try to catch my breath as people walk around me. Recovered, I get up and

For the first time since starting this desperate climb I can actually see the summit. And the thought of somehow reaching it, after weeks of languishing in an emotional abyss, makes my heart soar.

tackle the next series of switchbacks with as much momentum as I can muster, until fatigue, throbbing pain, and shortness of breath force me to sit down and rest again. Fearing someone will trip over my cast or step on my foot, I get up when the trail is clear of hikers and resume my struggle.

I am sweating profusely, just as I had the last time I climbed out of the Grand Canyon. But unlike the elation of that moment, I become more weary and irritable the higher I crutch up the mountain. The cast is chafing the inside of my right leg, and my left thigh is on fire from carrying the heavy cast. But I crutch on, one agonizing switchback at a time, locked into my own miserable little struggle. A broken shell of the healthy young man who ran up and down this same trail only weeks earlier, I decide I can't go any farther; I sit down to catch my breath before heading back down the mountain to lick my wounds and tend to my bruised ego. Maybe that sonuvabitchin' doctor was right, I mumble to myself. But before I can get lost in self-pity, a sweet voice calls out, "Are you all right? Can I help?"

"I'm fine. Thanks," I say gruffly, without making eye contact.

"Are you sure?" she asks.

"I said *no!*"

The young woman bounds past, and suddenly the warmth and kindness of her words sink in, and they encourage me on. I get up again and crutch up the next couple of switchbacks, chastising myself for being so rude to a stranger who was kind enough to try to help a gimp like me. "What a jerk," I tell myself.

The last switchback tops out on a small vista, and I use it as an excuse to sit down and rest. A Redtail hawk soars on a spring thermal, and a warm breeze fans my sweat-soaked T-shirt. To the north, I can see the trail snaking its way along a serrated ridgeline. I can rest on that stretch, I muse, before it climbs again, wrestle the next set of switchbacks, catch my breath again, then crawl the last quarter mile if I have to. I ache all over from weeks of inactivity, and my foot feels like it's going to explode from the blood pressure, but for the first time since starting this desperate climb I can actually see the summit. And the thought of somehow reaching it, after weeks of languishing in an emotional abyss, makes my heart soar.

Staring at the hard ground I've yet to cross, my thoughts drift back to Slavomir Rawicz's *The Long Walk*. The extraordinary tale of survival was required reading for all my students, and after my fall I sought inspiration from the book throughout my couch-bound internment. In 1941, seven political prisoners escaped from a grim Siberian slave camp near the Artic Circle. In an adventure of epic proportions, the group fled south on foot across Mongolia, traversed the Gobi Desert, and crossed the Himalayas before reaching India and freedom, nine months and more than four thousand miles later. The trail ahead of me was nothing compared to their incredible saga. And my own suffering, as painful and as emotionally debilitating as it had been for me, was nothing compared to what that heroic band of men and one woman endured for months on end in their quest for freedom. Yes, I knew about wilderness travel and survival, but I knew nothing about suffering or endurance on their scale. If I ever wanted to use my foot again, if I ever wanted to explore the frontiers of my own world, I would have to learn the art of suffering and endurance as they had. I would have to crawl before I walked again, and when I stumbled I would have to crawl again; and I'd certainly have to walk before I could ever run again. I had to start somewhere, and at that moment, reaching the summit was my shining path.

I struggle to my feet and start crutching my way up the mountain again. The pain is still there; it hasn't diminished for a moment since the fall, and I don't know if it ever will. I try to detach myself from it, I try to embrace it, I curse it venomously, but it never relents; it dogs me every step of the way as I continue crutching toward the summit. If I am going to cross the threshold back to who I thought I was before the fall, pain, I now realize, will be the price of admission.

I crutch on throughout the afternoon, slowly, methodically, one switchback at a time, until I reach the summit cap. A short scramble from the end of the trail up a chimneylike gully will put you, if you're whole, on top of the mountain. For me, it is the most dreadful stretch of rock I would climb—one slip, and I'd be back in the county hospital. My right leg has been chafed raw by the cast. My left leg feels as though someone has doused it with gasoline and set it on fire. My ankle is hexed with demonic pain. My armpits feel like they've been sandpapered then washed with salt water. And my hands are numb from being locked clawlike around the wooden handles of my crutches. I put both crutches in front of me, hop up, and clutch the black rock with one hand. I push the crutches up the rock overhead and, reluctantly, let go of them. I grab the rock with both hands, stand squarely on the toes of my right foot, and hold my left leg out in the air. I hop up to the next little foothold. I push the crutches up again, caress the next hold one hand at a time, and hop up again. I repeat this painful, awkward process until I can't go any higher. Suddenly, I can see over the other side. I am on the summit.

I stand up with my crutches and sway in the desert wind with joy and exhaustion. Tears are streaming down my swollen cheeks, and salt stings my eyes and sunburned lips, but I'm on top of the world. The valley is spread out far below. The red pyramid of Camelback Mountain floats in the distance. And golden peaks and ridges I've climbed with my students can be seen shimmering on the horizon. I've made it!

2

RUNNING WILD

From the Superstition mountain rose the Eagle;

From the sluggish-moving Gila rose the Hawk . . .

There I am running, there I am running.

The Shadow of Crooked Mountain.

Hawk Flying, 1904
Pima Indian festal song

FOR MONTHS, THE WORDS ECHOED THROUGH MY MIND AS I RAN ALONE THROUGH the desert night; they were simple words, ugly and final: "I fucked Ronnie. I want a divorce." They'd haunted me with grief and anguish; they represented dreadful spirits from a world I longed to flee. But tonight, still running alone in the stellar light of the dark heavens, they finally mean nothing. I let them go, and they float away as empty and meaningless as the lifelong promise Anna made to me when she said, "I do." When the County doctor said, "You'll never run again."

Stars flicker brilliantly as I run deeper into the dark night. I swing my arms in rhythmic unison to my breathing and periodically adjust my footsteps to the dirt surface of the pathway underfoot. Somewhere high above, a great horned owl hoots at my approach, but I can see nothing except the faint stark outlines of cottonwood trees as I stride past. They are enormous, cauliflower-shaped black shadows backlit against the dark horizon by distant, flickering lights of earthen dwellings still inhabited by Native Americans. For centuries, the peaceful Pima and Maricopa inhabited a vast ancestral land, which, in 1700, still comprised much of the central Arizona desert bordering the Salt and Gila Rivers. About that time, the fleet-footed Maricopa used paths along the Gila River to travel southwest far beyond their own territory during weeklong, 250-mile journey-runs to the Colorado River delta; there, they traded for many items with the Cocopa, including glycymeris shells the Cocopa collected from the Gulf of California and ʔuˑv ṣax, "rotten tobbaco," which the Cocopa brought from the Pai Pais living in the sierras of Baja to the west. But that was long before the white man tortured, subdued, and corralled the Maricopa like livestock on a small reservation with the Pima, a reservation bordered by the upscale Anglo community of Scottsdale. ("The home of fifty-cent millionaires," a crotchety old real estate instructor told us in class one night.) At the time, the dichotomy between those two communities was as striking as that between most bustling American border towns and the dirt-poor *colonias* of their desperate "neighbors" to the south. The obvious difference was that until Indian gaming the Pima and Maricopa hadn't lusted for the material life of greedy city dwellers to the west; their hearts longed to follow the natural pulse of their great rivers sucked dry by pork-barrel reclamation and irrigation projects sustaining unbridled Anglo developments, golf courses, and the unslakable thirst of farm crops like cotton. Like many Native Americans, they longed to roam freely across their vast ancestral lands. The paltry acreage that was parceled out to the Pima and Maricopa in the form of the Gila River Indian Reservation in 1859 was bordered by the desert heights of their sacred mountains: the Sierra Estrella, the Salt River Mountains, Pima Butte, and Superstition, or Crooked, Mountain. And today this land remains their refuge from a foreign culture that turned their traditional life and spirit ways on end—and in the process nearly drove them to the brink of extinction.

Admittedly, I was an uninvited guest, but the sparse lands of the Pima and Maricopa also became my refuge, albeit a fleeting one. But I wanted nothing from these Native Americans I could take away from them. I wouldn't make them promises I wouldn't keep. And I wouldn't even show

> I only wanted to run alone, sight unseen, at night, on the edge of the world that had also caused me so much pain. . . . It was here in the land of the Pima and Maricopa, that I learned to run again.

my face, lest they banish me from their unhurried land. I only wanted to run alone, sight unseen, at night, on the edge of the world that had also caused me so much pain. It was out here, near the western foot of Crooked Mountain, what early Pima once called *Kâkatak Tamai*, that I learned to distance myself from heart-shattering words and emotions and the power they held over my life in the other world beyond the reservation line. It was here that I danced with images from that other life, and they played out on a celestial screen that extended from one horizon to the other and as far back into my past as I dared delve. It was here in the land of the Pima and Maricopa that I learned to run again.

My feet continue padding softly along the desert floor, sending up powdery wisps of dust with each footfall. I suck wind in, I blow air out: *hih-huh, hih-huh, hih-huh, hih-huh, hih-huh.* My lungs heave in and out, charged by my swinging arms. Frogs croak from the narrow irrigation ditch beside me. The whistling scream of nighthawks can be heard as they swoop and dive for insect prey in the irrigated fields

> I was running east through the incandescent light of twilight toward Crooked Mountain . . . the coyote loped defiantly in front of me.

around me. Only occasionally do I feel a painful twinge in my ankle. My strides are full, flowing, as though I can't run fast enough.

But it wasn't always like that, even in the captivating realm of the Pima and Maricopa. One of the first evenings I ran out here, I chased a coyote—God's Dog, the Trickster, Coyote-Creator; it had many names, but it was an animal of great spiritual importance to Native American traditionalists. This coyote, however, was white, a pale white, with faint buff-colored markings, but white. It loped out of deep cotton, where it had apparently been lying in wait for dinner. The sun had just gone down, and I was running east through the incandescent light of twilight toward Crooked Mountain when I almost collided with it. Instead of sprinting away from me, though, the coyote loped defiantly in front of me, just out of reach, as I tried to catch up with it. I distinctly remember it looking back over its shoulder at me, playfully mouthing the lifeless bundle of a bloody, white-wing dove; it seemed to laugh at me as I limped after it, my leg sometimes buckling from the pain as I ran harder to catch up with it. But just as I would start to close the gap, it would trot ahead again, just out of reach, and start its game of catch-me-if-you-can all over again. When the coyote finally grew bored, it loped off the trail and became a blur of white burning through the creosote flats, whirling as effortlessly as a *remolina*, or "desert wind." In contrast, I limped along like a wounded animal several miles back to the college parking lot, my right leg carrying the burden of my left as I learned to do those painfully slow and difficult first miles of running. I needed an explanation for what had happened to me, so I went to tell my friend Gary what I'd seen.

"Are you sure it was white?" he asked, lighting an acetylene torch with a flick of his flint starter; he was at the college working on a new piece of metal sculpture, and I thought that with his artistic sensibilities he might be receptive to the image of a white coyote without too great a leap of faith from normal Anglo thinking.

"I'm sure it was white. I've never seen anything like it before," I said, almost pleading with him to believe me.

Gary swept back his long brown hair, pulled down his dark welder's goggles, and grinned, silently toying with the image of the white coyote in his head.

But I *hadn't* seen anything like it before. That's why I continued running on the reservation at twilight. I didn't have a basis of traditional Native American spiritual knowledge to understand what may or may not have happened to me. And I wanted to know if what I'd seen was real, if it was something else altogether, or if it was an apparition caused by pain, dehydration, and fatigue. When fever-struck prospectors trekked sixty miles down Kanab Creek in Arizona's forlorn Strip country during the 1870s for the gold rumored to be near its confluence with the Colorado River, many men dropped out from hunger and exhaustion; others pushed on into the depths of the western Grand Canyon "determined to 'see the elephant' for themselves after so long and fatiguing a journey," wrote canyoneer Walter Clement Powell in 1872. After a while, I began wondering if I'd seen the elephant, because, as much as I ran after the specter of the white coyote and searched for its physical reality, I never saw it again. What I did see in pursuit of it was pain, every shade of it. But with the pain came the glowing realization that my ankle was slowly getting better and that I could run on it again without limping or crying.

But it hadn't started out that way.

Not long after I crawled down Squaw Peak, Anna and I were married. I remember crutching up the sidewalk to the altar when one of my students grabbed me by the sleeve. Rex Woods was a bartender at a Scottsdale resort, and his wit was honed from years of verbal jousting with babbling "snowbirds," or winter tourists. Standing there in the midday sun, beads of sweat rolling down his forehead, he looked me in the eye and, only half jokingly, said, "John, it's not too late. I've got the car running." I should have listened. When I crutched up to the altar Anna had festooned with garlands of flowers, I watched, along with several hundred embarrassed guests attending the open air ceremony, as Anna tried to set two white doves free. On the verge of hysteria, she frantically shook the flowered cage. The frightened doves wouldn't budge, and the image of our love remained frozen there. That was my second opportunity to bail out. The third time came when Anna's father stormed up to the podium and—in front of God, my parents, guests, and passersby—harangued the crowd like a Third World dictator, telling them exactly what he thought about Anna and me getting married. Two and a half years later, he got his wish; his daughter's little adventure was over, and my heart was broken.

I was eighteen days into a 750-mile wilderness trek across Arizona when Anna broke the news to me, and unfortunately it stopped me in my tracks.

After crawling, crying, and hobbling around on my tender ankle for two years in preparation for the adventure, I realized the only way to prove my foot could stand the rigors of a full-time career in outdoor education would be to trek the length of Arizona north from the Mexican border to the Utah state line. I started planning for the trip the year Anna and I lived in the Arizona mountain community of Prescott, where I was both student and outdoor instructor at Prescott College; there, I had the good fortune of rubbing shoulders with bright-eyed, rosy-cheeked students and faculty who spun tales of their adventures around the world, from climbing the South Buttress of 20,320-foot Mount McKinley, the highest mountain in North America, to scaling the Diamond Couloir of 17,085-foot Mount Kenya in Africa. Crossing the canyons, mountains, and deserts of Arizona on foot seemed like a comparable adventure, and it became no less important to me than climbing Squaw Peak had been; I also felt our marriage sorely needed a new start, because without full use of my foot I often felt like only half a man. But this was no afternoon crawl up a desert peak; it was an arduous two-month trek across some of the most beautiful and intimidating terrain in the Southwest, and I'd have to train hard for it. The rugged, pine-clad mountains of mile-high Prescott were perfect for that. And when, degree in hand, I moved back to the valley with Anna, I focused much of my energy on training for the Arizona crossing. The reservation was the only place I ran, and the more I ran, the more my ankle improved. Even the county doctor expressed disbelief when viewing my new X rays: "I thought the talus would have died by now." The bone hadn't died, as he feared, but it was still painful to put in my daily ten miles in preparation for the trek.

And as the departure date drew nearer, I started having doubts about whether I was doing the right thing or whether I was going to fail miserably—as Anna's father predicted I would. Barely a week north of the Mexican border, however, my fears were dispelled. Carrying a heavy pack was still painful, but after a few hours of trekking, my ankle would warm to the occasion. As one sunset faded into the next, my ankle grew stronger, and my companion Jack Cartier and I kept bearing northwest through the heartland of the Chiricahua and Western Apache, across the pristine Chiricahua Mountains, through the seldom-visited Galiuro

Mountains, and along Aravaipa Creek, one of the only free-flowing streams in the Sonoran Desert. While hopping over a log in Aravaipa Canyon, though, Jack wrenched his knee and reluctantly fell back into vehicle support position as I continued to trek north.

A few days north of Aravaipa Canyon, I had Jack give me a ride to a pay phone. I wanted to give Anna a progress report before I entered the storied Superstition Mountains. I hadn't seen her for more than two weeks, and I was excited to tell her my ankle was holding up to the rigors of crossing Arizona. At last, we could have a new life together, free from the pain and uncertainty that had shadowed us since our marriage. I picked up the phone and dialed.

> The reservation was the only place I ran, and the more I ran, the more my ankle improved.

As soon as I heard her pick up the phone, I whispered, "Anna, I love you." There was a long silent pause. Maybe we had a bad connection. So I said it again. "Anna, I love you." Then, with no warning whatsoever, she said, "I fucked Ronnie. I want a divorce."

I was stunned, speechless. I felt like I'd been kicked in the stomach and hit in the head. For the second time in two years, my world came crashing down on me, and I was stopped cold in my tracks. I quit. I felt like dying.

When I returned to the valley, I sought relief from my pain and sorrow by running for hours on end through the tranquil land of the Pima and Maricopa. At first I wanted to flee Arizona altogether, maybe hole up in Telluride, Colorado; I had a small climbing school there a few years earlier, and I couldn't think of a better place to lick my wounds than in the snowcapped 14,309-foot Uncompahgre Mountains of the Southern Rockies, far removed from the grim reach of Phoenix's wasteland. But if I learned nothing else from my fall, it was that if I started running away from pain I'd be a transient prisoner of a broken heart. I'd have to stand my ground and deal with the terrible pain of divorce, day in, day out, the same way I had endured the pain of my ankle—by running.

That's where I was now.

The dirt path angled toward a full moon rising in the east, and I ran toward it with all my heart. My footsteps were gliding effortlessly, my arms were swinging smoothly, breathing came as easily as a desert wind. There was no pain, anywhere. At last I was free, and my path led straight toward the dark craters of the full moon rising behind the crest of the Superstition Mountains. I longed to visit that land of legend and mystery again; the last time I had, I was leading a charge of students from the back of a mustang. It was a stable horse, but nonetheless a sure-footed mustang that had no need for horseshoes, the wrangler assured me at the trailhead. He was right; it climbed rocky La Barge Canyon like a goat. But midway into our trek through the canyon, the cinch on my saddle broke, and I was dumped hard on the desert floor, helpless with my leg still encased in plaster. But that mustang never left my side, and when I fixed my saddle he carried me with ease all the way out of the Superstitions. Those days, though, were gone now, and as I ran I could see the future stretched out before me, unbound by torment and pain, linked only by soft footsteps, which continue to leave their faint marks on the desert floor. I hoped to visit those mountains again, as the ancient Pima had when elder Hawk Flying sang: "From the Superstition Mountain rose the Eagle; From the sluggish moving Gila rose the Hawk . . . There I am running, there I am running. The Shadow of Crooked Mountain." I longed to visit Crooked Mountain again, running wild as I now was through the heart of an ivory moon.

II.

SEVEN MONTHS LATER, I RUN OUT THE OTHER SIDE OF THAT DESERT MOON, A SLIP-stream of diaphanous images whirling in my wake. I've emerged from the desert realm of the Pima and Maricopa and am now running through the ancient mountain sanctuary of the ʔpača, "people," (known as the Yavapai). A vertical mile above the Sonoran Desert, theirs is a world dominated by statuesque granite boulders and crystal-blue skies, airbrushed with the piney scent of swaying ponderosas.

It is January. A cool winter sun is crawling out of the horizon, slowly burning the thin layer of frost off the path in front of me as I run deeper into the Granite Mountain massif. Dense clusters of piñon and juniper trees mask the horizon to the north, and prickly pear cacti shower my bare legs with hundreds of tiny arrowlike glochids as I brush past. I tear over a low rise, kicking up small rooster tails of dust and dirt behind me. I suck in deep drafts of cold mountain air and fly down the other side of the hill, unconsciously flapping my arms to slow my descent. But it's too late. My feet slide hopelessly on the decomposed granite surface, hundreds of ball bearings of coarse stone catapulting me toward a bone-rattling wreck. I tumble out of control and soar through the air. Fortunately, I land in a sandy wash winding around the bottom of the hill like a lazy snake, and the impact is not as punishing as I expect it to be. *Whhoosshh!* Sand explodes everywhere. I spit cold, damp sand out of my mouth and spray the ground in front of me with stringy tails of mucus and sand as I blow out each nostril. I brush sand off my face and shake it out of my hair. But suddenly, I hear a chorus of ugly grunting. I jump to my feet and see that I'm surrounded by a leaderless band of a dozen or more saber-tusked peccaries stampeding blindly around me. Brandishing razor-sharp incisors as long as bear claws, they root up the ground around me with small, black hooves, grunting: *huug, huug, huug, huug, huug.* I stand there breathless, looking for a tree to climb for fear these near-blind desert pigs will strip my bare legs of flesh. But there is nowhere to run and nowhere to climb; I stand there like a scarecrow, convinced any animal that relishes eating the needle-covered pads of prickly pear cactus would have no problem munching on my spindly legs.

> I'm surrounded by a leaderless band of saber-tusked peccaries . . . any animal that relishes eating the needle-covered pads of prickly pear cactus would have no problem munching on my spindly legs.

Fortunately, they don't see me. The pack of rodent-looking pigs resumes its noisy foraging along the dry wash as I begin running toward Granite Mountain Saddle, trying to shake off the fear of imminent bruises. At one time, 7,626-foot Granite Mountain lay within the boundless ancestral lands of the Yavapai. Like many Native Americans in the Southwest, the Yavapai were fleet of foot, making prodigious journeys throughout their homelands. During June, they ventured from their cool forest environs into the appalling summer heat of the Sonoran Desert in order to collect saguaro fruit. In early autumn, they'd visit Granite Mountain to harvest juniper berries, acorns, walnuts, and even the manzanita berries that adorn the slick, red-barked bush many Anglos like to cut down and spray paint silver for Christmas decorations. No doubt the Yavapai's foraging trips into Granite Basin were also linked to their spiritual beliefs, because one anthropologist reported that her informant said Yavapai spirits "inhabit Granite Peak."

Running toward Granite Mountain Saddle, wearing little more than a pair of shorts and a wool sweater to protect myself from the elements, it's easy to understand the power and sanctity the area held for the Yavapai. They also used the mountain as a natural granite fortress to elude white men who hunted them like dogs during the 1870s. Even famed, territorial "Indian tracker" Al Sieber was quick to admit the frustration of trying to track the Yavapai in a place like Granite Mountain, or nearby Granite Dells, because it entailed "scores of miles of the most backbreaking travel, and if any sign at all was uncovered, you were lucky, so elusive was the enemy. It was discouraging." Fortunately.

Were it not for the modern trail hacked out of brush and blasted out of hard rock, my running through their stony domain would also be discouraging. But I had not come to disturb the Yavapai spirits that may still be dwelling in a region that has become a modern rock climbers' haven and is now fenced and labeled by Anglos as wilderness. I had come for a glimpse of how this mountain might once have been seen by an indigenous people who lived in harmony with it, who, unlike the white man, did not view it as wild.

One of the first Native American elders to address the Euro-American concept of wilderness was Chief Luther Standing Bear. Although the ancestral land of his own people, the Oglala band of Sioux, lay 850 miles to the north of the Yavapai's, the Sioux chief articulated the concept eloquently. With their timeless wisdom, Standing Bear's enlightening words left an indelible mark on me. I didn't realize, while studying them by the light of a campfire the week before, that they would change the way I viewed the Anglo concept of the the land, wilderness, and Native American ancestral ground I would run through in the months and years to come:

> We did not think of the great open plains, the beautiful rolling hills, and the winding streams with tangled growth, as "wild." Only to the white man was nature a "wilderness" and only to him was the land "infested" with "wild" animals and "savage" people. To us it was tame. Earth was bountiful and we were surrounded by the Great Mystery. Not until the hairy man from the

east came and with brutal frenzy heaped injustices upon us and the families we loved was it "wild" for us.

I adjust my stride and breathing to the gradient of this well-trod trail as it climbs out of the headwaters of Granite Creek toward the rocky saddle high above.

Built during the Depression by homeless men using black powder and steel tools, the trail I'm running up bears little resemblance to the ancient footpaths early Yavapai people etched with ceaseless footsteps during their nomadic wanderings. No other indigenous group in Arizona thrived, as the Yavapai reportedly did, in such a challenging and diverse spectrum of life zones and environmental extremes, which ranged from the snow-covered Bradshaw Mountains of central Arizona to the sun-scorched deserts of western Arizona. Based on ethnographic accounts of other indigenous groups, one can only surmise that the Yavapai also ran in order to cover great distances across an ancestral region that once encompassed twenty thousand square miles, just as other Southwest peoples had done; the Mojave, the Chemehuevi, the Hopi, the Paiute, the Pápago, and the Apache were but a few of the Native American groups that ethnographers and historians tell us could run upwards of a hundred miles a day, day after day, more easily than I now can as these hand-tooled switchbacks grow steeper and the pain of the ascent grows more labored.

My lungs burn from the altitude, and my throat feels red and raw from the cold. I pump my arms harder, but my thighs, covered with a sheen of cold sweat, also burn from the steep climb. I shake my gloveless fingers as I run, then blow on them; they too have grown stiff and numb with cold as I pass beneath the huge rock wall of Granite Mountain. I try to warm myself in the brittle morning air by running faster. Only momentarily are my thoughts drawn to the cracks, chimneys, and faces of the great white wall, which has provided me—and other climbers from throughout the country—with hours of exhilarating climbing during the pleasant days of Indian summer. Why Tony and I hadn't climbed this immaculate shield of rock instead of a Phoenix slag heap named after pioneer Arizona's failed camel experiment is only a flicker of a thought before it vanishes. I crest the cold, windswept summit of Granite Mountain Saddle, panting billowing puffs of hot, moist air.

An ice cap of wind-hardened snow blankets the saddle, and a north wind whistles south through the pines, threatening me with stone-cold feet if I venture beyond. My immediate thought is to turn tail and flee back the way I came. I know the route now. It is safe. It is certain. It's also downhill. I'd only have to wait a couple of hours for my friend Chris to pick me up, once she realized I hadn't gone over the saddle to our scheduled rendezvous on the other side of the mountain. I peer over the north side of the saddle; if I'd enjoyed the visceral warmth of the winter sun on the south side of the saddle, it looks bleak, snowy, and dangerous to the north. Worse, I can't find the trail indicated on the topographical map I'm clutching in my cold hands. Still, I'm tempted to see what's on the other side, if only because this is the first time I've attempted to traverse a mountain by running it; I won't have any idea how Native American runners (among them messengers, traders, hunters, and warriors) crossed mountains unless I run it as well. The twelve-hundred miles I've run since moving to Prescott, trying to adapt to the rigors of altitude, hills, and trails, have led me to this point. I know what's behind me; curiosity and the unknown push me to the edge, but I have no idea what lies beyond.

My lungs burn from the altitude, and my throat feels red and raw from the cold.

I plunge downward, but I immediately begin post-holing in the crusty snow with all the finesse of a bawling calf caught in a deep snowdrift. The steep descent and sheer gravity carry me downward as I slalom through black-barked pine trees like a hunted man. The sharp crust of the snow scrapes my bare legs as they perforate the crust, but the depth and compactness of the snow aren't enough to slow my descent. My speed increases. I grab wildly at the branches of small pines, but they are cold and wet and their slick green needles slide through my hands like small frozen fish. My momentum snowballs until I am no longer post-holing but sliding downward atop the ice-encrusted snow. I plop down on my haunches before crashing headlong into a tree. I put my feet out in front of me to break my descent, but the soft rubber heels of my shoes won't bite into the hard crust, and for the second time today I careen toward a bone-breaking wreck. Now desperate, I swing around and slide head-

> I plunge downward, but I immediately begin postholing in the crusty snow. . . . The steep descent and sheer gravity carry me downward as I slalom through black-barked pine trees. . . . I grab wildly at the branches . . . I plop down on my hanuches before crashing headlong into a tree.

first on my stomach toward a small pine tree in hopes of grabbing it before I fly off the abrupt drop that looms ahead. *Whack!* My armlock momentarily holds as I take the brunt of the impact across my right collarbone, but the momentum of my legs swinging across the steep ice in a wide arc jerks me loose and the bark-covered branch of the pine tree slips out of my grasp. Suddenly, I'm avalanching toward the drop again. I flail wildly at anything I can grab, and a lone branch tears and burns through my right hand until a cluster of pine needles anchors itself in my palm. I stop in a spray of ice.

My slushy wet feet skate wildly on the ice as I scurry back up to the small tree; I manage to wrestle around it until I'm on the uphill side again. This small pine is all that stands between me and the drop below, a drop, I now see, over a granite step that would have ended in broken bones, blood, and ice. Before the cold overwhelms me, I quickly plot my course around this drop, and a half dozen other backbreakers lurking below, and pick out a small ridgeline leading down to Williamson Valley. I post-hole over to the shaded ridgeline through thigh-deep snow. The crusty stranglehold at the bottom of each step tries to wrench off my icy shoes, but I've knotted my laces for the worst, and when I finally reach the ridgeline, still wearing both shoes, I'm breathing like a sled dog.

My feet are cold, almost numb. So I run downhill through the snow with wild abandon, frequently plowing through deep drifts as fast as I can in hopes of restoring circulation and warmth in my feet; when it finally returns, I break out of the trees in a dreamy haze.

"Annerino, over here!" I hear a voice in the distance crying out. It's Chris Keith, my friend and, today, my shuttle driver. I've survived, not with much grace, but the ensuing adrenaline rush only boils my blood to run wild again.

III.

THE NEXT TIME I RUN WILD, I'M ALONE IN THE 7,663-FOOT GALIURO MOUNTAINS. It is a cool, clear day in March; a brisk wind rustles out of the north. My legs feel strong, and I feel confident I can run fifty miles across this isolated mountain range in a day. That's only half the distance the Chiricahua and Western Apache reportedly ran between sunup and sunset through the mountain islands and intervening valleys of southeastern Arizona during the height of the United States' "Apache wars." That's what lured me to the Galiuros to begin with—the idea of running, as I now am, carrying little more than a knife, flint and steel, and some rations.

I suck wind in, I blow air out: *hih-huh, hih-huh, hih-huh, hih-huh, hih-huh.* My lungs heave in and out, my legs charge toward the power I hunger for—*gaɫkeʔhoʔndi,* what Western Apaches called running power. In *Western Apache Raiding and Warfare,* Apache elder David Longstreet described this supernatural power to anthropologist Keith Basso: "A man who has this power can run long distances, and even on the shortest day could run from Fort Grant to Fort Apache and get there in mid-afternoon."

An 1881 military map from the court-martial case files, on record at the National Archives, shows this Apache trail: as the crow flies, it's eighty miles from the north end of the Galiuro Mountains to the foot of the 11,420-foot White Mountains; factor in the endless twists and turns of the rugged topography, and you're looking at a hundred miles. In a day. A hundred miles in a day! What was it like for the Apache to run such distances? No one but these fleet-footed *Ndee,* Apache people, knows for certain. Native Americans have a great oral tradition of recording events and tribal history, so non-Indians can only imagine what early Apache runners dreamed of or what it felt like physically to run a hundred miles wearing a pair of knee-high leather moccasins, painted with wind tracks to make their legs light, and a traditional breechcloth, with their long black hair, bound by a red bandanna.

One case documenting a daring 170-mile escape by two Apache women in 1865 sheds light on their remarkable endurance. In 1931, Apache scout David Longstreet recounted how his mother and several other Apache women were abducted by U.S. troops and Pápago trackers after a bloody raid on their mescal gathering camp at the foot of the Santa Teresa Mountains. They were brought to Tucson, but while the Pápago celebrated the spoils of their attack, Longstreet's mother and another woman escaped and vanished into the night. Said Longstreet: "They stayed in the Santa Catalinas that night and the next day traveled toward the Galiuro Mountains, making camp about halfway to them. The next day they got to the Galiuro Mountains. Here they saw some tracks, but they said, 'These are of the Aravaipa Apaches, and they are no good, so we will stay away from them.'" That they did, bivouacking at night without blankets and surviving on roasted mescal hearts until they reached their village near Goodwin Springs. But the single most telling piece of evidence from Longstreet's account came at the end of their difficult journey when his mother was recognized by one of the U.S. officers who'd raided their camp. Said Longstreet, "The officer shook hands with her" in admiration. "He wanted to know how she got home. She told him her legs were like horses!"

That's how my legs still felt ten miles into the Galiuros—that they were carrying me like horses. Averaging 250 miles of running a month since crossing Granite Mountain, I had few worries, other than fatigue, about trying to run half the distance the Apache historically ran. Four miles later, however, my legs are seized with cramps. I walk peg-legged for a few minutes and guzzle a liter of water from one of the two bota bags I'm wearing crisscrossed on my chest *villista*-style. I cinch down my camera to my survival belt and start running again, trying to shake out the rigid cramps with a flick of each step.

But the trail I'm running up is covered with blowdown, fallen trees and logs, and to make any progress I have to climb over or slither beneath them on all fours. These guerrilla movements, however, combined with my abrupt ascent out of the Sulphur Springs Valley, exhaust me by the time I reach the East Divide seventeen miles out. My thighs are screaming, and my eyelids are starting to droop with fatigue. I'm spent. I can't go any farther. I should turn back; it's all downhill. But I can't; there's no place to run back to. Once the domain of the *tseijin*, "dark rocks people," or Aravaipa band of Western Apache, I've been dropped off on the southern end of one of the most remote, unforgivingly rugged, and seldom-visited U.S. Forest Service wilderness areas in the Southwest.

Sitting alone atop that Galiuro ridge, halfway between hell and gone, I can see Eagle Pass between the Santa Teresa and Piñaleno Mountains. Geronimo and the *dè'ida*·, "enemy people," band of Chiricahua Apache often crossed that divide in the 1880s, returning to San Carlos after their audacious, fleet-footed raids into Mexico's Sierra Madre 250 miles south. But I quickly lose that train of thought because I feel weak, unnaturally so. I must have a low-grade infection. My face feels flushed, and the recovery I'm patiently waiting for never occurs. I look at my maps; I have no options. The shortest distance to any kind of help is my rendezvous point at Power's Garden sixteen miles north. Somehow, I have to make it there by nightfall. Like Longstreet's mother, I'm not carrying any kind of sleeping gear, but unlike that brave Apache woman, I've never survived off roasted mescal hearts. It's too cold to spend the night in the open with-

> I stick my fingers in my mouth and try to vomit, in hopes of ridding myself of the debilitating bug that's infected me. But I only gag and spit up a vile, bitter-tasting phlegm.

out food or bedding. Sick or not, somehow I have to run it; wearing knee-length wool socks and a natty old wool sweater, I'm too lightly clad to move any slower.

I stand up, stretch my legs, and start running due north along the high-line spine of the Galiuro Mountains. In terms of natural direction finding, I visualize the seven-thousand-foot high range as a capital H lying on its backside. I am running along the lower right leg of that H and have to reach Power's Garden, situated in a deep cleft of the canyon between the two upper arms of the H. But the narrow, slippery path I'm following is heavily overgrown with chaparral and manzanita bushes, and they shove me back and forth across the ridgeline like an unruly mob. Consequently, it takes all my concentration to maintain a run.

Feeling weaker by the yard, I'm not sure how much longer I can main-tain the awkward lurching of a condemned man, so I try daydreaming about the rock climb I'm going to attempt with George Bain and Dave Ganci in the Grand Canyon two months from now. But that thought doesn't hold my attention either. A degenerative fatigue and malaise overcome me, and I repeatedly fall to my knees as I continue staggering toward 7,663-foot Bassett Peak.

When I reach what looks like a mirage of that peak, dots are swirling in front of my eyes and I feel like heaving. I stick my fingers in my mouth and try to vomit, in hopes of ridding myself of the debilitating bug that's infected me. But I only gag and spit up a vile, bitter-tasting phlegm. I want to turn back, but there's no place to turn back to. I want there to be an easy way out of here, but I can't fly like the Redtail hawk now does, soar-ing dreamily overhead. I need running power. But Apache didn't come by *gaɫkeʔhoʔndi* easily; the young people were taught many forms of run-ning by their elders and *di yih*, or "medicine men." As children, they were taught to run fast enough to catch butterflies and birds burdened with heavy wet feathers after monsoon rains. As young men, they ran as part of their sweat-bath ritual, singing sacred Apache curing songs as the hot rocks hissed with steam. When young women came of age during the four-day-and-night puberty ceremony of White Shell Woman, they ran in the four cardinal directions to ensure a long healthy life. The Apache ran to trade with the distant Mojave far to the west and the Pueblo people far to the north. When mounted government troops hunted them like dogs, they out-ran their horses over the long pursuit, and, when they were starving, they ate their enemies' horses. As a non-Indian, I now realize, the knowledge and power of ga𝘭ke?ho?ndi are not within my grasp. I want to cry.

I wonder if mountain man and trapper James Ohio Pattie cried when he descended the flanks of the Galiuro Mountains somewhere near here while traversing the range between March 31 and April 2, 1824. Wrote Pattie:

> On the 31st, we reached the top of the mountain, and fed upon the last meat of our beavers. We met with no traces of game. On the morning of the first of April, we commenced descending the mountain, from the side of which we could discern a plain before us, which, however, it required two severe days to reach . . . we had nothing to eat or drink. In descending from the icy mountains, we were surprised to see how warm it was on the plains. On reaching them, I killed an antelope, of which we drank the warm blood; and however revolting that recital may be, to us it was refreshing, tasting like fresh milk.

The abundant herds of antelope that once thrived in the San Pedro and Sulphur Springs valleys were killed off without ceremony by white men not long after Pattie explored the region, and none remain in view to quench my own thirst, even if I'd carried a gun for survival rations. But I'd given up hunting with guns not long after my grandfather died and resolved only to carry a knife while traveling alone in the bush. I am low on food, but I am too sick to hold anything down anyway. My bota bags have been sucked dry, and my lips are cracked and bleeding. I keep running, through dirt, ice, and snow, unaware of when I'd started running again; my lungs heave in and out: *hih-huh, hih-huh, hih-huh, hih-huh, hih-huh.* A whirling blur of rocks, leaves, foliage, pine needles, emory oak, Mexican piñon, and Apache pine trees shrouds me for hours on end as I continue panting through the snow and undergrowth. Catclaw and buckthorn rake me, shredding my arms and legs with long, painful blood-streaked scratches and punctures. My movement is more atavistic than conscious. I keep running. I've got to find the sign. I'm now drooling.

By the time I reach the weathered trail marker sticking out of the brush like a sawed-off street sign, I'm reduced to whimpering. But the block letters notched in the brown wooden sign prove that, despite the fear and doubt I had traveling blindly through the underbrush, my dead reckoning was right on the mark: RATTLESNAKE CREEK. There it is, my ticket back from beyond! I think.

> I vomit, but I am too cold and nervous to stop and clean the foul slime off my tattered sweater.

I start mumbling with joy as I gallop off the west slope of a peak called BM 7,099, confident that I know the way to my rendezvous. I am nothing more than a runner now; I no longer have a personal identity. I am merely movement from one physical clue to the next. And each time I sniff out a blaze mark etched into the gnarled bark of an alligator juniper tree, an old section of trail, or a small cairn, I cry out, relieved that I'm tying this incipient track together through the upper reaches of Rattlesnake Creek.

I follow the serpentine path back and forth into the underbrush until it dead-ends in a vicious cluster of catclaw. "Yeooww!" I scream. I backtrack, always running, but they're all dead ends now. I vomit, but I am too cold and nervous to stop and clean the foul slime off my tattered sweater. So down I go, hopping from one boulder to the next, moving not like the runner I once knew but more like a coyote pup trying to make sense out of the tenuous footing along the sharp rocks and narrow walls of the creek. This is treacherous ground, even if I wasn't sick. One slip and it'll be an agonizing and bloody crawl out of here to God knows where. But if I think about the consequences—breaking a leg or reinjuring my stiff ankle—my subliminal fears will turn into reality. All I can do now is move, instinctively running.

Gravity and the angle of my descent control my running speed, until I am going faster and faster; the painful jarring shudders through my legs as they whip across the ground. *Whap! Whap! Whap!* But I can't stop. A furious series of steep drops unreels before me, and I continue leaping wildly until I suddenly realize I'm making seven-foot jumps back and forth across the creek, and it's running with water. Running with water? I stop frequently and gulp the cold water with my scratched, cupped hands but never for more than a few moments at a time. Running is everything now.

The setting sun is shrouding Rattlesnake Canyon with a cold shadow just as I reach the old Power's Mine Road, and my running becomes a race with that shadowline. If I can somehow stay ahead of it before I reach Power's Garden I'll be all right, but if that dark veil eclipses my arrival, well, I'm scared. It's not even a thought process, only an atavistic reaction to the tenuous threshold between daylight and darkness.

It's twilight when I finally reach Power's Garden; I'd been promising myself all along that this was the end of the trail. "Chris!" I scream. No answer. "Chris! . . . Chris!" Still no answer. Frenzied, I start racing around the old line shack still used by cowboys working the rough interior of the Galiuros, but it's bolted shut. Signs warn to stay the hell out. To take my mind off my fears, I try to busy myself with the history of this homestead. The time was 1918. And the tragic shoot-out that erupted here on February 10 over a warrant served by the local sheriff posse to brothers John and Tom Power for draft dodging was the catalyst for the largest manhunt in Arizona history. No one knows who drew first blood, but when the smoke cleared two minutes later three posse members lay dead and the young men's father, Thomas Jefferson Power, lay in the throes of death. Wounded in the shoot-out themselves, the Power boys dragged their father's body into the mine and, with former cavalry scout and paroled horse thief Tom Sisson, rode the dead men's horses out of the

Galiuros and headed for Old Mexico along the Chiricahua Apache trail. When the trio was finally captured south of the border twenty-seven days later, Sisson and the Power boys had, according to one historian, "eluded a thousand posse members and eight troops of the U.S. Cavalry." Incredibly, they'd covered the last 170 miles of their exhausting escape on foot, after abandoning their stolen mounts in the former Apache redoubt of the Chiricahua Mountains.

"Chris! Chris!" I yell again. But there is no answer. I don't know where she is, and I imagine the worst.

I'd first met Chris in the Valley of the Sun a year earlier. Her reputation as a photographer preceded her, and we frequently talked by phone. Our friendship grew, and we decided to join forces when we moved back to Prescott and split expenses. The most respectable studio we could find was located next to a funeral home, and it was agreed that I would use the kitchen to pound out a terrible first novel while Chris remodeled the small bathroom into a darkroom.

During frequent visits to Chris's darkroom, I discovered the depth of her ability to capture the essence of people in her portaits. Hanging dripping wet from a spiderweb of stainless steel wires were masterful black-and-white prints of people from a world I hadn't known before: an eight-year-old girl carrying her month-old sister in a rebozo through the streets of Antigua, Guatemala; a Mao tribesman trading opium on the Burmese border of northern Thailand; El Zarco, a Chicano sculptor, firing a Zuñiga-influenced bronze in Tepoztlàn, Mexico. These were the exotic locales Chris had ventured to alone, and from those travels she brought back soul-stirring images that needed no explanations. I didn't know it at the

The setting sun is shrouding Rattlesnake Canyon with a cold shadow just as I reach the old Power's Mine Road, and my running becomes a race with that shadowline.

time, but my intense exposure to Chris's formative body of work made a lasting impression that would change the course of my own career from that of a camera-starved actor laboring on the novel he only dreamed of starring in to a photojournalist who, like Chris, longed to capture the people, places, and events that continue to shape our lives and the worlds in which we live.

> Running ten miles a day through the six- to seven-thousand-foot-high mountains . . . was entirely different from running the creosote flats and farmlands of the Sonoran Desert

Chris had also studied a difficult form of Buddhist meditation called *vipassana,* or "mindfulness," while living in Chiang Mai, Thailand, a few years earlier; part of the practice required her to walk for hours across a teakwood floor of a small, empty room called a *gutee,* meditating solely on the acts of walking and breathing and their individual components. And Chris was far more adept at working within the constraints of our small studio than I. So I frequently broke out of my confines and roamed the Bradshaw Mountains, Sierra Prieta, and Black Hills of Prescott looking for new and exhilarating places to run the daily ten miles I tried to maintain. That was the magic number. I don't know where it came from, but one night while running through the land of the Pima and Maricopa, I figured that if I could run ten miles a day I could do anything. But running ten miles a day through the six- to seven-thousand-foot-high mountains surrounding Prescott was entirely different from running the creosote flats and farmlands of the Sonoran Desert, and that made for daily adventures that ultimately led to my crossing Granite Mountain.

Once I had survived that wild twelve-mile run, as clumsy and ignorant as I'd been, I embarked on a series of other wilderness runs in hopes of building on the knowledge of running wild I was attaining both by the trial and error of running through the canyons, mountains, and deserts of

Arizona and by studying ethnographic accounts, government monographs, anthropological papers, and histories I'd ferreted out during painstaking, often enlightening hours of research at university and museum libraries and special collections. One nugget I'd unearthed was about the Western Apache, who used a running power . . .

But that's why I was now in over my head.

I break down as I run and stumble along the boulder-strewn canyon bottom, but I'm too dehydrated and exhausted to cry. Tears won't form, and my legs are in too much pain to move voluntarily; they are controlled by something beyond me now. Maybe it's fear. Darkness completely engulfs me as I continue thrashing down the flood-swept black gash of Rattlesnake Canyon.

The sound of rushing water screams at me. Tree limbs lash me like a penitent. Brush tears at me. Logs trip me. Rocks stop me just long enough to let me know that something other than conscious thought is controlling my movement, as though I'm outside myself watching someone else struggle through the oil-black, thigh-deep torrent. I feel weird and unworldly, as though I've never been here before; but I *have* been here before, while trying to cross Arizona with Jack Cartier. The water's cold, I know it

> I feel like a cold husk of blood, muscle, and bone. I struggle desperately to focus long enough to ignite the fire.

is, but it doesn't feel that way, just wet. The only thoughts I have now are that somehow my eyes are still open and my body—not me—is still running. And it won't, can't stop!

A dark wind is gusting across Power's Hill, and I'm shivering violently with cold, wet chills when I finally crawl out of Rattlesnake Canyon and head across the black plain toward Aravaipa Creek. I have to stop and start a fire now, or I'm going to die. I hastily gather black shapes of wood and agave stalks, but my hands tremble as my stiff fingers strip damp bark away from the dry tinder beneath; without it, there will be no fire tonight, only death by hypothermia. Shaking uncontrollably, I pile the tufts of tinder, tiny pieces of kindling, into a small tepee sheltered from the wind by my body, which has grown rigid with cramps; squatting on my haunches, I feel like a cold husk of blood, muscle, and bone. I struggle desperately to focus long enough to ignite the fire.

One strike. Another. Nothing. The wind is howling around me, and my body continues to wretch and shake uncontrollably. I take a deep full breath, then slowly exhale in an attempt to control my spastic shivering; it doesn't help. I strike the long knife along the flint again. Nothing. I strike it again and again, scraping the razor-sharp steel down the length of the flint, showering the ground with a celebration of dying sparks. Nothing. I try again and again. Finally, a single spark takes hold of the dry yucca fiber, and, still shaking in fits and stammers, I add bits of kindling to the small miraculous flame, afraid I'll snuff it out if I add too much fuel too quickly. Piece by piece, I slowly pile on more and more wood, until the sudden eruption of flames singes my mustache and eyebrows and my body slowly begins to warm. When it does, I know that I'm going to survive and that Chris, mindfully pacing somewhere out there in the middle of the night next to her car, has been unable to ford Aravaipa Creek, swollen with the same runoff that boiled down Rattlesnake Canyon. Dreaming the fire, I no longer have any idea what *gaɬkeʔhoʔndi* is.

3

THE MIDNIGHT CRACK

We are the first and doubtless will be the last

party of whites to visit this profitless locality.

Lieutenant Joseph C. Ives, April 3, 1858,
upon entering the Grand Canyon

It is May. The hour is late. Snow has begun to fall, and the wind will not let up. We have come prepared for the heat, the kind of skull-numbing heat that sweeps over the inner Canyon this time of year like a simmering mirage, not the last vestiges of a brutal winter still frothing down off the alpine heights of the North Rim.

Standing there shivering on a small ledge, 4,370-odd feet above the muddy Colorado River, I have to make a decision: continue climbing for the summit in hopes of finding enough firewood to survive a freezing bivouac at 7,123 feet or attempt a long and dangerous retreat down the Southwest Face of Zoroaster Temple in the dead of night. That's where the three of us are perched now, on a majestic sandstone temple in the heart of the Grand Canyon, and we're burning what little daylight remains. Worse, we are anchored to a confusion of nylon rope, our teeth are chattering from the cold, and we are hopping in place like old men on a blustery winter night.

I look at my partners.

Dave Ganci, the bearded pioneer among us, had been here two decades earlier, when he and Rick Tidrick pulled off the audacious first ascent of Zoroaster Temple. In the process, Dave and Tidrick not only climbed what is arguably the most magnificent temple in the Grand Canyon but also proved that rock climbing techniques pioneered by John Salathé during the golden age of climbing in Yosemite Valley could be used to climb what were once considered the Canyon's unscalable summits below the rim. So a first ascent of the Southwest Face wouldn't be as important to Dave as it was to me—even if he hadn't been doubled over from the debilitating effects of giardia.

George Bain, my other partner, was a Colorado River boatman and a veteran Grand Canyon climber with an enviable list of Canyon ascents to his credit, including a new route up Zoroaster's north side the year before. If push came to shove, he could live with that for another year or so.

Me, I'd never climbed anything as mesmerizing as Zoroaster before, except in conversation over a brew with these two lads. But having been touched by the magic of a temple named for the Persian deity of Zoroastrianism, I am now drawn to its summit like a moth to a flame and little else seems to matter—with the exception of the safety of my partners. That's why I'm fretfully trying to sort out the pros and cons of continuing, given that I per-

> By climbing the Southwest Face I hoped to be able to determine the path I was truly destined for: Himalayan climbing or running wild—I couldn't master both.

sonally have a lot riding on Zoroaster. It's the first difficult new route I've attempted since my fall. And I knew that if my ankle could stand the rigors of the rugged, two-day approach to Zoroaster I could at least entertain the possibilities of a career of Himalayan climbing. But if my ankle fell apart en route to the climb, I always had running, *running wild,* I thought. But shortly after crawling out of the Galiuro Mountain fastness of the Aravaipa Apache, I had doubts as to whether I'd be able to take running wild to the limits I'd first imagined. Tossing and turning around the dying embers of that lonely Galiuro bivouac fire, my ankle had been seized with such pain I felt like I was back on Squaw Peak with crutches. Come daybreak, I needed an agave stalk to hobble another dozen miles out to my rendezvous with Chris on Aravaipa Creek. The Galiuro run had driven me to a troubling crossroads in my life, and by climbing the Southwest Face I hoped to be able to determine the path I was truly destined for: Himalayan climbing or running wild—I couldn't master both.

If I decided to push on, the three of us would be drawn into another dangerous race, a race against darkness. We'd already lost the first race with our dwindling water supply. Natural springs and perennial streams are as scarce in the Grand Canyon as they are difficult to reach; so most of the water we needed for this weeklong adventure had to be carried: a gallon a day per head, eight and a half pounds a gallon. Combined with enough climbing gear, ropes, and food to attempt an ascent of what had repulsed several other strong parties, the staggering weight and unwieldiness of water sloshing around in our packs made our knees buckle—and my ankle scream. Even so, we knew three gallons of water each wouldn't be enough to reach Zoroaster, do the climb, and descend all the way back to Phantom Ranch at the confluence of Bright Angel Creek and the Colorado River. So once we established an advance camp at the base of Zoroaster, we replenished our marginal supply with water George had cached above the Redwall formation the year before and water Dave and I collected from a tinaja, "rain pocket," below neighboring Brahma Temple. But when Dave pressed his lips to that shallow water pocket, he sucked out a nasty intestinal amoeba called giardia, and it dogged him like a marked man throughout the day.

We'd been on Zoroaster Temple since sunup, slowly and methodically free-climbing our way five rope lengths up of this monolithic rock pinnacle. At high noon, the fossilized sand of the Southwest Face absorbed the warm rays of the Canyon sun like an upended beach. We stripped down to our T-shirts and savored each airy pitch, because we were climbing in a great inverted mountain range that stunned us with its scale and thousands of feet of heart-stopping exposure. But none of us had had any water since noon, and that had only been a few mouthfuls each. It is now 5:28 P.M., and the severe fluid deficit is beginning to take its toll.

But the dark pall of night is my biggest worry now; never mind my fear that these wind-whipped snow flurries might turn into a merciless storm

Southwest Face of Zoroaster Temple. George Bain composes himself after taking a 25-foot lead fall during the first ascent. (Photo by John Annerino)

that could bury us on our perch. If night lies down on us before we reach the Toroweap summit blocks, neither George nor I will be any more fit to lead than Dave is now. I wasn't sure about George, but up until now night climbing had not been my specialty.

George and Dave wait silently for my decision; their eyes say everything: they can go either way. Just make the call. But I'm tired and distracted, and precious minutes tick by as I'm held rapt by the scene before us. Staring back across the immense gulf of the inner Canyon like an awestruck tourist, I can see the imposing escarpment of the seven-thousand-foot Coconino Plateau; it tumbles off the South Rim like a tsunami of rainbow-hued rock collapsing en masse atop the thin silver strand of the Colorado River a vertical mile below. As heavily laden as we'd been during the approach, it had taken a full day to reach the river from the South Rim through that brink, though the declivitous South Kaibab Trail provided the quickest route through the Toroweap, Coconino sandstone, and continuum of neapolitan rock walls that would have otherwise proved insurmountable. But once we headed north from Phantom Ranch, we had had to rely on Dave's and George's recall of a route that ascended the glass-black Vishnu schist, the rotten Redwall limestone, and the bloodstained Hermit shale. In the process, we had climbed nearly a vertical mile to reach the foot of this magnificent, flat-topped horn of Coconino sandstone. Yet, Zoroaster Temple was not the only temple of the Grand Canyon lost to the modern world; before us and all around us stood dozens of other supernal spires and buttes that also resembled the dwelling places of deities. Part of the allure and fascination of climbing in this stupendous gorge was that many of its temples had been named by geologist and cartographer Clarence E. Dutton after temples he'd visited in the Orient during the 1800s; they were too sublime to be named after mere mortals, Dutton had rightly concluded. Better to name them Tower of Ra, Angel's Gate, Confucious, Buddha . . .

"Annerino! What do you want to do?"

Startled from my twilight reverie, I turn back and ask George if he has any matches. I know he does, but I just want some reassurance that if we manage to climb to the summit in the dark we can at least build a bivouac fire.

"Yeah," George says. The word hangs there momentarily, before being swept into the depths of the Canyon by a chill wind.

"All right, I'll make you a deal," I tell him.

"What's that?" George yells above a gust of wind.

"You lead that," I say, pointing to the dangerous pitch looming above, "and I'll lead that."

His orange parka flapping wildly in the wind, George eyes the two tomb-sized blocks we'd seen earlier; it doesn't look like it'd take much to dislodge them and squash us like roadkill. Faced with such a prospect, I have no illusions about trying to make the delicate nerve-jangling moves around them myself. George isn't enchanted with the prospect either, because, if he blows a move on this pitch and doesn't dislodge those blocks, he will take a bone-crushing pendulum against the opposite rock wall. A long fall down a smooth rock face or a screaming bounce into an overhang were acceptable risks I was willing to take, but the throbbing pain in my ankle was a potent reminder to avoid unprotectable leads above ledges and such.

Having apparently worked out the sequence of delicate moves in his head, George peered beyond his lead into mine. "You want it bad enough to lead *that,* in the dark?" he asks me.

"I'd rather climb at night than rappel at night," I tell him, and as soon as I do, I realize there isn't any other option; if we're going to survive the night without caving in to hypothermia, we have to climb. Our hand has been forced. Unlike climbing, which ideally melds mind and body to rock in a series of fluid movements, rappeling requires a climber to rely almost entirely on the mechanics of rope anchors and a rappel harness. And the history of mountaineering and rock climbing has been tragically marked with the corpses of world-class climbers who, at one distracted moment, fell screaming to their deaths because they'd accidently unclipped the wrong carabiner while rappeling.

"You lead the traverse, George. I'll do the rest," I tell him.

Each of us holds the key for the other; without them both, the door to the summit will remain locked, and the three of us will be forced to rappel one frightening rope length after another into the dark and who knew what kind of fatal mistake awaiting below. Clad in flimsy parkas and heavy sweaters, we are too cold to remain at an impasse. Buffeted by strong, erratic gusts of wind, George starts up. Snow pelts his thick red beard, and his gold earring swings back and forth like a soundless wind chime.

"You got me, Annerino?"

"I got ya, George!"

Climbing in the bewitching depths of this awesome gorge began circa A.D. 1000; that's when archaeologists tell us Native Americans first climbed 7,646-foot Shiva Temple. The *anaasàzi,* or "enemy ancestors," climbed the forested, mesa-topped summit of Shiva for flint embedded in the Kaibab limestone that crowns it. Evidence had also been discovered that the Anasazi climbed Wotan's Throne, Elaine Castle, and Guinevere

Castle; who's to say how many other temples, spires, towers, and buttes they climbed, whether in search of flint, to elude marauding enemies, or in sacred quest of manhood?

Not the scores of fever-struck prospectors who arrived at the South Rim during the late 1800s. Responsible for constructing the eighty-four miner trails that once snaked their way into the Canyon—many of them along the precipitous paths of the Anasazi—these argonauts were too busy prowling the Canyon's depths for gold, silver, copper, and asbestos to address such concerns.

Once their glory holes played out, or they realized it was going to cost more to pack their pay dirt out on burro trains than the low-grade ore was worth, miners like Captain John Hance and William Wallace Bass discovered it was more profitable to guide tourists down their hand-forged trails. And with this influx of the Canyon's first tourists came recorded ascents of Mount Huethawali, Coronado Butte, Apollo Temple, and other temples not requiring hemp ropes and ironmongery.

> If we're going to survive the night without caving in to hypothermia, we have to climb.

It wasn't until Harvey Butchart visited the Grand Canyon in 1945 that climbing in it got serious. Before his recent retirement, the ninety-year-old canyoneer made 83 ascents of remote canyon temples (largely by perilous scrambling without ropes, keen route finding, and endurance), and discovered 116 rim-to-river routes (in 1882, Clarence E. Dutton estimated there were only four, each within a day's journey of the next), traced out 164 breaks breaks in the formidable Redwall formation, by tracking the incipient routes of the ancient Anasazi.

It wasn't until Dave Ganci and Rick Tidrick arrived at the South Rim in 1958 to climb Zoroaster's Northeast Arête, however, that the Grand Canyon's first real rock climb was made. Having repulsed four other expeditions, Zoroaster Temple fell to Ganci and Tidrick, who launched their attempt to coincide with the August monsoons that periodically recharge the Canyon's ephemeral water sources.

After spending a drizzly night camped at Phantom Ranch, Ganci and Tidrick forded rain-swollen Bright Angel Creek and climbed toward the base of Zoroaster Temple, car-rying sixty-five-pound loads and a gallon of water each. The extend-ed forecast called for four days of rain, and they were confident

> If he makes the moves across wafer-thin footholds, we'll gain a stance at the bottom of the final pitch; if not, he'll take a shocking sixty-foot fall, pendulum into the wall, and probably dislodge those two huge blocks above us.

they could fill their empty five-gallon metal gas can with rainwater on their journey through the stifling inner Canyon desert.

By the time they started up the nerve-racking break in the Redwall, dehydration brought on by one-hundred-plus degree temperatures had taken its toll. Wrote Ganci: "Realizing we had drunk three quarts of our two gallons of water, we decided to start rationing the precious liquid, still expecting to collect rain. The clouds cleared that night and the star-ry night was an unwelcome sight."

Too anxious to wait for the forecasted monsoons, Ganci and Tidrick bivouacked high above and decided to attempt Zoroaster at dawn the fol-lowing day. But dehydration and fatigue caught up with them halfway up the Northeast Arête, and they were forced to bivouac again, this time huddled together on a narrow ledge. Still stiff from the cramped, uncom-fortable bivouac, the pair negotiated an exposed traverse the following morning and surmounted the Northeast Arête's crux summit crack. Shortly after 11:00 A.M. on September 23, 1958, Ganci and Tidrick reached the summit of Zoroaster Temple and built a four-and-a-half-foot-high cairn.

If we could be half as lucky to trade the cold for the heat, I thought.

"Annerino! . . . You got me?!"

A nerve-rattling half hour later, George is on the crux. If he makes the moves across wafer-thin footholds, we'll gain a stance at the bottom of the final pitch; if not, he'll take a shocking sixty-foot fall, pendulum into the wall, and probably dislodge those two huge blocks above us.

I'm scared. Dave gives me one of those what'd-we-get-ourselves-into looks. We both remember the twenty-five-foot lead fall George took earlier in the day; the force of it jerked me up in the air so violently, it nearly uprooted the three bushes Dave and I were anchored to. It was a thin line between survival and hurtling into the yawning drop, all roped together, toward our water cache in Sumner Wash three thousand feet below. A masonry bolt would have prevented that near disaster, but we were trying to climb clean.

"You got me, Annerino?" George screams again.

"I got ya, George!"

In the falling snow and failing light, I can barely discern the dark image of George as he stretches across the crux. It's an awkward and desperate move. The key handhold must be just out of reach, maybe an inch, maybe two. Dave and I can't see clearly. But George pauses for a moment, steeling himself against the fear of not putting the delicate moves together. There won't be a second chance. At that moment, I try to detach myself from the reality of a long lead fall; if he takes one, there's nothing I can do except hold on and pray none of us is killed. Dave seems equally resigned at the moment. As for George, I can feel the tension of his right leg resonate down the length of rope into my cold hands. Or maybe it's simply the wind trying to dislodge the human spider tenuously clinging to the wall above.

George has to make the move now, before he's overcome with fear. As if prompted by some atavistic cue, George stretches farther across the wall and grasps the hold to make sure it won't slough off in his cold fingers. When he knows it is sound, I can feel the relief reverberate back down the length of rope. He steps across the dark heavens and screams, *"Yowwweee!!!"* He's done it. He's crossed the Twilight Traverse, and he was the only one among us who could have put those desperate moves together tonight.

"Guess it's my turn," I tell Dave. He nods silently, still doubled over with cramps.

George ties off and puts me on belay. I start climbing up his perilous vertical puzzle, confident I'm safeguarded by his taut rope above. With night almost upon us, there is no time to remove the anchors George had carefully placed on this difficult stretch. So I climb past each dangling nut and make the crotch-ripping stretch beneath the two huge blocks. I grasp what remains of the gear rack from George and sling it around my neck and shoulders.

"Your turn," George says, puffing on his stogie.

"Glad I didn't lead that," I tell him, half hoping he'll be swept away by the camaraderie and volunteer to lead my pitch as well. But George has earned his stogie-lit perch; I, alone, have to earn mine high above.

"Wait till you see the off-width," he says, trying to laugh off the last of his fears and rush of adrenaline.

"I don't want to look at it till I get there," I tell him. George laughs again, and we wait, ritually passing the stogie back and forth between us, the brightness of the burning red ember a gauge to measure the depth of the darkness and the cold that will dictate my own movements above.

It's nearly midnight when Dave finally reaches us. The wind is still blowing, dusting our legs and eyelashes with dry spindrift, a promising sign that we may have escaped hell's fury. Dave ties off next to George. Based on how long it's taken him to jumar and clean the pitch, I assume giardia has left him weak so I don't broach the subject of his leading the last pitch.

I grab the plastic flashlight and stick it in my mouth. It's my lead, Dave's belay. There is no time for backslapping. Darkness has already beaten us to this perch, and we are losing a grim third race to cold and fatigue. George has since climbed out of the blowing snow and crawled lizardlike between two boulders. He knows I won't sprint up the "midnight crack."

Tentatively, I start up. The small battery-powered beam shines the way, but I don't need the light to know I'm groping through a layer of Permian sea sludge that forms the mortar between the Coconino sandstone and the Toroweap limestone; it is too soft and crumbly to permit a solid purchase with my fingers or slick-soled climbing boots. The sharp steel ice hammers and rigid twelve-point crampons of an alpine climber would have been more suitable for this appalling layer, but who could have guessed that while viewing the Southwest Face from the distant South Rim vista four days earlier? We hadn't. So I take the climbing a foot at a time, aware that Dave may be dozing on and off, unable to stave off the irresistible pull of sleep.

> There is no time for backslapping . . .
>
> Darkness has already beaten us to this perch, and we are losing a grim third race to cold and fatigue.

Carefully removing my right hand from a crumbly hold, I take the light out of my mouth and shout into the black void below.

"Dave! . . . Hey, Dave! . . . You awake?!"

" . . . huh . . . yeah, I gotcha!"

I tug at the rope and continue groping, as though I'm spelunking out of a dark, muddy cavern. Fatigue is enveloping me in a deadly embrace, and it feels like I'm about to be yanked into the abyss. I want desperately to sleep. Cold is slashing at me like Galiuro catclaw. I don't want to be alone, but I feel as though I'm on the edge of the world and about to tumble into an endless free fall through black space. I have to stay awake long enough to finish the lead. I mouth my upper lip between my eyeteeth and the flashlight; whenever fatigue darts in from its ominous orb, I bite down until I can feel the pain, the salty trickle of my own blood. I am climbing for my life.

With each grungy foot I gain, I yell back down to Dave, flashlight in mouth: "Dave! . . . Hey, Dave, you awake?"

But it always takes the second or third cry to get a response out of him: " . . . Yeah . . . yeah, I gotcha."

I'm not sure how much rope I've run out, but once I climb over the crumbly edge of mud, I arrive at the base of a chimney and decide to place a bolt; under normal, daylight conditions, it wouldn't be necessary, but fear has me on a tight leash. I'm high above my sleeping belayer with no reliable anchors between us. I fumble for the bolt driver and commence hammering, occasionally hitting my left hand instead of the aluminum drill, but it is too cold to feel the steel hammerhead bruising my bare knuckles. The bolt placed, I clip into it and fight my way into the base of the chimney. I'm safe in here, I think to myself once inside; there's no exposure. There's no exposure at night, anyway, so what are you thinking? I'm getting groggier; I bite down on my lip again. With my knees and the palms of my hands pressed against the wall in front of me and my heels, buttocks, and shoulders wedged behind me, I shinny up. Wriggling awkwardly, it feels like I'm going to be spit out of the crack at any moment because, for every difficult foot I gain, I slip a half foot back.

Temporarily wedged, I shine the light at the black catacomb above and see several sinister-looking chockstones that look like they're going to fall on me. But as I struggle through this natural bomb bay, I carefully thread each of those chockstones with nylon webbing and clip my carabiners and rope to them, wondering how much of a fall it would take to avalanche them on top of me. Cursing and grunting, I struggle upward a few inches at a time, knowing I wouldn't fall far before the chockstones permanently wedged my broken legs and back between the narrow walls of this tomb.

If I'm lucky, the chimney will widen above and end in a womblike cave leading to the summit blocks. I follow it, hoping this fantasy will play out. But the higher I climb, the more disoriented I become. It's so dark, I have no real sense of up or down; I only know *this* is the way I entered the chimney, so *that's* the way I continue struggling against gravity—headfirst, until I smash my helmet on the pointed ceiling. When I do, my worst fears are confirmed: dead end. Fear races me back down thirty feet of the most desperate climbing I've done. As long as I control my breathing, though, I don't have to down-climb; my body, pulsating like a snail in its shell, prevents me from falling.

I can see nothing below me except the black hole I once knew as the Grand Canyon; I can see nothing above me except blackness. If I'm about to die, I want to do it climbing as I never have before. Above me, I know, is the off-width George laughed off earlier. Too narrow to chimney in with my body and too wide to jam-climb with my hands and feet, it is the crux of the Midnight Crack, and it defies me to climb it.

Convinced I'm about to take a killer fall, I thread the last chockstone with a nylon runner, insert my left hand and arm into the overhanging fissure, and contort them until it feels like a ten penny nail is sticking in my shoulder. I try to focus all my energy in my pain-racked left arm, and when I pull down on it with everything I've got, it feels like I'm going to pull Zoroaster down on top of me. When I realize the temple is not going to tumble, I stem my right leg against the wall in front of me, but I repeatedly miss the crucial nubbin with my quivering right foot. I begin shaking all over. My left arm feels like it's going to dislocate, and I feel myself start to slip. I scream and begin sobbing until the pitiful cries stop as quickly as they'd begun.

"I gotcha, John!"

"Get us off here, Annerino!"

But their voices are from another world, both of them straining to see that which they cannot: a fading pinprick of light crawling toward the dark, starless heavens.

I never could do a one-arm pull-up, so I take in a deep breath and grab my left forearm with my free hand to prevent my shoulder from dislocating. Hanging by my fist, I relax my right leg as best I can under the torque and strain, then point the toe of my boot at the small nubbin of rock, now dimly lit by the small flickering beam of light. The batteries are starting to fade, and I can taste the salt trickling out of the side of my mouth. My leg quivers like a wand bending in the breeze, but my boot kisses the nubbin. Once, twice, I can feel it, and when the light comes back on I can see it again. I press against the nubbin, caressing it to make sure it won't flake off; slowly it takes the pressure of my weight. I stand up on it and relieve the torturous strain on my twisted arm.

Peace surges through me like a warm, gentle wave when I realize I'm negotiating a crux I could never really see; but I rein in this small feeling of pleasure before it leaves me stranded thirty feet below the summit. I dig furiously into the crack above with both arms. I brace my bruised left knee below, push off with my right leg, and move up again. Just a few more feet and it's over . . .

When I crawl over the edge of the summit block, I spit the flashlight out of my mouth and collapse. I fall into a fitful doze. I don't think about freezing to death in my sleep; it's just that it seems so passive in the cold, and I welcome the rest, at long last.

"Annerino! . . . Hey, Annerino! You awake?!"

I hear voices. Someone's calling me from my dreams: I blink my eyes, but I still can't see anything. It's suddenly bitterly cold and voices are screaming.

"Annerino! . . . Hey, Annerino! You awake?!"

I draw up my left leg, which had been dangling over the edge, crawl on my hands and knees to the nearest bush, and anchor the rope. I remember wiping blood off the side of my mouth before yelling into the center of the earth: "All right, we're up!"

II.

WE ARE LOST IN THE STEEL-GRAY MIST OF FIRST LIGHT, THREE SMALL FIGURES HUDDLED next to the damp, smoldering coals of a dying fire. We are drowsy but anxious. At any moment, the life-giving sun is going to erupt out of the towering precipice of the Desert Facade far to the east; when it does, glorious rays of brimstone burn across Blue Moon Bench and cast us in an ethereal orange mist that stirs the drifting smoke of a fire that stoked our dreams with magic throughout the night. We are groggy, and our bodies are cold and burned: our faces, eyelashes, and whiskers are scorched from restoking the fire through the waning hours of darkness; and our loins are knotted with cramps from turning our backs to the hungry teeth of the wind. We are stiff, sore, ravenous, and thirsty. My ankle feels like a wolf's been gnawing on it. But we are alive, atop the supernal crest of Zoroaster Temple, and we are enshrouded in a holograph of the rising sun, where time, distance, and pain are momentarily suspended.

Levitating in the midst of this Canyon dream, the sun slowly bakes the deep chill out of our haggard bodies, and I gaze into the last burning embers of our fire while George and Dave rustle awake from their own half sleep. I've been dreaming the fire off and on throughout the night, and I've seen a recurring image: that of a man, running alone through the Grand Canyon. I'm not sure who he was; it was just a wisplike figure dancing in the crimson flames as my head drooped on and off my chest and saliva ran down my chin. But he—it—was trailing the arc of the sun, running east to west through the Grand Canyon as far as I can now see through titian clouds that unveil the reality of the dream. From the mouth of the Little Colorado River Gorge, where it spills its turquoise waters into the muddy Colorado River, the tiny figure ran west along the broad, undulating platform of the Tonto formation, 150 stories above the mighty river . . . and he—it—didn't stop running until reaching the sea blue cascades spewing out of Havasupai on the west end of the Grand Canyon.

That's all it was, an image of a man running through a Canyon dreamscape, any man, everyman. But the image stays with me as the three of us rope down the Northeast Arête to the foot of Zoroaster. As soon as I shoulder my heavy pack, I know who that figure was, because pain dogs my left foot the two days it takes us to reach the South Rim. During our journey out of the inner Canyon, I am frequently tempted to share my dream with Dave, George, or even with Chris, who'd kept the vigil of expedition photographer at our advance camp throughout the night. But it seemed too private, even sacred an image, or maybe preposterous, to share. How would they understand the dream if I didn't, and how could I trust them to see the reality of it: running end to end through the timeless realm of the same canyon I was struggling out of.

I wait until I return to Prescott, where I'm soothed by the warm winds of summer blowing through the ponderosa pines outside my mountain cabin, before I phone Tim Ganey. He will tell me if I've gone off the deep end or if somebody—anybody—could run through the Grand Canyon of the Colorado River.

I'd first met Tim in high school when a beautiful girl spun us both around in a lovesick wake. Kathleen had long, brown wavy hair she sometimes festooned with ribbons; she had a warm smile that made my knees weak, a hearty laugh, and a discreet voluptuousness that outclassed her peers. But Tim had the schoolboy charm and Redford good looks, and he stole Kathleen's heart without a fight. Instead of butting heads over her, though, Tim and I became friends, drawn together by the same unending flow of adolescent dreams and ideas. But there was another force at work between us that we could never explain; some might call it mental telepathy, but we didn't know about such phenomena then. More often than not, each of us already knew what the other was thinking without having mentioned it. As a result, I came to trust Tim's judgment and perspective implicitly. If anybody could grasp the incredulous concept of a lone man running through the Grand Canyon, Tim could. I rang him up.

"What do you think, Tim? Honestly!"

"I think it's a great idea."

"But nobody's ever done it before," I protested.

"John"—Tim always used your first name like an exclamation point if he wanted your undivided attention—"That's exactly why we should do it."

Without my even asking, Tim had volunteered to embark on this quixotic journey with me; his enthusiasm was contagious, and Craig Hudson, a close friend of Tim's, was soon drawn in. So the three of us rendezvoused in my Groom Creek cabin to sort the whole thing out. Was it really possible to do what, to our knowledge, no one had ever attempted before? Was it an impossible dream? Or was it a visionary quest you couldn't believe unless you embarked upon it yourself? And if it was possible, could a lone runner survive the extraordinary odds of running through the Grand Canyon? We try to answer those formative questions when we roll the three-foot-long Grand Canyon National Park topographical map across the pine-dusted cabin floor. When we do, it's as though we've pried open a dark, jagged crack in the earth's crust that exposes my deepest fears. Sitting there gaping into the brown, two-dimensional abyss, we wonder what would happen if, instead of viewing this Brobdingnagian fissure as a canyon, we looked at it as an inverted mountain range in the Himalayas. Could we, having been inspired by the mountaineering feats of Hermann Buhl, Maurice Herzog, Reinhold Messner, and others, employ those same Himalayan tactics to running

> He will tell me if I've gone off the deep end or if somebody—anybody— could run through the Grand Canyon.

end to end through the Grand Canyon? Viewing the Canyon as a mountaineering objective, we thought we saw a way to resupply a runner, using the same strategy the legends of the climbing world used to tackle their Himalayan dreams. But instead of using a base camp and advance base camp at the foot of a mountain to support a continuous string of camps leading to a bold summit push, we could establish a roving base camp atop the South Rim and, from it, send support crew members into the inner Canyon to set up one-night spike camps as the runner journeyed east to west through the heart of the Grand Canyon.

In theory, it seemed like a sound approach. And instead of our meeting falling apart under the preposterousness of the idea, Tim and Craig saw a way to reach out for what I believed was far beyond my mortal grasp. When they did, they grew serious; if I was willing to commit to it, they'd do whatever it took to resupply me through the Grand Canyon. All they wanted was to be part of a team that pulled off the impossible.

> The potential hazards of running end to end through the Grand Canyon . . . dehydration, heatstroke, hypothermia, drowning, flash floods, falling, rockfall, rattlesnakes, scorpions, black widows, cactus daggers and thorns, or breaking an ankle in between water holes.

Coming on the heels of our Zoroaster ascent and my painful struggle out of the inner Canyon, it didn't take me long to commit to running the Grand Canyon. My ankle, I was beginning to realize, might never recover sufficiently to climb an eight-thousand-meter peak. I knew I could endure the pain of the two-week approach marches required to reach most Himalayan base camps. But what would happen, I wondered, if my ankle was suddenly frozen with pain while front-pointing up the

Northeast Ridge of 26,795-foot Mount Dhaulagiri, or the Second Step below the summit of Everest? What kind of death trap would I be climbing into? Worse, what kind of icy tomb would that seal my teammates into? Contemplated from that perspective, running the Grand Canyon became my shining light; if my foot couldn't stand the torturous burden of carrying seventy-pound loads up a series of high-altitude camps, I could attempt to run through a canyon that was on the same otherworldy scale as a Himalayan giant. And if my ankle blew apart en route, I'd be the only one facing the risks, because I'd be running the redline solo.

Still, I had no real way to gauge the immense physical scale of my undertaking, so I was continually drawn to the epic ascents of Buhl, Herzog, and Messner, among others. In one of the most remarkable adventures in the annals of Himalayan climbing, French mountaineers Maurice Herzog and Louis Lachenal climbed to the 26,545-foot summit of Annapurna on June 3, 1950; theirs was the first ascent of an eight-thousand-meter peak, and they made it without the use of supplementary oxygen. So did the Austrian Hermann Buhl when he climbed the 26,660-foot Nanga Parbat on July 13, 1953; he also made his legendary first ascent without oxygen, but he climbed to the summit solo after an unprecedented high-altitude bivouac. No stranger to extraordinary odds, bivouacs, and heights was Reinhold Messner; on May 8, 1978, he and fellow Tyrol climber Peter Habeler were the first to climb 29,028-foot Mount Everest without oxygen. Two years later, Messner returned to *Chomolungma*, "mother goddess of the world," as the Nepalese call Everest, to make the first solo ascent of the highest mountain on earth, once again without oxygen. These were the epic tales of men in the Himalayas that helped me put the physical scale of the Grand Canyon into perspective. In so doing, I realized I might not be cut from the same cloth as the Buhls, Herzogs, and Messners of the world and that there was a strong possibility I could die trying to run the Grand Canyon. At the time, an average of one in ten climbers who went to the Himalayas perished from falls, avalanches, seracs, rockfall, crevasses, storms, frostbite, exposure, edema, exhaustion, or simply disappeared. And the potential hazards of running end to end through the Grand Canyon were no less intimidating, among them dehydration, heatstroke, hypothermia, drowning, flash floods, falling, rockfall, rattlesnakes, scorpions, black widows, cactus daggers and thorns, or breaking an ankle in between water holes.

Faced with such prospects, I commenced training (see Appendix) with the knowledge that I was about to face the Everest of canyons and that any one of a handful of dangers could snuff out my life in the wink of an eye. Averaging sixty to seventy miles of running a week through the ancestral realm of the Yavapai, my routes ranged from the level, antelope-covered plains of Coyote Springs at the foot of the Black Hills to the steep mountain roads and trails that climbed the forested heights of Hassayampa Creek, Spruce Mountain, and the Sierra Prieta. Salted in with my running, I maintained a climber's regimen of sit-ups and pull-ups, but I mostly focused on bouldering to prepare myself for any unroped cliff climbing I might be faced with in the Canyon. I also made a frequent practice of running along a three-inch-wide, quarter-mile-long log fence in order to develop the fluid balance and agility I'd need to run the narrow, treacherous paths of the inner Canyon.

> I make a frequent practice of running along a three-inch-wide, quarter-mile-long log fence in order to develop the fluid balance and agility I'd need to run the narrow, treacherous paths of the inner Canyon.

As one week faded into the next, I increased my daily running mileage so that by the time I departed for the Canyon I could confidently run thirteen miles a day of rugged mountain or mesa trails, or roughly one-third to one-half the distance I anticipated I'd need to cover each day between resupply points and the Canyon's life-sustaining water holes. When I wasn't rock climbing on weekends to maintain a psychological edge for dealing with the frightening vertical exposure of running along the cliffs and rim tops of the inner Canyon, I ran in canyon-, mesa-, desert-, and mountain-wilderness and roadless areas to simulate the diverse environmental conditions, physical obstacles, and spiritual challenges I might encounter in the Canyon. In the process, I steeled myself for the loneliness and psychological uncertainty of running unfamiliar terrain without companions or logistical support.

Fortunately, most of these wilderness runs didn't turn into the life-and-death struggle the Galiuros had; in crossing the hard ground of the Aravaipa Apache, I realized I'd made too big a leap too quickly. So I increased the length of my wilderness runs until I could comfortably run twenty-five to thirty-five miles at a crack without caving into fatigue. But one run stood out from all the others in a way that made me reexamine

my motives for running wild in general and for running the Grand Canyon in particular.

Running Paria Canyon, a principal migration route used by Pueblo Indians circa A.D. 1100. The author ran the length of many wilderness areas such as Paria Canyon in preparation for his first Grand Canyon run.

III.

It was a warm sunny day in February, and I was running through the wind-whipped creosote flats of Organ Pipe Cactus National Monument on the U.S.-Mexico border. Pushed by a strong tailwind, I was gliding south across the *bajadas,* "lowlands," that fan out from beneath the volcanic cusp of 3,197-foot Kino Peak when I noticed two sets of footprints; they were headed north across the thorny desert, but whoever made them had to be desperate because both sets of prints were made by bare feet! I knew I was following a border smuggler's route that wound its way toward Phoenix via the desolate back roads of the Pápago Indian Reservation, but what I didn't learn until later was that the tracks I followed south another fifteen miles to the ancient Sand Pápago encampment of Quitobaquito Springs on the Arizona-Sonora line were those of Mexican citizens. They were headed north across the deadliest desert in North America, which patiently waited to swallow them alive. The reason was simple and tragic. The hardworking men who attempted those desperate 50-to-120-mile-long treks most often did so during the summer when farm labor jobs were most plentiful, yet when the desert was at its cruelest. Many did not survive this killing ground, and a terrible death toll mounted into the hundreds of those who perished "commuting to work."

This empty quarter of southwestern Arizona was the same merciless desert the Hohokam crossed circa A.D. 1000. That's when they made ritual two-hundred-mile journeys to the Gulf of California to gather precious glycymeris shells for making jewelry. Perhaps they came from the pueblos near Squaw Peak, Camelback, or Superstition Mountain, but once they ventured south of the Gila River they entered a prehistoric no-man's-land that received less than four inches of rain a year when it received any moisture at all. From the Gila River, the ghost bands of Hohokam tracked south from one petroglyph-covered trail shrine to the next across the forlorn Growler Valley and the bleak lunarscape of the 4,236-foot Sierra del Pinacate before entering the daunting fifty-mile-wide swath of towering sand dunes now known as El Gran Desierto. This desert forms the largest sand sea in North America, and it was the last formidable barrier the Hohokam had to cross before reaching the lifesaving fresh water springs gurgling into the Gulf of California. Upon the Hohokam's return to the valley, many of their blue shells were fashioned into sacred pendants, while others were traded north—perhaps via the *sinagua*, "without water," and the Cohonina people—before they finally reached the Anasazi in the Grand Canyon. It's not known what these ancient traders dreamed of or endured as the sacred blue shells were passed from one hand to another across 350 miles of the most desolate and forbidding country in the Southwest. So one must look to the Pápago to glean any insight into the ocean power the blue shells held for these ancient desert cultures, because half a millennium after the Hohokam made their last journey to the big water, the *tóhono ʔòʔodham*, "people of the desert" (formerly called the Pápago), embarked on their own sacred journeys to the Gulf of California to gather salt along distant trails that shadowed the Hohokam's. Tribal elder José Lewis Brennan wrote of their vision quest in 1897:

Many people
Are just run for miles and
Never get any power
From the ocean.
I suppose there are but very few
Who make their luck and become somebody
Or know something.

Running for miles. To get power. To know something! A spiritual quest for knowledge. These thoughts stayed with me as I continued tracking the bare footprints through the ancestral lands of the O'odham. This fearsome tract of Sonoran desert, what Spaniards called a *despoblado*, "uninhabited land," was also the crossroads for another kind of trail. And none was more feared by non-Indians than the *Camino del Diablo*, "road of the devil." Since 1699, when Padre Eusebio Francisco Kino first crossed the parched, sun-blasted ancestral lands of the *Hía Ced ?O'?odham*, "people of the sand" (called the Sand Pápago), to the west, the 150-mile-long Camino del Diablo claimed hundreds of

> Unless I could discover something of substance about the dawn of Native American running that would infuse my own running with meaning and spiritual renewal, I began wondering what was the whole point of it?

lives. During the 1850s alone, historians estimate that at least four hundred gold seekers—many of them Mexican nationals—died of thirst en route to the California goldfields. By the turn of the century, the Boundary Commission put the death toll at a thousand and stated it was a record without parallel in North America. It still is. What, I wondered, running through the cool winter sands, did the border country's modern gold seekers endure during the height of summer? How did they survive an ancient path of fire that crossed the Devil's Road and followed the timeless tracks of the Hohokam shell trail and the Pápago salt trail on grueling ultramarathon-length ordeals most athletes wouldn't survive? I wasn't sure. But those bare footprints opened my eyes to the human struggle of crossing historic routes and prehistoric trails, as well as to the ancient ways of Native American running and knowledge. Where did each of their pathways lead to? Why and when were they used? What did they see and dream of? And what could it possibly have been like to run them?

When I returned home, my mind swept clean by running through the desert borderlands, I added to the files of ethnographic and historic sources I'd started collecting not long after moving to Prescott, and I came to realize that a mosaic of ancient trails and trade routes still crisscrossed the American Southwest and the frontier of northwest Mexico. I began using these materials to retrace the history of Native American running back to its source.

As a result, I became more and more disenfranchised with a national running craze being hyped by magazines, books, and big-budget advertising of marathons and 10Ks that paid little, if any, heed to the vibrant cultural traditions and history of Native American runners. What, gonzo journalist Hunter S. Thompson asked in *The Curse of Lono,* "would cause 8,000 supposedly smart people to get up at four in the morning and stagger at high speeds through the streets of Waikiki for 26 ball-busting miles in a race that less than a dozen of them have the slightest chance of winning?" Would these same good people be running, I wondered, without the convenience of paved roads? And if their running wasn't linked to their own culture, or a natural lifeway in which running was used for trade, travel, hunting, war, spiritual knowledge, or cultural indentity and survival, what would prevent this modern running boom from going bust? Cold beer, bland spaghetti, and free T-shirts? And where would millions of these same joggers, runners, and racers be five, ten, fifteen years down the road—crippled by the tortuous effects of pounding through asphalt jungles, hobbling around on blown-out knees, riding bikes, or walking? Retracing those bare footprints across the stark desert was a turning point for me, and I posed those same questions to myself. Unless I could discover something of substance about the dawn of Native American running that would infuse my own running with meaning and spiritual renewal, I began wondering what was the whole point of it?

Yet, as much research as I did and as hard as I trained, I was never sure it was enough. Historically, Native Americans grew up running long distances, but I was only a recent convert to it. So I ran harder and longer through the forested realm of the Yavapai, until sometimes I would just "dorph out" after a run and stare mindlessly at the food on my plate, my brain reeling from endorphins, the body's natural opiate. When I discovered the dorph factor, though, I realized that no matter how stiff my ankle might be at the beginning of a run at some point the endorphins would kick in, the pain would disappear, and I would feel as though I were running on air.

I was running so much at seven thousand feet above sea level that I began having vivid dreams about just that—running on air. The dream always started out the same way. I'd be running through the fog-shrouded woods up the road from my cabin, and, ever so slowly, my strides would get longer and longer, and I would stay aloft a moment or two longer with each footstep until eventually I was floating, running above the ground. If I'd used drugs or smoked dope, I would have understood why I was having these astonishing dreams, but I didn't; coffee, aspirin, orange juice, beer, and mountain spring water were the elixirs I used to prepare for or come down from long-distance running. Maybe the dreams had something to do with the fact that I was hypnotized by my research into the Tibetan trance runners called *lung gom-pas* and the teleportation that Chemehuevi runners reportedly used; they were two mystical forms of running that didn't fit within the Western concept of running, and perhaps the esoteric imagery carried over into my dreams. There was no explaining it. But each time I had the flying-running dream—and I had it more and more frequently as the date of my departure for the Grand Canyon drew nearer—I would have sworn I'd actually, physically, run two to three feet above the ground, f-l-o-a-t-i-n-g.

It was too overpowering to focus on the Grand Canyon and running it in its entirety, but, when broken up into segments, its scale became manageable.

I was going to need some kind of spiritual edge in order to pursue my dreams even midway through the Grand Canyon. So I began visualizing the course of my inner Canyon odyssey, the same way I'd envisioned my route through the Galiuros—day after day, until there wasn't any section of it I couldn't clearly call up to memory while running. Only, I didn't just visualize each topographical stretch of the inner Canyon route, I envisioned myself running along a narrow, crumbly ledge high above the roaring Colorado River through an endless V-shaped tunnel that twisted and turned into eternity. It was too overpowering to focus on the Grand Canyon and running it in its entirety, but, when broken up into segments, its scale became manageable—at least psychologically.

That's the way many of the Grand Canyon's early travelers took the immense canyon, in sections. The prospectors who arrived at the Grand Canyon during the 1870s, for instance, were convinced they'd unearth the mother lode somewhere in the depths of what they viewed as an open-pit gold, silver, or copper mine. To reach their pickin's and glory holes, however, they had to forge trails down from the lofty heights of the North and South rims—eighty-four in all—into what for some became a "trap, a prison, or even a grave" and for many others was the last place on earth they should have tread: "Before us frowned hideous escarpments, and on each other walls

> Whether any of the region's indigenous groups ran end-to-end through the Grand Canyon was not known.

hemmed us in . . . a chasm which seemed to fairly yawn for victims . . . the glad sunshine refused to follow us into this gloomy cavernous depth . . . a tremendous gash in the bosom of nature." Such nightmarish perceptions were the antithesis of the sacred visions of the Hopi and Hualapai Indians who revered the Grand Canyon as the opening through which mankind originally emerged.

Many of the miner trails followed the ancient footpaths first made by the Anasazi circa A.D. 850. The Anasazi trekked in and out of the inner Canyon on a seasonal basis to grow food on the fertile deltas along the edge of the Colorado River, to hunt desert bighorn sheep along the precipices of the inner gorge, and to gather agave hearts and hunt deer on the forested rims high above. But the faint trails of the Anasazi, those of the region's later indigenous peoples—including the Paiute, Hopi, Navajo, Havasupai, and Hualapai—and the miner trails that, for the most part, followed their paths plunged off the edge of the Grand Canyon directly into its depths in rim-to-river fashion. Records that the Anasazi undoubtedly traveled east to west through the inner Canyon along its narrow terraces, or even along the broad bench of the Tonto formation, to reach the twenty-five hundred Pueblo-style cliff dwellings they inhabited at the height of their civilization were difficult to ferret out.

The record is held by an old man . . . who ran to Moencoppi, nearly fifty miles away, and back each day throughout the summer, spending an hour there working in the fields.

Although anthropologists and historians had reliable records of people like the Shivwits band of Paiute crossing the western Grand Canyon and Colorado River from the North Rim to the South to visit and trade with the Havasupai, the only people known to enter the Grand Canyon from the east and to travel any distance to the west were the Hopi. In their own words, the Hopi of the Coyote, Sand, and Sun clans periodically made sacred salt pilgrimages from their villages on Third Mesa to the mouth of the Little Colorado River Gorge a hundred miles west. Paying solemn reverence to their deities en route, the Hopi followed the deep tributary chasm of the Little Colorado River Gorge west into the hidden recesses of the Grand Canyon to their sacred salt mines. It's not known for certain if—during journeys unrelated to their salt pilgrimages—the Hopi ever ventured farther west through the inner Canyon along the Colorado River and Tonto formation to their mines on Horseshoe Mesa, where they collected blue copper ore for ceremonial face paint, or, if they did venture that far through the inner Canyon, if they continued farther westward along the Tonto formation to the Havasupai living at Indian Gardens. Nor is it known whether the Indian Gardens' band of Havasupai ever followed the Tonto formation into the setting sun to reach their distant village of Havasupai on the west end of the Grand Canyon or whether they also limited their east-west travel to the ancient Hopi-Havasupai trade route atop the South Rim to link key access points into the Canyon's depths. Constructed by miners during the 1880s, the seventy-two-mile-long Tonto Trail traced the paths of the Anasazi across this broad inner Canyon terrace. If fever-struck Anglo prospectors could follow it, what was to prevent the region's indigenous people from using the Anasazi trail system? These were some of the questions I'd hoped to answer.

Whether any of the region's indigenous groups ran end to end through the Grand Canyon was not known, either, but each came from a strong, often sacred running tradition. The early Hopi, for one, were formidable long-distance runners. An enlightening account was published in the August 1909 edition of *The Border*; in an article titled "Life and Its Living in Hopiland," Kate T. Cory wrote:

> It is doubtful if any tribes of Indians or any groups of white men in the country can average with the Hopi in running: it is instinctive with him; wherever he goes afoot, if any distance, he runs, striking a rapid springy trot, the right arm crooked, and working back and forth as he speeds along; and he seems not to know what it means to tire.
>
> Thirty miles a day to Keams Canyon is an any day jaunt for him; and the railroad, sixty-five miles away, he makes if a good runner easily before sunset. The record is held by an old man, now in the happy hunting ground (the "Skeleton House" the Hopis have it) who, so the story goes, ran to Moencoppi, nearly fifty miles away, and back each day throughout the summer, spending an hour there working in the [corn] fields.

The ancient trade route traversing the seven-thousand-foot-high Coconino Plateau on the Canyon's South Rim linked the Hopi villages with the Havasupai two hundred miles west. During his travels throughout the region in 1775–1776, Spanish missionary and explorer Francisco Tomás Garcés first documented the Hopi use of this route to trade with the Havasupai, but it's not known how frequently it was used or during which seasons. If they needed to follow the route during the winter to barter for precious seeds, bighorn sheepskins, herbal medicine, or red ocher paint and it was buried under snow, was there an alternate route? If so, wasn't it most practical to follow the Little Colorado River Gorge westward through the balmier depths of the Grand Canyon along the ancient paths of the Anasazi along the Tonto formation to reach the Havasupai? And if any of the region's indigenous people did make use of an inner-Canyon trade route, wouldn't running have been the most efficient way to cover such distances?

> An Indian has been known to carry a letter from Guazapares to Chihuahua and back again in five days, the distance being nearly eight-hundred miles.

Without the benefit of oral histories or written records to draw on, I turned my attention to Mexico's Sierra Madre Occidental six hundred miles southeast of the Grand Canyon in hopes of shedding some light on these questions. There were many historic—and more recent—accounts of Chihuahua's *rarámuri*, "foot runners" (commonly known as the Tarahumara), running for days on end through the mile-deep *barrancas*, or canyons, of the Barranca del Cobre region, an area reportedly larger than the two-thousand-square-mile extent of the Grand Canyon of the Colorado River. One of the most enlightening accounts of the Tarahumara's running prowess came from Norwegian explorer and anthropologist Carl Lumhultz; he spent five years journeying throughout the Western Sierra Madre during the 1890s to witness the Tarahumara, Tepehuán, Huichol, Cora, and Tarascan Indians in their ancestral domain. Of the Tarahumara runners, Lumholtz wrote:

These runners show a remarkable endurance. An Indian has been known to carry a letter from Guazapares to Chihuahua [city] and back again in five days, the distance being nearly eight hundred miles. In some parts where the Tarahumaras serve the Mexicans they are used to run in wild horses, driving them into the corral. It may take them two or three days to do it, sleeping at night and living on a litle pinole. They bring in the horses thoroughly exhausted, while they themselves are still fresh. They will outrun any horse if you give them enough time. They will pursue deer in the snow or wild dogs in the rain for days and days, until at last the animal is cornered and shot with arrows or falls easy prey from sheer exhaustion, its hoofs dropping off.

Using the Tarahumara as a yardstick, it seemed probable that any one of the Grand Canyon's indigenous groups had the stamina and intimate knowledge of water holes, topography, and survival to run through the inner Canyon. Each came from a rich tradition of running: Havasupai children were taught to get up at dawn and run toward the rising sun as far as they could before turning back. Paiute runners were one of the only groups of Native Americans reported to run antelope to death, and when Mormon pioneers were accompanied by a group of eighteen Paiute rabbit hunters they recalled they trotted easily alongside their horses without tiring. During the four-day Navajo puberty ceremony of *kinaaldá,* "changing woman," young women were instructed to run to the four directions while the medicine man chanted the sacred verses of the Navajo Emergence Story:

My little one, they run out shouting, they run out shouting,
My little one, they run out shouting,
My little one, they run out shouting, they run out shouting,
My little one, they run out shouting.

However, while running was the most efficient means for the Tarahumara to travel long distances within Mexico's own Grand Canyon,

I couldn't locate oral histories or anthropological records of the Navajo, Paiute, Havasupai, Hualapai, Hopi, or Anasazi having run end to end through the Grand Canyon. If any of them had, that sacred knowledge was lost. What could it have been like, I wondered, for an ancient Native American to run—as the Tarahumara

> Tonight, I would come to know this memorable path by feel.

still do in their own rugged barrancas—through the Grand Canyon? What was the most practical route to follow? When did they run it? And if they made such a journey, wouldn't they go in winter or spring, when the Canyon's marginal water sources had been recharged by precipitation— as indigenous trails and trade routes were traditionally followed throughout the arid Southwest and northwest Mexico?

These were some of the hypothetical questions that helped me look at the Grand Canyon from a human perspective. If I looked at it solely from the standpoint of tackling an inverted Himalayan mountain range, running the Grand Canyon seemed so far beyond my grasp I never would have considered stepping off the rim and into the heart of stone. But if I looked at it in the light that somebody might have made the fleet-footed journey before—whether in prehistoric or more recent times—it was conceivable not necessarily for me but for someone to run the Grand Canyon of the Colorado River. With Tim and Craig standing squarely behind me, I was willing to run the gauntlet.

I thought about that as I ran along the historic wagon route marked by the Senator Road. The night was coal black, and it was snowing heavily. Large feathers of icy snow frosted my face and body as I galumphed through deep, soft snow that buried my tracks as quickly as I made them. It was surprisingly warm for a snowstorm; I could feel sweat, mixed with melting snow, drip down my neck. Winter had just about played itself out, and spring was nearly upon us. I was headed toward the headwaters of Hassayampa Creek; during spring runoff it roared through the forested breach of Spruce Mountain and Mount Union, and it marked the turnaround point for the daily fifteen miles I tried to burn up and down this historic trail in preparation for my inner Canyon journey. In the process, I'd logged so many miles on this route, which roller-coastered through the lush stands of ponderosa pine, spruce, and fir, that I knew every twist and turn, every blind corner, and every vista: the gnomelike clusters of granite boulders I spent hours climbing, the spike camps still held down by prospectors trying to hit pay dirt, the tall pine tree I was chased up by a sow javelina, the summer camps city dwellers used to cure their ills in the wilds. Tonight, I would come to know this memorable path by feel.

That's what I was doing now, running blind through a blowing snowstorm, because maybe there was one last lesson to glean from the Bradshaw Mountains before I dropped over the edge of the world or maybe I just needed to shake out my Canyon jitters. The snow crunched underfoot as I padded along what felt like a wet wool blanket. My lungs heaved in and out, my arms pumped. I breathed in snowy drafts of mountain air, the snowflakes dissolving on my tongue and throat with each deep breath: *hih-huh, hih-huh, hih-huh, hih-huh, hih-huh.* Nothing could stop me tonight; I felt so strong and alive. This was my own sacred realm, and I'd come to revere it the only way I knew how—by running. I just hoped what I'd learned here and elsewhere throughout the Southwest could be shape-shifted along my inner Canyon path.

Soon, I will be running wild through what was the last frontier in the American Southwest to be explored by non-Indians.

I wasn't sure, but I knew I was headed toward the site of the old Walker camp, kicking small white footballs of snow out in front of me with each step. Made up of thirty-four prospectors, the Walker party was led into the rugged Bradshaws by legendary mountain man Joseph Reddeford Walker in May 1863; the six-foot Tennessean guided them into the heart of the Bradshaws, after a roundabout two-thousand-mile journey, in hopes of hitting the mother lode. That they did, and the rich placers they discovered led to the founding of Prescott as Arizona's "wilderness capital." Wrote one expedition member: "We considered our long journey at an end [near the headwaters of Hassayampa Creek], for at last we were in the unexplored regions of central Arizona, the place of our destination."

When I finally reach the vicinity of their rustic camp, I am covered from head to foot with a half-inch layer of snow. The night has somehow grown darker, and I am alone in these black mountains, alone in my dream of running the big canyon. Standing in ankle deep snow at the edge of Hassayampa Creek, still silenced under winter's embrace, along the very route Walker's "Hassayampers" used to escape the deadly clutches of the Sonoran Desert, I cannot hear a sound except for my breathing, and all I can see is the dream of the canyon journey beyond. Soon, I will be running wild through the last frontier in the American Southwest to be explored by non-Indians. I only hope it won't prove to be my own final destination. I didn't know, but I was about to find out.

4

THE ABYSS

You must write yourself off before

any big climb. You must say to

yourself, 'I may die here.'

Doug Scott,
Himalayan climber

ONE MOMENT I AM STANDING ON THE EDGE OF THE 7,360-FOOT-HIGH COCONINO Plateau, staring into the fearsome depths of the most magnificent canyon on earth, my nerves raw with dread and awe; the next moment I am free-falling into the abyss, plunging downward, endlessly down, down, down toward the very center of the earth. The irrepressible force of gravity has swept me off my precarious perch, and what emerges before me as I continue floating down a steep, dusty trail on the eastern end of the Grand Canyon is a mirage of dreams that commences with the thundering hooves of horse thieves riding hell-for-leather 150 miles across this corrugated terrain to Utah and the edge of frontier justice. Unarmed except for a knife, carrying two bota bags of water, and a small rucksack, I trail that image like a posse until it dissipates into the whirling dust of a *remolina* spinning through the depths of the Canyon far below.

As I plunge deeper through unfathomable layers of geological time and run farther beneath towering walls of stone, that image fades into the next: That of the great Navajo warrior Manuelito. Known to his people as *nabááh jiłt'áá*, "warrior grabbed enemy," Manuelito led a frightened band of western Navajo down this same treacherous path in 1863 to escape the scorched earth campaign of Colonel Christopher Kit Carson. And they spin out their own whirling dervish of dust, screams, and sacred dreams to destroy their enemy on the pathway before me:

Enemies that shall die,
Of the coyote that shall eat them,

Of the crow that shall eat them,
Of the magpie that shall eat their flesh,
Of the wolves that shall eat their flesh
And carry away every part of them.

But the *diné*, "the people" (commonly known as the Navajo), weren't the first to descend into the Grand Canyon near here. Led to the South Rim by Hopi guides, who used Tanner Canyon as the western path to reach their sacred salt mines, García López de Cárdenas was thought to be the first non-Indian to see the canyon in 1540, when he determined the Colorado River did not look so far away. But after three days of fruitless struggling toward the same river I now see winding out of Marble Canyon into the gaping chasm of the Grand Canyon, Cárdenas's three scouts were forced to crawl back out, prompting Cárdenas to write later in his journal: "What appeared to be easy from above was not so, but instead very hard and difficult." That's why I tried not to focus on the reality of what I was doing—attempting to run from one end of this incredible canyon to the other. I just had to step off the edge of the Coconino Plateau and jump feet first down the Tanner Trail in hopes of outrunning my fears into the depths of the Canyon—the fear of failing at such an extraordinary quest, the fear of having to crawl back out of the Canyon along the route of Cárdenas' failed expedition to reach the *río tizón*, "firebrand river."

These were the thoughts and images that whirled around me and through me as I whipped into the stony basin between Cárdenas and Escalante Buttes, following a trail of dreams also used by a host of early settlers. Seth B. Tanner, for one, was said to have rebuilt "an old Indian trail" in 1889 to reach his copper mine near the river's edge. Married to eighteen different women, Mormon polygamist John D. Lee also used this trail to hide his legendary cache of lost gold. So did moonshiners who, during Prohibition, used this same trail to reach their stills in order to line their pockets and soothe the parched throats of South Rim tourists. But this last thought dissolves as I slowly regain my composure on this historic spoiler's route.

Crisscrossed on my chest like bandoliers, my bota bags swing in rhythmic unison with my breathing—*hih-huh, hih-huh, hih-huh, hih-huh, hih-huh*. My footsteps float on an incandescent cushion of red dust. My running is effortless, *hih-huh, hih-huh, hih-huh, hih-huh, hih-huh*. I have hit my stride, and, physically, I feel indomitable. Yet, as I streak across the hard red ground of the Supai sandstone, kicking up dust with each footfall, I am suddenly seized by the stark realization that there is a very good reason no one, in recent memory, has run end to end through the Grand Canyon: the utter feeling of insignificance that overcomes me. Did the Anasazi experience a similar feeling of being swallowed alive? If so, did they stare into the eyes of this fear while singing for power on a rocky promontory during a lone vision quest *"Aye na-ya-ya-ya, aye na-ya-ya-ya, aye na-ya-ya-ya, aye-na-ya-ya-ya."*? Or did they revere the living power of the great canyon with other pueblo members, their gaunt faces lacquered with red ocher and deer grease paint, their necks adorned with blue shells the Hohokam carried from the ocean, their lithe bodies covered with the sacred plumes of eagle feathers, as they danced throughout the night by the light of ceremonial fires? I don't know.

> I just had to step off the edge of the Coconino Plateau and jump feetfirst . . . in hopes of outrunning my fears into the depths of the Canyon.

So I stop a short distance ahead, remove my rucksack, and crawl into a small cave. Carefully, I begin digging with my fingers in the powdery red dirt for the straw sandal I know is beneath. I'd found the ancient relic lying on open ground years ago, and after showing it to my students, I'd reburied it in secret so other backpackers or scientists wouldn't steal it. When I feel the coarseness of the matted straw, I carefully remove the fragile remnant and watch tiny cascades of red dust spill off it onto my sweaty legs. I stare at it and wonder who wore it? Was he carrying a crude pack on a trump line? Did he run into the Canyon, or did he run *through* it, as the Tarahumara still do, wearing handmade *guaraches* (leather sandals), in the deep barrancas of the Sierra Madre far to the south? What did he dream about? Did he have a spirit song he chanted during his sacred journey into the earth's core, so near the Hopi's hallowed *sipápuni,* the opening through which their ancestors emerged from the Underworld? Was he Anasazi? Or was he Hopi, using the western path to reach the sacred salt mines? I

I am suddenly seized by the stark realization that there is a very good reason no one, in recent memory, has run end-to-end through the Grand Canyon:

don't know. But holding the matted-straw sandal, I know I am no longer on a historic trail but on an ancient pathway that will lead me to my own. The sandal is tangible, physical proof of what esteemed anthropologist Robert C. Euler discovered in the Canyon not so long ago:

> Four thousand years before Major Powell's men tumbled through the Grand Canyon in their wooden boats, before geologists and archaeologists investigated its lessons and records, before photographers adjusted their focus and tourists stood on the South Rim in awe—four thousand years before all this, human beings had wandered the Canyon's depths.

As I now was, only I was running through the chartless spiritual realm of the Desert Culture and, later, the Anasazi; yet, in this fragile sandal that once guided calloused feet through the stony domain of the inner Canyon, I had a tenuous spiritual link to the past that indicated I was on the right path, a path that would undoubtedly raise more questions than I could answer, a path that could snatch away my life like the flicker of a chuckwalla's tongue. But it was my quest, and my path, and I now had to follow it, wherever it might lead me and however it might end.

I carefully rebury the sandal, and, as I step backward, I whisk away my footprints with my sweat-stained red bandanna; I am brushing out my telltale tracks, as border phantoms do far to the south, so that the ancient sandal might remain sealed in the red earth, undisturbed for the next millennium.

I start running again down this ancient pathway, my tiny tracks mere pinpricks beneath the mile-high wall of the Palisades of the Desert to the east. I am alone. I am insignificant. My movement within this canyon is inconsequential to the Canyon itself, to world events unfolding far beyond the reach of the South Rim, but at last I am emerging from the dream of running the inner Canyon into the reality of it.

Descending the Tanner Trail to the Colorado River like a tumbling drop of water, I'm struck by the realization that I have finally stepped across the threshold from illusion to what I imagine is real. And what I imagine is real is that I've fallen nearly a vertical mile within a linear distance of eleven, and my pummeled, blood-gorged thighs tell me I've run it too quickly. But any pain I feel is eclipsed by the fact that I've reached the Colorado River at Tanner Rapids at twenty-seven-hundred feet above sea level. And as benign as the churning waves look to me, I know that the river and the natural forces that created it are responsible, in part, for carving a canyon that the best scientific guesses estimate to be 1.7 billion years old—far beyond my own comprehension of time and space. What I do understand, dripping with sweat and mesmerized by the ceaseless ebb and flow of the river, is that the Colorado River rises on the west slope of the Continental Divide, near 10,175-foot La Poudre Pass in the Rocky Mountains of Colorado. And try as modern man has to tame this mighty river with engineering marvels of concrete and steel, it continues to flow all the way to tidewater at the head of the Gulf of California, some fourteen-hundred miles downstream from its source.

Barely a dozen miles into my own journey, I have reached River Mile 68.4 (measured downstream from River Mile 0 at Lee's Ferry). It was here in 1959 that an unidentified boy tried to save himself after his trip leader fell to his death and his young companion died of thirst while attempting to hike rim to river and back via the Tanner Trail in a single day. Faced with death by dehydration if he followed their path, the boy made a desperate attempt to float on a log all the way to Phantom Ranch twenty miles down-

> Running through the tammies, I am repeatedly flogged and swatted and jabbed with sharp, brittle branches.

stream. Fortunately, he was rescued before he was swept into the deadly maelstrom of Hance Rapids and added to the Colorado River's voracious toll. Before 1950, the *Río Colorado*, "Red River"—as it was called by Spanish explorer Juan de Oñate in 1604—had already claimed the lives of thirty-eight people by the time the first hundred Grand Canyon explorers and adventurers had successfully navigated it.

Here, at Tanner Rapids, I turn left and head west through the Mojave Desert scrub toward the forbidding entrance to the Upper Granite Gorge; this was the endless V-walled tunnel I'd envisioned running along, during my training, high above the roaring Colorado River. But temporarily coursing through it, along the south side of the Colorado River, is a heavily beaten path used by hundreds of river runners who plunge through the frothing rapids and legendary big drops of the Colorado River each year. The trail follows the edge of the river through virile stands of "tammies," or tamarisk trees which have been strangling the river since they were introduced to Arizona from the Middle East at the turn of the century. Running through the tammies, I am repeatedly flogged and swatted and jabbed with sharp, brittle branches. But there is no escaping this punishing thicket of tammies until I reach Cárdenas Creek three miles later. When I do, I'm covered with irritating green needles and nettles and showered with tammie dust, and the salt burns the blood-streaked webs of scratches that cover my arms, legs, and face.

I stop, remove my pack, and immerse my body in the frigid river. Historically, the temperature of the Colorado River averaged between seventy-five and eighty-five degrees during the late summer months, so it was easier for horse thieves to swim their horses across the low-water ford upstream at Lava Canyon and for the Shivwit Paiute and Havasupai to cross the river on their inter-Canyon trade route far to the west. But that was during pre-dam days. Spewing out of the chilly depths of Glen Canyon Dam, the river temperature at this point now averages between forty-five and fifty-five degrees. And when I dunk my hot, sweaty body into it, it feels as though I've fallen through a hole in the ice. I shudder and shake vigorously then grab the base of a tammie before I'm swept hopelessly downstream. Revitalized, I drag myself out and, still dripping with Rocky Mountain snowmelt, shoulder my pack and bota bags and start running again, sloshing through the sand in wet shoes and socks up a steep trail that leads to a perch of Anasazi ruins atop Unkar Hilltop.

Situated on a high bluff overlooking the bold sweep of canyon both upstream and down, this cluster of ruins is one of twenty-five hundred ancient dwellings recorded in the Grand Canyon that date back one thousand to four thousand years. Like the ancient sandal, these small stone dwellings are, for me, a trail shrine that connects my inner Canyon pathway. Seeing them fortifies me to plunge farther into the reality of the dream of running end to end through the Grand Canyon, but they also pose questions: Did the Anasazi use the same route I used to reach this pueblo from the South Rim? Did the Anasazi follow what has been described as the "prehistoric Indian route going north from the Tanner Trail over the pass between Escalante and Cárdenas Buttes," a steeper, more direct approach? Or did the Anasazi, like the Hopi who later followed their ancient footsteps, travel west through the inner Canyon along routes from the Little Colorado River Gorge or Tanner Canyon? These were questions I hoped to answer by running.

But before I run farther along this ancient pathway, I lie down on my stomach, grab the edge of the precipice with both hands, and peer straight down at the green river boiling through Unkar Rapids far below. River Mile 72.3 is yet another historic milepost along the Colorado River. On May 26, 1955, canyoneers Harvey Butchart and Boyd Moore were crossing the river on air mattresses, near the Hopi's sacred salt mines far upstream, when Moore fell off and drowned. His body was never recovered, but his pack was eventually found below Unkar Rapids. Fortunately, Moore's tragedy didn't prevent Butchart from becoming the Grand Canyon's eminent non-Indian canyoneer, and in 1962 a Welshman named Colin Fletcher looked him up. Fletcher had seen the Canyon and was so moved by the experience he dreamed of walking through it from one end to the other, but he was uncertain as to the exact route to follow. Butchart provided the missing links for Fletcher's dream. Two months after leaving Hualapai Hilltop, Fletcher completed his odyssey and became "the first modern man to have gone the whole length of the National Park [walking]." But when Fletcher, backpacking west to east through the inner Canyon—contrary to the direction I was traveling, reached the foot of Unkar Rapids, he was able to make his way along the bottom of the immense head wall I was staring down; at the time, the river was flowing at a mere trickle of 1,250 CFS (cubic feet per second). But today the river is so high, pummeling the arching red wall of Dox sandstone with six-foot waves, I've been forced to take this breathtaking detour.

I get up. And with more uncertainty than ever, I start running along this promontory until I find a way back down to the river on the other side and the route I'd planned to follow downstream through the Upper Granite Gorge to Hance Rapids. I know this difficult leg of the route parallels Fletcher's, and Tim, Craig, and I had discussed that fact at length. But we decided it was best not to try and compare the two journeys. While Fletcher used Butchart's extensive experience to guide him along each stage of his route, Fletcher was the first known person to tie Butchart's marathon-length weekend sorties together in one continuous trek. And while my own route would follow in the footsteps of these two men, and those of Anasazi and indigenous Canyon dwellers who preceeded them, I was trying to compress a two-month backpacking adventure into a weeklong journey by honing down the quest to its most basic element: that of a lone man running. And because we were categorically opposed to using air support for food drops, as Fletcher had on three separate occasions, our food drops were to be carried into the inner Canyon on foot. And had we not known of Fletcher's successful journey, we still would have plunged headlong into our quixotic adventure together—precisely because of what we didn't know and because we were pulled by the same irresistible forces that lured Fletcher into stepping across the brink from his own dream into the reality of crossing the inner Canyon on foot.

> I'm now faced with two dangerous option: I can backtrack . . . or I can attempt an unnerving hand-traverse along a narrow ledge above the icy river.

But this isn't merely a dream, because, when I reach the river again on the other side of Unkar Hilltop, the route I try following along the river-bank disappears in heavy stands of tammies, deep sand, and slippery ledges of red shale. It's terrain that probably should be walked, but I am still trying to define what may have been possible for the Anasazi to run and what was not. So I carry on, hopping from ledge to ledge, drifting in and out of a blur of green tammies and pockets of sand dunes.

I stop when I reach Seventy-five Mile Rapids; it's eleven in the morning, and the route ahead is blocked by a series of impassable cliffs jutting out over the river. I'm stuck. If there is an Anasazi route around this Cenozoic barrier, I don't know where it is. But I've got to find a way. I had told Craig when he dropped me off at the head of the Tanner Trail to wait one hour; if I didn't crawl out of the Canyon with my tail between my legs by then, he was to tell Tim to gear up for the next three resupply points and then begin hiking down the Grandview Trail to upper Hance Creek. That's where I'm supposed to meet Craig tonight for the first food drop.

But I'm now faced with two dangerous options: I can backtrack to Unkar Hilltop and look for a route that courses high above the river, but that would sap what little energy I have left—if I didn't perish from thirst along that grim stretch. Or I can attempt an unnerving hand-traverse along a narrow ledge above the icy river, in hopes I can maintain a more direct route along the river, my only source of drinking water.

The choice is obvious, or so I think. But my mind is so fuzzy from the heat and from having daydreamed through several hours of running that I don't realize what I've done until it's too late; fifteen feet along a narrow catwalk, the consequence of falling twenty feet into the icy river hits me. I try to backtrack, but I'm too nervous with fear to safely reverse the moves. If I fall, I'll plummet like a stone with this pack on, and I'll be dragged to the bottom of the river to meet what seasoned river guides call the "green slime" and get trapped in its deadly embrace before I can shed my pack and kick and fight my way back to the surface to breach for air.

I begin groping blindly with my fingertips, but each hold I test breaks off in my hand. Clinging by my fingertips and two narrow toeholds, I feel myself start to to slip. The pack and bota bags are dragging me off. I slip, my right leg barn-doors, and I lunge desperately, sinking my left hand in the jam-crack above; it's solid. Dangling above the river by my clenched fist, my feet temporarily riveted to a pinch of rock, I squeeze the water out of my bota bags with my free hand and blow them up with air to act as a crude flotation device, in case I peel off. The strength draining from my left shoulder, I unclip the waistband from my pack as gingerly as possible, slide off the right shoulder strap, then let the left strap slide down to my elbow. Unharnessed from this deadly anchor, I'm ready to move again.

But Hance soon discovered, as other prospectors had, that there was more money to be made guiding tinhorns into the Canyon than hauling low-grade ore out of it.

Reaching blindly around the right corner, I pull off another handhold. I try again, more frantic than before; as I do, I slide the inside edge of my right foot around the hairline ledge to support my probe. I stretch farther, teetering, but I manage to latch on to a good handhold; at least it feels good, but after my fall I've never trusted rock like this. Now I have to, or I will fall, freeze, and drown. I release the fist jam and commit to the move; I swing across—and the traverse goes!

I breathe a deep sigh of relief as I scramble back down to the river and trot along the intermittent sand and rock to the mouth of Pápago Creek. Here I'm faced with a second airy traverse above the river, but it proves less difficult and dangerous than the first. Once I complete it, I'm relieved the rest of the route to my first resupply point won't entail any more rock climbing.

By the time I reach the mouth of Red Canyon, however, I'm dripping with a nervous, foul-smelling sweat, and I'm dizzy with fatigue. For the first time, I'm having serious doubts about running with a fifteen-pound pack, but I wasn't sure how else to carry the marginal supply of food and bivouac gear I'd need if I couldn't make it to the first resupply point before nightfall. Yet, I'm reluctant to leave anything behind.

So I crawl into the sparse shade of a white boulder near the junction of the Hance and Tonto Trails in hopes of escaping the brunt of the ninety-degree heat. I feel nauseated, too nauseated to eat, and my head is spinning. The fact that I'm laid up next to the cacophonous twenty-eight-foot fall that Hance Rapids makes through the Upper Granite Gorge, one of the Colorado River's legendary big drops, hardly registers. I suck down water and drift in and out of a haze.

I dream of Hance, not the rapid—which has become a soothing, resonating background hum surging through the rugged black walls of the Upper Granite Gorge—but the man; "Captain" John Hance he liked to call himself. He came to the Canyon from Tennessee in 1883 and rebuilt an Anasazi trail down Red Canyon to reach his asbestos mine on the other side of the river. But Hance soon discovered, as other prospectors had, that there was more money to be made guiding tinhorns into the Canyon than hauling low-grade ore out of it. As a result, Hance spun tales as big as the Grand Canyon itself. And many tourists believed his stories, especially those fogbound on the South Rim. That's when the bearded canyoneer would walk up to a group of unsuspecting tourists and say, "Fog's about right to cross." Hance would then lace on a pair of snowshoes, tromp over to the edge of the Canyon and test the consistency of the fog with one of his snowshoes; then he'd turn back to the puzzled tourists and say, "It's just right for crossing. But it's shorter to the North Rim if I start from Yaki Point. Watch tonight and you'll see my campfire over there." The lanky Tennessean would head into the woods and wouldn't show his face until the next day, then he'd ask them, "Did you see my fire on the North Rim last night?" If they had, he'd give them a wink and a wry smile; if they hadn't, he'd tell them, "Well, I couldn't see your lights over here, either . . . The fog was pretty thick going over and I made good time. But coming back was different. The fog was thin and it sagged under me at every step. It was like walking on a feather bed and now I feel plumb wore out. Guess I'll take a nap before supper. If any of you folks would like to try it, I'll be glad to lend you my snowshoes next time she fogs up good and solid."

That's what I was hoping for, for it to fog up good and solid, because I no longer felt like running on hard brittle rock. I longed to run on the same pillowy ground I'd crossed during the Hassayampa Creek snowstorm only weeks earlier, even if I had to run the Canyon at night. But there isn't a cloud in the sky, and the white sun hammers me as I trudge up the Tonto formation through the skull-numbing heat. Situated near the four-thousand-foot level, fifteen hundred feet above the Colorado River and three thousand feet below the South Rim, the terrace of Upper Sonoran desert I'm running along begins here at Red Canyon, in the eastern half of the Grand Canyon, and ends more than ninety miles to the west. I'd envisioned this terrace as the most ideal inner Canyon route for the Anasazi to use in order to reach distant pueblos—as well as other fleet-footed traders—primarily because it's the broadest bench coursing east to west through the Grand Canyon. It was along this seemingly flat bench that promoter Robert Brewster Stanton had also envisioned laying tracks for the Denver, Colorado Canyon, and Pacific Railroad at the turn of the century, had he received funding; fortunately, he did not. What has been laid down over the ancient sandal tracks of the Anasazi, instead, is the Tonto Trail, and it slithers its way along the Tonto formation like a hydra-headed pit viper. I was planning to make a beeline along the Tonto all the way to the South Bass Trail, where I'd connect with another ancient trail network that would guide me the rest of the way to Havasupai. But today, the Tonto formation is overrun with feral burros, beasts of burden turned loose by prospectors like Hance, Louis D. Boucher, and others, the kind of animals naturalist John Muir liked to call "hooved locust." And throughout the long afternoon, I run, then repeatedly backtrack, along a confusing network of wild burro trails that frequently branch off the main stem of the Tonto Trail and end in debilitating culs-de-sac.

There are no crowds, and there is no aid station fanfare, when I struggle into our first resupply point in the blistering desert sun late that afternoon. I'm totally spent, and Craig is stretched out on a foam pad, dead to the world. "Craig!" I whisper. He looks at me, startled, as if he's seeing an apparition; but I can't believe what I'm seeing either. We'd planned to rendezvous here, at this exact pinpoint in the middle of the Grand Canyon—on paper, in theory—but neither of us can quite believe that we have done it.

> But here we are, shocked by the fact that we somehow reached our first rendezvous point together.

It's not that we doubted each other's ability to reach this rendezvous on time, it's just that neither of us had ever done anything like this before. But here we are, shocked by the fact that we somehow reached our first rendezvous point together.

I drop where I stand and begin rummaging through Craig's pack for a beer. If the Tarahumara, long heralded as the greatest long-distance runners in the world, spent a third of their time preparing, drinking, or recovering from the effects of a milky-white corn beer called *tesgüino*, we figure we deserve a brew for our own efforts. I rip open the tops, and hot foam jets everywhere, we carry our sudsing beers into the shade of a cottonwood tree sustained by the trickling waters of Hance Creek.

Green leaves and white clouds flutter together overhead and I soon lose myself in them, hypnotized by the poetic movement, thirst, and fatigue. But I can't stomach the bitter ale and instead relish drinking the sweet, gnat-infested creek water that soothes my feet as the mirage of leaves and clouds flutters faster and faster, spinning my head around and around, until I hear Craig say, "Didn't think you'd make it here today."

"I didn't, either," I tell him.

"How was it?" he asks.

"Craig, it happened so fast, it was like watching a movie. But it was strange, 'cause it seemed like it took a week . . . know what I mean?"

"Yeah."

But he doesn't know what I mean anymore than I do. It's just mindless chatter, trying to express what can't be said . . . until the mirage of green leaves and white clouds whirl faster, and faster, and I rest my head on the ground in hopes of stopping the endless spining of the earth, sky, and canyon. I can't. So I clutch at the dirt with my fingers and hang on to keep from being swept away.

II.

IT'S HALF PAST SEVEN, AND THE FIREBALL OF DAWN BURNED OVER THE EDGE OF THE
Canyon ages ago; a monotonous veil of gray clouds blots out the sun,
extinguishing the flaming pastels that once painted the soaring red cliffs.
The air is suffocatingly humid, and I feel as though I'm running through
eternity—*hih-huh, hih-huh, hih-huh, hih-huh, hih-huh.* Endless footsteps
nibble away at the Tonto Trail, a mere two and a half to three and a half
feet at a time. I am nothing more than an ant being charging through a
great gash in the earth. And my mind is too clouded with fatigue to accept
the fact that I'd run the day before what it would have taken me three to
four days to trek. Nor does the Canyon's exalted scenery awaken me from
my sleeprunning, as I continue winding in and around flying buttresses of
Redwall limestone—a five-hundred-foot-thick layer of 335-million-year-
old marine fossils, that's gouged by deep caverns and streaked with curtains of iron oxide: *hih-huh, hih-huh, hih-huh, hih-huh, hih-huh.* My only
conscious thought is linear motion: what will it take to run around the
deep travertine drainages, which cleave the Tonto formation in five different sections between me and the South Kaibab Trail, my next resupply
point and, if need be, my only escape route out of the Canyon twenty
miles west? I don't know. Cut by eons of headward erosion, the dark, dangerous tributary drainages of Cottonwood Creek, Grapevine Creek,
Boulder Canyon, Lonetree Canyon, and Cremation Creek form often
impenetrable side canyons, and they are further incised by precipitous,
sometimes overhanging, sub-drainages and canyons. Together, the gauntlet of canyons that stands between me and the South Kaibab Trail, and the

Grand Canyon's seventy-odd other tributary canyons, funnel spring snowmelt and summer monsoon rain into the Colorado River from the rim world a vertical mile above. In so doing, these canyons within the Canyon will prevent me from making what I envisaged in the crimson firelight atop Zoroaster Temple as an arrow-straight run through the heart of the Grand Canyon. Then, that dawn vision was an illusion to the reality of

Before I have time to consciously react, I'm leaping over the striking pit viper.

following the trail of the Anasazi across the Tonto formation, which geologist Edwin McKee described in *The Inverted Mountains*:

> The airline distance between those places Red [Canyon in the east] and Garnet [Canyon in the west] . . . is not many miles, but the actual travel distance is unbelievably great, for it is necessary to skirt around the heads of innumerable canyons and many branches to each of these. Frequently one sees one's goal a half mile or so ahead but has to travel two to three miles to attain it.

The illusion and the reality of running the inner Canyon: were the Anasazi wizards at time traveling, as the Chemehuevi runners of the Mojave Desert far to the west were said to be? I'm not. And as I continue heading west, running in and around the unending branches of these dark, serpentine crevasses—through black brush scrub, yucca, and agave—a dull stream of images whirls around me: Craig's knee-wrenching descent down the Grandview Trail; his lung-searing crawl, cigarette in hand, back up the ancient Hopi trail to coordinate the next food drop; his unwavering belief that I'd deliver on my next promise—"I'm not sure how, Craig, but I'll make it to the South Kaibab tonight." These are the images that whirl around me as my body continues to float across the Tonto, drawn deeper into the clutches of the unknown, pulled by the illusory forces of the Canyon itself.

The cold fangs of reality lash out at me when I round the western escarpment of 5,236-foot Horseshoe Mesa. Coiled like the tail of evil in front of me is a Grand Canyon Pink, or Mojave rattlesnake. But before I have time to consciously react, I'm leaping over the striking pit viper. My foot lands; the fangs whip at me; a puff of dust whooshes up my bare leg. And the next moment I'm back in ICU, at the bedside of my snakebitten sister. On the brink of death, her left thigh is a hideous blue and so swollen with edema it looks like it will burst. Her calf is gridelin, and her foot has turned a ghastly hue of black.

I focus on the tangible physical elements of running: the sweat dripping down my sunburned cheeks; the salt burning my cracked lips; the pasty saliva coating my tongue; the rucksack slapping my back . . . the path . . . where one misstep means a deadly drop a thousand feet or more.

Her black, leathery toes look like they'll fall off to touch, and her entire leg—well, it doesn't look like a leg anymore—her entire limb is oozing with pus-filled lesions and pocked with ulcerous cavities dissolving blood, muscle, and bone from the ravenous hemotoxin of a Diamondback rattlesnake. "Mrs. Annerino, would you please sign this release? We need to amputate." Thank God she stood her ground again and told them, "No, absolutely not!"

The strike is complete. The ivory white, hypodermic fangs fold back into the sheaths of the serpent's mouth. The Mojave coils again. And I escape by a hair'sbreadth the horror of my sister, who hobbled away from surgeons' knives with all but a few toes intact.

Rattled awake by this brush with death, I pick up my pace in hopes of shaking off these haunting memories as I continue striding endlessly to the west, wondering if perhaps this snake was from a world still unknown

to me: *hih-huh, hih-huh, hih-huh, hih-huh, hih-huh.* For Navajo traditionalists, the Grand Canyon is *Áshiih,* the sacred cave of Salt Woman.
And if such spirits still dwelled in the Canyon, as Native Americans have
long known and revered them to do, were they all benevolent or were
there others that could bring me harm? If they could, would running
through the sweat lodge of the inner Canyon cure me? Or would it take
the sacred cane of a *toxó buaxant,* a Southern Paiute snake doctor, or the
hand-trembling, visions, and sand paintings of a Navajo *Hataaĺíí,*
"singer," chanting a Holyway ceremony to cure me:

Aye na-ya-ya-ya, aye na-ya-ya-ya, aye na-ya-ya-ya, aye na-ya-ya-ya . . .

Rub your feet with pollen and rest them.

Rub your hands with pollen and rest them.

Rub your body with pollen and lie at rest.

Rub your head with pollen and put your mind at rest.

Then truly your feet become pollen.

Your hands become pollen.

Your body becomes pollen.

Your head becomes pollen.

Your spirit will then become pollen.

Your voice will then become pollen.

All of you is pollen.

And what pollen is, that is what peace is.

The long trail ahead is now a beautiful trail.

Long life is ahead, happiness is ahead.

Aye na-ya-ya-ya, aye-na-ya-ya-ya, aye na-ya-ya-ya, aye na-ya-ya-ya . . .

As my footsteps crunch through the sand, gravel, shale, and coarse,
shoe-ripping Muav limestone, I focus on the tangible physical elements
of running: the sweat dripping down my sunburned cheeks; the salt burning my cracked lips; the pasty saliva coating my tongue; the rucksack
slapping my back with a thump-bump every time I take a step; the path
and how it traces the black, crumbly edge of Tapeats sandstone, where

one misstep means a deadly drop a thousand feet or more into the Upper Granite Gorge. But the Canyon, the Grand Canyon of the Colorado River, and the omnipotent force it exerts over all my senses, deprives me of what tenuous contact with physical reality I'm able to maintain with these simple thoughts. And throughout the hypnotic morning hours, which slowly dissolve into the dreary noontime hours, I feel as though I'm nothing more than an ant being whose progress through the Canyon is controlled by forces far deeper than my own cognizant drive to run through the Grand Canyon. *Aye na-ya-ya-ya, aye na-ya-ya-ya, aye na-ya-ya-ya . . .*

During epochs lost to Western thought and modern memory, Cremation Canyon was believed to be used by prehistoric Native Americans who burned their dead in blazing funeral pyres on the rim thousands of feet above. As I stride through this aboriginal burial ground, an eerie unworldliness of shadows and darkness overcomes me. I can hear the promordial screams and resonant chanting of shamans echoing off the canyon walls as they hurl fire falls of corpse powder, burned chips, and splinters of bone upon me, *aya' na-ya-yah eh-eh-eh, aya' na-ya-yah eh-eh-eh, aya' na-ya-yah eh-eh-eh,* showering the chasm with the charred, smoldering remnants of their spirit-kin, while I fight to escape the grip of this fearful ground. Was it taboo to even be here? It felt like it, but I had no warning, unless the rattlesnake was a sign; but I did not have the spiritual knowledge to interpret it as one. Was this sacred ground for the Navajo, Hopi, Paiute, Havasupai, or Hualapai? The U.S. government did not think to ask the Grand Canyon's indigenous people before forcefully displacing them to create a national park for non-Indians in 1919. Instead, what appears on the U.S. Geological Survey topographical map is a simple and telling name for those who know how to read it: Cremation Canyon. Anglos and Native American "progressives," however, have been sternly lectured from childhood on not to believe in such matters, but traditionalists who have seen the Great Spirit, been touched by the Holy Ones, been blessed by the *katcinas,* or been hunted by the Skinwalkers know the power and sanctity of sacred ground. There is no explaining it. They are messages carried on the winds of nature and indigenous man, often in ceremony: *aya' na-ya-yah eh-eh-eh* . . .

Struggling alone through the heat and miasmas of this ancient burial ground, I find my pack is a burden I can no longer bear. I stop. A zephyr of dust swirls around me and spirals up in the hot yellow sun. *Whoosh!* Suddenly, I'm staring at the great white horn of Zoroaster Temple towering four-thousand feet above the Inner Gorge of the Colorado River. Huddled around our summit bivouac fire, there was no better place to view the dream of running the inner Canyon than from the loftiest perch in the Grand Canyon; now, but a pilgrim struggling at the foot of that great temple, I know the reality no longer coalesces with the dream, and my efforts to run the loose talus and rock scree out of Cremation Canyon are pitiful. Fortunately, I have the ancient route of the Anasazi to lead me the rest of the way out; as long as I can stay upright, moving, I will not be seized by ghostly visions of Skinwalkers blowing corpse powder in my face. *Iissshhh!*

In *The Grand Canyon of Arizona*, photographer and writer George Wharton James wrote:

> The old Tonto Trail—the trail made centuries ago by mountain sheep [desert bighorn], small bands of which are still to be found in the remoter corners of the canyon, then followed by the Indians, whose moccasined feet made less impression upon it than did the hoofs of the sheep. And in the two or three decades just passed, a few white men trod it.

As I now did, leaving even less of an impression with my feeble efforts to run a pathway to self-discovery almost a century later.

The midday sun has burned a hole in the cloud cover, and I am flaccid with fatigue and heat stress by the time I reach the junction of the South Kaibab Trail. A major milepost on my journey, this heavily used trail is one of the only rim-to-river trails that did not follow the natural sandal- and moccasin-beaten paths of Native Americans or the hand-forged trails of prospectors laid down on top of them. With the hard labor and sweat of Havasupai trailblazers, the National Park Service chiseled and dynamited this declivitous trail into the Canyon in 1925; park officials wanted an alternate to the nearby Bright Angel Trail, because hostel-er Ralph Cameron had the gumption to charge a dollar a head for any-one who wanted to use his trail.

Standing here in the middle of the Grand Canyon, my body festering in the sun like the blisters on my feet, I can easily envision the "gigantic squirming centipede" march of two mules and fifteen Havasupai dragging five-hundred-foot strands of shoul-der-burning steel cable into the depths of the Canyon, in order to hang the Kaibab Suspension Bridge like a gangplank across the Colorado River. With more than fifty-thousand people hiking to the bot-tom of the Grand Canyon each year, the Havasupai weren't the last to put their faith in that vital inter-Canyon link. The fastest among the new wave of inter-Canyon visitors was Allyn Cureton. Hailing from the nearby lum-ber town of Williams, Cureton ran like a deer twenty miles across the Canyon, via the North and South Kaibab Trails, in less than three hours and eight minutes; his record crossing was made on well groomed canyon trails, but it entailed a vertical descent of 5,740 feet, followed by a punishing vertical ascent of 4,810 feet.

> I'm repeatedly forced to stop and drink in hopes the putrid water will stave off heat exhaustion. But I'm feverish and dizzy, and my thighs are flamed out.

I take a long pull from my bota bag; the water is hot and putrid, and I feel like gagging. I cross this historic thoroughfare, then strike out for Indian Gardens another five miles distant, ancient home of the *havasúwa ʔapača*, "people of the blue-green water" (commonly known as the Havasupai). I know this short leg is the most well manicured stretch on the entire Tonto Trail, not only because it provides backpackers with a vital link between the South Kaibab and Bright Angel Trails, but because presumably it's the flattest stretch of the Tonto formation between Red and Garnet Canyons. It's so level that in 1922 Commander R. V. Thomas of the British Royal Flying Corps barnstormed off the South Rim and landed his puttering, single-engine Thomas Special near Plateau Point, screeching to a stop in a cloud of dust on a hastily built runway fifty feet from the edge of a deadly plunge into the Inner Gorge. But what was white-knuckle flying for the World War I ace is dreary labor for me. I'm repeatedly forced to stop and drink in hopes the putrid water will stave off heat exhaustion. But I'm feverish and dizzy, and my thighs are flamed out. So I stumble into the lean shade of a boulder and pass out on the ground until I feel strong enough to run a few hundred yards farther. Then I'm forced to sit down again and stare at the ground, my cramped and clammy legs stuck to the mud-, silt-, and sandstones of the Tonto like a fly in ointment. I repeat this debilitating process over and over, until I've finally covered the interminably long and monotonous two-and-a-half-mile stretch to Pipe Springs Canyon.

I'm met there by Ginny Taylor and, difficult as it is for me to focus, my eyes still stinging from the heat and sweat, I can see she is beaming. In the winter of 1976, Ginny and her companion Chris Wuerhman became the first known canyoneers to trek end to end through the Grand Canyon below the largely trailless, seldom-explored North Rim; in terms of modern Canyon exploration, it was the next frontier to cross after Colin Fletcher's South Rim trek. And it's an enormous stroke of luck to have this lithesome blonde on my support crew, because Ginny has the ability to read the Grand Canyon's scale and natural lines of weaknesses better than anyone I've met. Holding me up with both arms, she notices my vital signs, and, without allowing me to cave in to the emotion of our reunion, she pumps fresh water down me in an attempt to stave off heat exhaustion; she does. Shadowing me like an old range hand, she drives me the rest of the way into Indian Gardens, home for the night, I think.

After Cremation Canyon, this former Havasupai encampment is the next ancient link along my inner Canyon pathway. It was within this oasis of cottonwood trees, sustained by soothing perennial water, that the kaθadevhé, "coyote tail," band of Havasupai sought refuge after being displaced from their eastern homelands in the Little Colorado River Valley. During his exploration of the Painted Desert and Grand Canyon region at the turn of the century, George Wharton James saw the small plots of land the Havasupai had under cultivation at Indian Gardens; he also penned a telling passage that may be the only record of this inner Canyon route being used by the Havasupai: "This [the Bright Angel Trail]—as were all the trails from the Little Colorado River to Havasu Canyon—was used first long ages ago by the Havasupais."

Any intention I'd had of staying at this historic Havasupai encampment turned Park Service heliport and backpacker way station is aborted, because Dick Yetman has other logistical plans from Tim and Craig. After cracking us each a bottle of Mexican beer, Dick and Ginny push me the next couple of miles along the Tonto formation to Horn Creek. There, Chris May, a former student of mine, has our camp set in a hollow beneath an overhanging roof of Tapeats sandstone. Chris has learned his lessons well, because he plies the three of us with a sumptuous meal of quesadillas, canned oysters, strawberries, and hot black coffee.

> All I want to do is stay in the safety of my sleeping bag and forget I'm trying to run through the Grand Canyon . . . I've got the dry heaves, and my ankle feels like a ball of fire.

Lying on my back, staring at the fluted Canyon walls soaring overhead, I'm slowly recovering from the day's struggles, but it's difficult for me to hold back the tears; after two days of struggling alone through the inner Canyon, it feels strange to have the companionship and camaraderie of friends. I couldn't be more grateful, and I welcome their warm, encouraging words well into the moonlit night, which shrouds the Canyon in a lunar mist. Still, our rendezvous seems more illusion than reality; none of us is quite able to grasp that, together, we're running through this mystical canyon of stone and light. While there have been fleeting moments of clarity and reality throughout my journey, it still feels as though the run never really moved from the dream to the reality of it. Then, maybe that just isn't possible in the Grand Canyon. As one writer wrote: "Men began to make marks in the canyon, and the canyon marked them in return, for no man can truly see the Grand Canyon and afterwards be entirely the same." I wasn't.

"John, wake up; it's time to go."

Early the next morning, I hear Chris May's deep voice muffled outside my sleeping bag. I pull the covers back over my head and blot out the Canyon because I no longer have the will or desire to expose myself to it. It's just out there waiting, a living entity, waiting to consume whatever energy, emotion, and dreams it didn't suck out of me the first two days. But Chris nudges me again.

"John, you've got to get going."

I don't want to get going. I know it's late; flies are already buzzing around our lair, a dangerous sign the heat is already reflecting off the looming Canyon walls.

But all I want to do is stay in the safety of my sleeping bag and forget I'm trying to run through the Grand Canyon. As Dave was so fond of saying after our Zoroaster climb, "I

The pain I thought I'd finally escaped has rendered me helpless . . . I cannot—do not want to—continue. It's beyond my capacity to endure.

feel like I've been eaten by a wolf and shit over a cliff." I'm nauseated, I've got the dry heaves, and my ankle feels like a ball of fire. But Chris and Dick drag me out of my sleeping bag, and, after dressing, I reluctantly start heading west again, in the footsteps of the Anasazi, along the endless Tonto.

Any freedom of running I'd felt the previous two days is now restricted to a debilitating hobble-run. My right leg, the workhorse of the pair, takes the brunt of the torturous jarring every other step I take. But it's not enough. Each time my left foot kisses hard rock, a searing pain knifes through my leg, and tears and sweat roll down my cheeks. For the first time in years, I hear myself repeating those awful words: "You'll never run again . . . never run again . . . never again . . . "

After six years, I thought I'd grown callous to the pain, proving to myself that if I couldn't fulfill my dreamy lust of climbing Himalayan peaks I could seek my vision and limits of self-discovery through the wondrous, airy dance of *running wild*. Because I'd learned, often the hard way, how to stay beyond the reach of pain. But this time, I've crossed the line, and the pain I thought I'd finally escaped has rendered me helpless in the maw of this great abyss.

I cannot—do not want to—continue. It's beyond my capacity to endure. I stop hobbling and woefully consider my plight: failure. What will it taste like? How will I live with it, today and in the years to come? What will these friends think, who've put their own lives on hold to help me? Not much. How could they? But before I'm overcome with self-pity, Dick nudges me from behind. Reluctantly, I take the bamboo cane he offers and hobble a few more steps. It feels as though I'm running on raw nerve endings, and I stop again. I'm aware of nothing other than this miserable, throbbing pain. My pain. Not even the Grand Canyon, in all its hoary power and majesty, can eclipse it. Yet, Dick knows which buttons to push: he toys with my misery by threatening to photograph me if I so much as look as if I'm going to stop and walk. For a while (I'm not sure how long) his taunts prove too much for my pride and I accept his challenge by painfully running ahead—until the pain finally severs my will to go on.

Desperate, I reach down deep for inspiration, but there was only one story I knew of that could put my plight into perspective: that of Thomas L. Smith. The year was 1827. The Kentucky-born mountain man was reportedly "shot by an Indian" while trapping beaver on the east slope of the Rocky Mountains. But the camp cook couldn't stomach the thought of amputating Smith's leg with a swift whack of a bowie knife across a tree stump. So Smith drank a bottle of whiskey and, with the help of Milton Sublette, cut off his own leg below the right knee! Smith was carried on a stretcher to the Green River, a principal tributary of the Colorado River, where he wintered over in the care of his three Indian wives; one was said to be a Snake, another a Utah, and another a Shoshone. The herbal poultice Smith's wives repeatedly dabbed on his bloody stump proved a near-miraculous cure, because the following spring *We-he-to-ca*, or "Peg Leg," was strong enough to ride seven-hundred miles southwest to the Mexican border. There, Peg Leg and his companion, French fur trapper Maurice LeDuc, headed through "the weird, frightening Algodones sand dunes west of what is now Yuma [Arizona], where the furnace-like heat sucks moisture out of a man's body." Peg Leg and LeDuc led their packstring of pelts, stolen from their boss Ewing Young, west across this searing, hardscrabble desert in hopes of trading them in the small Spanish coastal settlement of the Pueblo de Nuestra

> Having whimpered and hobbled nearly every step of the way today, I have trouble believing . . . I'm going to race through the Canyon even faster than our most optimistic projections.

Señora de los Angeles. Some historians believe the pair was in the grip of the Mojave Desert, between the Borrego Badlands and the Cargo Muchacho Mountains, when Peg Leg and LeDuc discovered, scattered atop "three golden hills," a mother lode of black gold nuggets. Their claim, disputed to this day, became the legend of the Lost Peg Leg Mine; fact or fancy, the whiskey-loving, bar-brawling, pelt-and-horse-thieving Peg Leg came from an era of wooden ships and iron men.

Still hobbling one peg-legged step after another, I realize my pain couldn't possibly be worse than hacking off your own leg with a bowie knife. And should I succeed on my own quest, which now seems remote, the end would eclipse my torment and pain. Stumping along the Tonto one leg at a time, I only hoped that my gamble to cross this inner Canyon desert would pay off, as Smith's had in crossing the Mojave desert.

By the time I reach Hermit Creek, still stumping ahead of Dick, I know I'm going to do whatever it takes to reach the end of this journey, if I have to crawl on my hands and knees through the rocks, cactus, bur sage, and agave to do it. It can't possibly get any worse.

But Prescott climber Brian Gardner is waiting for us at Hermit Creek, and he bears strange news. "Tim is skipping the Hermit [food] drop and headed to the South Bass," he says, stabbing the air with his cigarette.

Having whimpered and hobbled nearly every step of the way today, I have trouble believing that my resupply crew, moving like chessmen atop the game board of the South Rim, thinks I'm going to race through the Canyon even faster than our most optimistic projections. By way of the Tonto Trail, and the wearisome maze of feral burro trails that stray from it, the South Bass Trail is forty to fifty miles away! Without the Hermit food drop, the South Bass Trail is far beyond my striking distance. And Dick knows it. There's only one option: send a messenger. Without asking, Dick says goodbye and starts running up the Hermit Trail—a steep, cobblestone stairway that climbs a calf-torquing thirty-five hundred vertical feet in seven miles—in hopes of catching the resupply crew before it heads to the South Bass.

Between 1912 and 1930, Hermit's Camp was a one-night stopover for dudes who'd ridden into the Grand Canyon on Fred Harvey mule trips. For the rest of the afternoon, I soak my weary legs in a rock tank of slime-green water below this old mule skinner's outpost at the foot of 4,871-foot White's Butte. I marvel at the ease with which water spiders glide across the shimmering surface of this Canyon pool and wonder what it'd be like to run through the inner Canyon so effortlessly. I'm also left wondering whether Dick's long shot will pay off. I know I wouldn't have made it this far today without his help. And when Tim Ganey and Margie Erhart finally show up at sundown, I know my journey may have ended right here if Dick hadn't made a heroic sprint for the South Rim.

With darkness enveloping the inner Canyon, it's too late to cover the next eight miles to Boucher Creek, my original destination for day 3. So Tim breaks open the first of several six-packs, and the four of us pass the evening under the starry canopy of the Milky Way, trying to forget the improbability of success on a journey that's momentarily linked us all together. Snippets of conversation drift past me as I nod on and off from fatigue: something to do with news releases being sent to the Arizona dailies and the progress reports Tim and Craig are airing live each morning with Phoenix deejay Bill Heywood, but none of it really sticks. And the next thing I know, Tim is saying, "John, get in the bag."

"Yeah, okay, Tim."

A friend from the past, the brother I never had, Tim tucks me into my sleeping bag as though it's the most important thing he could be doing. I watch him take a pull from his beer, voices wish me well, and the starry canyon night fades to black.

III.

THE SOOTHING MELODY OF HERMIT CREEK RIPPLING IN MY EARS AWAKENS ME LONG before first light the next morning. Squinting through the moist, narrow slits of sand-blasted eyelids, I'm mesmerized by the twinkling heavens still showering the Canyon with stellar dust. Falling stars streak across the heavens trailing luminescent tails of phosphorous light from the shadow wall of the South Rim through the black hole of darkness formed by the North Rim. In the background, I hear the Canyon rhapsody of crickets and the mellifluous cooing of mourning doves as they flutter their damp, dewy wings in the brittle branches of a mesquite tree. I fumble for my small flashlight and begin surveying camp for other signs of life. The long, narrow beam of light swings back and forth across the dark ground, revealing clothes, gear, canteens, boots, socks, and cooking pots strewn about, as though our camp has been ransacked by raccoons or ringtailed cats. Puffy faces squinch out of sleeping bags, not quite ready to leave their wombs. One by one, I focus my light on each of them: Tim, then Brian, Margie, and Ginny. Their haggard flashlit faces are masks of fatigue, sunburn, and, for Tim, the indefatigable leader, stress. It's obvious they've each paid dues to get me this far. I flick off the light and stare at the constellation of Aquarius, the Water Bearer, but it's too late to start dream-traveling among the heavens now. I don't know what to do. It's obvious I can't hold up my end of the bargain to run the Grand Canyon. My ankle failed me yesterday, and I have no idea what I'm going to do about it today.

Reluctantly, I wiggle my foot, the same way I've done every morning for the last half dozen years. There's been no more accurate a barometer than this simple test to tell me what kind of day I'm going to have, whether I'm going to hobble around like an old man or whether I'm going to dance down the street like Bojangles himself. But I don't feel a thing. There is no pain. Nothing. Fearful that I'll awaken a monster, I slip out of my sleeping bag, carefully put my bare foot on the ground, and stand on it. But the only sensation I feel is the soothing pressure of moist sand conforming to my flesh. I lift my right foot off the ground and hop up and down on my left. Still no pain. I run in place. Nothing. I slap my foot down hard on the ground. Nothing. The pain has vanished.

> Aye na-ya-ya-ya, aye na-ya-ya-ya, aye na-ya-ya-ya,
> aye na-ya-ya-ya . . .
> Then truly your feet become pollen.
> Your spirit will become pollen.
> All of you will become pollen.
> The long trail ahead is now a beautiful trail.
> Aye na-ya-ya-ya, aye na-ya-ya-ya, aye na-ya-ya-ya,
> aye na-ya-ya-ya . . .

I suck in the cool morning air as traces of first light brush the fire-hardened black rims of the Canyon lavender and pink. I want to scream out and blast the Canyon awake: I'm whole, I'm alive again! But I sense that frantic tingling again, my nerves suddenly exposed to the same dread and awe I had when I plunged down the Tanner Trail three days earlier. I have forty-five miles of no-man's-land to cross by nightfall, the equivalent of the Galiuro Mountains laid down in the heart of the Grand Canyon—only this daunting leg of my inner Canyon route is completely walled in by the imposing brink of the South Rim, imprisoning me in an escape-proof corridor formed by the unbreachable Redwall formation to the south and the black chasm of the Inner Gorge to the north. Beyond Boucher Creek, there's no way out of the Canyon that I know of until I reach the South Bass, and I simply do not know whether I can run that far between sunup and sunset after what I've endured to reach this point.

I slip into my running shoes and lace them on like dancing slippers; once again, I crisscross my bota bags on my chest like bandoliers. I lash a rolled-up parka (prepacked with rations and survival gear) around my waist like the wide leather belt of a holster. I kick the rucksack aside in hopes someone will burn it. I turn around and start running, glancing back at the four sleeping bags squirming in the sand like multicolored grubs. My support has no idea what they've done for me, and today, live or die, I will run for them.

Ten minutes out of camp, however, one of my bota bags ruptures, douching my legs and feet with two precious liters of cold, chlorine-treated Hermit Creek water. But there is no turning back today for any reason. I'd promised myself yesterday that if, by some remote chance, fate smiled on me today, I would burn my bridges and risk everything to reach the South Bass Trail, the next resupply point and escape route intersecting the Tonto formation to the west. But reaching the South Bass represents more than that now; if I have any hopes at all of running in the footsteps of ancient traders through the Grand Canyon, I have to run this corridor virtually non-stop. So I hastily scrawl a note on a torn piece of map and leave it with the dead bota bag on a trailside boulder: "Bag broke. Don't worry. Feel great. Should be plenty of water en route. See you in church, amigos. Annerino."

> I's obvious I can't hold up my end of the bargain to run the Grand Canyon. My ankle failed me yesterday, and I have no idea what I'm going to do about it today.

According to Tim's weather reports, the high for the inner Canyon today is predicted to reach the mid-nineties, give or take ten degrees for the Tonto. Still, I'm confident I'll find enough seasonal water en route to the South Bass to replenish my remaining bota bag with the two to three gallons of water I've been drinking each day. That was one of the main reasons Tim, Craig, and I agreed the best time to attempt running through the inner Canyon would be late April: Nighttime temperatures would be mild enough to survive a bivouac in the open if, for some reason, I couldn't make it to the next resupply point between sunup and sunset. (That posed an interesting question in itself: with twenty-five hundred dwellings scattered throughout the Grand Canyon, would ancient traders have had to cover such distances

> My bota bag is my hourglass, against which time and life are now measured in precious mouthfuls.

between pueblos, kin, and food—if they'd made such journeys? I doubted it.) Yet, the most important reason for choosing late spring was that, ideally, most of the major tributary drainages would still be running with snowmelt, permitting me to run from water hole to water hole through this inner Canyon desert the way Native American runners and traders had done elsewhere throughout the desert Southwest—provided my other bota bag didn't break. But I couldn't be certain about that, so I just keep running through the golden light of dawn as it paints the towering walls, hanging alcoves, and amphitheaters of stone with a warm glow that, in a matter of hours, will turn into a searing heat.

As I run, a song plays in my head; there's no stopping it, and it drums me for miles across the Tonto:

It is night, my body's weak, I'm on a run, no time to speak, I've got to ride, ride like the wind to be free again,
And I've got such a long way to go, such a long way to go, to make it to the border of Mexico.
So I run like the wind, run like the wind . . .

I run, run like the wind, dancing with joy along a pathway that arcs like a rainbow from one end of the Canyon to the other. The running is pure fantasy; it is the running-flying dream come to life; there is neither effort nor any hint of pain. It is pure flight. I suck in deep breaths of crystal morning air; I blow heavy drafts of carbon dioxide across my lips. My arms swing back and forth in graceful cadence to my legs, which bound and fly over the terrain: *hih-huh, hih-huh, hih-huh, hih-huh, hih-hih.* It's here, somewhere in the reverie of the Tonto, with the sun slowly burning over the edge of the Desert Facade far to the east, the silver strand of the Colorado River roiling and glimmering below, the multilayered tiers of stone stair-stepping from rim to river, that I realize I am having the finest hour of running in my life. If I go no farther than Boucher Creek, this incomparable feeling of flight is the payoff for all the pain and torment I've ever felt, because, now, finally, I'm *running wild* through the Grand Canyon, floating through my dream.

Named for French Canadian Louis D. Boucher, Boucher Creek is a small, pristine oasis at the end of what was called the Silverbell Trail in 1891. For me, there's never been a more beautiful and secluded spot to just sit and while away the hours than this secret haven tucked into the deep folds of the Tonto, because it was here that the white-bearded hermit, who was said to "ride a white mule, and tell only white lies," supplemented the meager pickin's from his copper mine with a small orchard of peach, pear, and apple trees and a verdant garden of chilies, tomatoes, and melons. It was here that I first introduced my students to the timeless wonders of the Grand Canyon, and it is here I want to stop and immerse my body in the mesmerizing waters of Boucher Creek as it gently winds its way through the hermit's Eden down to the Colorado River. But I simply cannot. My bota bag is my hourglass, against which time and life are now measured in precious mouthfuls; the sun will have climbed too high and the precious water will have drained away, if I stay here longer than a few moments.

Like a water spider skating across a canyon pool, I keep running, effortlessly. But something is strange. It feels like someone is staring at me. They *are*—backpackers. And when I finally notice them, I see them sitting like a row of mummies, leaning against orange nylon packs; they are wearing khaki shorts and trousers, floppy white hats, and dark sunglasses; zinc oxide covers their noses, and little silver cups dangle from their belts. There's an unworldly feel to the scene. Not that I didn't expect to see hikers, even in this remote sanctuary a ten-mile drop off the South Rim; it's just that, except for the handful of hikers I saw clustered around the South Kaibab and Bright Angel Trails, the inner Canyon has been surprisingly devoid of people this spring. But the expressions of this group betray their collective disbelief that they're looking at a lone man running from where to who-knew-where? For a moment I'm tempted to stop and explain, until one lady remarks, "Why, what a lovely place for a morning jog." *A what?* I think to myself. I turn, keep running, and don't look back.

Once I regain the Tonto formation on the west side of Boucher Creek, I make a mental checklist of the daunting canyons and travertines that await me beyond. River guides call them "the gems" for the namesake rapids they create at their confluence with the Colorado River: Topaz Canyon, Slate Creek, Agate Canyon, Sapphire Canyon, Turquoise Canyon, and Ruby Canyon, followed by Serpentine Canyon. As with the gauntlet of canyons that had to be run to reach this point, there are no easy shortcuts around these dark serpentine crevasses, and each has to be completely contoured sub-canyon by canyon in order to proceed west across the Tonto formation in the footsteps of the Anasazi. Today, however, Topaz Canyon and Slate Creek are easy marks, and both are running with water. Still, this is the first day I refuse to look back to see how far I've come— I'm so intimidated by the hard ground and the incomprehensible scale and distance I've got to run by sundown. More importantly, I don't want to break the point of focus that might be propelling me forward.

By the time I stride into the head of Turquoise Canyon, however, I'm on the verge of "hitting the wall." I'm dorphed out: I can't do simple math without a pencil; and I'm hungry enough to eat a bar of soap. I start wolfing through my meager rations, two foil-wrapped bean burros, in hopes the carbo load will replenish my depleted glycogen reserves before I start running again. But before I can swallow the last mouthful, my eyelids droop closed. I lie down on the bare ground, curl up like a stray dog, and go to sleep, belching as I doze.

Canyon dreams dance in my sleep, those of ancient hunters, bounding from boulder to boulder beneath the towering red walls. They are running in deerskin moccasins, traditional breechcloths, and beaded buckskin shirts. Crude metal knives dangle from concho belts, and mountain lion quivers loaded with reed arrows swing back and forth across their backs. Each carries a bow in one hand and water in small pine-pitch-covered baskets that bounce up and down. They run like the wind, their shoulder-length black hair swept back in the breeze, as they float through the canyon singing:

A-ye-he, a-ye-he, a-ye-he-e-e-e-á, A-ye-he, a-ye-he, a-ye-he-e-e-e-á, A-ye-
he, a-ye-he, a-ye-he-e-e-e-á, A-ye-he, a-ye-he, a-ye-he-e-e-e-á . . .
He dreamed he was in another country,
where a cooling wind blew,
and girls in a little circle danced:
A fresh wind in that land
girls circle around.
He dreamed he went to a strange land,
where men continually danced
while singing this song:
Go away somewhere, hungry.
Go away somewhere, hungry.
Go away somewhere, hungry.
A-ye-he, a-ye-he, a-ye-he-e-e-e-á, A-ye-he, a-ye-he, a-ye-he-e-e-e-á, A-ye-
he, a-ye-he, a-ye-he-e-e-e-á, A-ye-he, a-ye-he, a-ye-he-e-e-e-á . . .

When I finally wrest myself from sleep, my legs are knotted with cramps and paralyzed with lactic acid. Worse, my stiff, leaden body tells me my physical collapse point has been reached. But I have no choice; I have to keep running. Perched two thousand feet above the Colorado River and three thousand feet below the South Rim, I can't go up, and I can't go down. I can only go west. Except for the refried beans still clinging to my teeth and mustache, I'm out of food, I'm midway across this inner Canyon frontier, and I'm completely locked onto this hanging terrace, until I reach the South Bass.

I crank myself back into a standing position and focus on forty-two-hundred-foot high Shaler Plateau, a scorpion-shaped buttress poised above the Tonto formation that looks like it'll devour anything that passes within its grasp. I run toward it; it is nothing more than an illusory barrier to run through and beyond. I try not to let any other thoughts or visions enter my mind other than the mental image of a canyon dweller running unscathed through the cluches of this monument of stone.

Throughout my research, there have been Eastern thoughts and concepts that did not fit on the same page as the Western notion of running or within the cultural realm of either the Grand Canyon or Native American running. One such discipline was that of Tibet's running lamas, or *lung gompas,* who once mastered a mystical and psychic form of running called *rkang-mgyogsngosgrubs,* "success in swiftness of foot"; they did so in order to embark on religious pilgrimages that required practitioners to run virtually nonstop

> These astonishing running monks reportedly chanted their mantra . . . until they'd completely dissociated themselves from the physical act of running . . . actually teleporting themselves through their spiritual landscape.

several hundred miles across a twelve-thousand-foot-high plateau called a *chang-tang,* or "wildland." As these dervishes ran, they focused their thoughts and energy on a distant point, such as the snowy flanks of twenty-two-thousand-foot high Mount Kalias, their most sacred mountain. In Alexandra David-Neel's enthralling *Magic and Mystery in Tibet,* she wrote:

> It is difficult to understand that a training which compels a man to remain motionless . . . in strict seclusion in complete darkness, which lasts three years and three months . . . can result in acquisition of peculiar swiftness.

Moreover, it must be understood that the lung gom method does not aim at training the disciple by strengthening his muscles, but by developing psychic states that make these extraordinary marches possible.

These astonishing running monks reportedly chanted their mantra, sacred words of power, until they'd completely dissociated themselves from the physical act of running—to the point, some believe, where they were actually teleporting themselves through their spiritual landscape.

Running through the geographical and cultural landscape of the Grand Canyon, however, where Anasazi, ancient traders, Native American runners, and Spanish and Anglo explorers have come to life in my dreams, is a world apart from the *lung gompas*. And I have no idea why such thoughts have come to me now, or, for that matter, the faintest idea of how to apply the lost esoteric discipline of *rkang-mqyoqsnqosqrubs* to my inner Canyon journey. But whatever slivers of insight I might have gleaned from studying David-Neel's account and Lama Anagarika Govinda's *The Way of the White Clouds* throughout the long snowbound Groom Creek winter I hoped would help me form some kind of mental strategy if my body fell apart in the Canyon as it had now. I didn't plan it, but strange as it now seemed, while following the path of the Anasazi, visions of the *lung gompas* have suddenly surfaced. And I wonder if this was the same conceptual dilemma geologist Clarence E. Dutton faced when he named many of the Grand Canyon's magnificent temples and Native American spiritual landmarks after Eastern deities instead of using the names of the *yeibechei*, the masked gods of the Navajo, the *katcina*, the living spirits of the Hopi, or the mythical beings from the spirit world of the Paiute, Havasupai, and Hualapai? I don't know.

Nor do I know where the phrase comes from that starts playing itself out as I wind around Shaler Plateau into the hideaway of Ruby Canyon: *major domo, major domo, major domo* . . . I'm no longer running, I'm floating outside my body watching myself run, hypnotized by the image of a man running beneath soaring Canyon walls.

I'm on the verge of hallucinating when this image slowly dissolves into the rubescent glow of the Redwall formation sweeping around the head of Serpentine Canyon. The sun is going down, and tiny white lights are dancing in and out of my peripheral vision. I take that as a warning I should bivouac before I float off the edge of the Tonto and plunge into the black gneiss of the Inner Gorge. But dark, ambling silhouettes merge with white lights dancing on the horizon; they appear to be threading the narrow Tonto Trail on the west side of Serpentine Canyon, and the nearness of those silhouettes floating across the yawning abyss leads me to believe I can stay coherent long enough to reach the South Bass. But first, I must stop. I

> I'm no longer running, I'm floating outside my body watching myself run, hypnotized by the image of a man running beneath soaring Canyon walls.

unshoulder my empty bota bag and refill it under a cool rivulet of water. I can't help but wonder if those silhouettes are hikers or if they're the small stony shadows of the *amíye*, "spirits," of the Havasupai, dancing through the heat of a shimmering mirage. I have to find out. I get up and start chasing them. Slowly, they get closer and closer, until I'm surrounded by bobbing shadows—but they're real; at least I think they are. All nine of them. And these dark shadows hastily go about the worker-bee movements of setting up camp before the last light of day burns off the edge of the planet. Out of the corner of my eye, however, I see a lone silhouette break off from the others and float toward me; it's a young woman, and she appears to be in her early twenties. That's all that registers until she asks, "Are you the runner?"

I nod, not knowing how such news has reached the inner Canyon, then look back up, transfixed by the miniature cascade of water pouring out of my bota bag into my mouth. I purposely avoid making eye contact with her because I'm afraid if I do, the spell, the dreamy trance, whatever I've worked myself into in order to reach the South Bass, will be broken by the flood of emotions that would come pouring out with conversation.

"You're camped here," she says, "aren't you?"

"No, I've got to make it to the South Bass tonight."

Her words are a warm bouquet. My response is disconnected and emotionless.

"Why don't you stay here? It's getting too dark to . . . "

"I don't have a sleeping bag," I tell her, wondering why I'm explaining myself to this stranger.

"You can stay in mine," she says softly. Her words hang there between us, but my mind's playing tricks on me. I didn't really hear that, did I? And for the first time, I look into the deep, dark brown eyes of this dear stranger. In the afterglow of sunset, her soft complexion has a weathered effervescence that comes from traipsing around the red-rock mesas and slot canyons of the Colorado Plateau. Her dark brown hair is loosely knotted in the back, trailing two long, thin braids. Her body is firm, yet lithesome. And her supple breasts are molded by a white T-shirt emblazoned with FRIENDS OF THE RIVER.

"With me," she says.

Now I know my mind is playing tricks on me. She didn't just say, "with me," did she? If she did, I don't believe what I'm hearing—or seeing. So I can't possibly answer her. This *is* an hallucination, and she's simply a wonderful apparition of everyman's Canyon dream. But there it is: "with me." Here I am. And there she is. Serendipity and temptation in spirit and flesh—and it's beyond my grasp. I want to laugh. I want to cry. A flood of emotions threatens to engulf me where I stand. I want to hold her in my arms and be held fast in her passionate embrace by all the worldly security she represents. Yes, your wonderful presence in this dark, lonely abyss is proof I'm back in the land of the living, after miles of trance-running through this canyon dreamscape. But something far deeper than my own cognizant drive to run through the Grand Canyon has taken hold of me again, *aye na-ya-ya-ya, aye na-ya-ya-ya, aye na-ya-ya-ya, aye na-ya-ya-ya,* and it's not going to let go of me until I reach the South Bass. This force, wherever it comes from, prevents me from lingering, even for so beguiling a canyon mistress. Or was she? Or was this perhaps the same wisplike fox spirit that Buddhist scholar John Blofeld described in *The Secret and Sublime*, the fox spirit who consumed a man's very life force in the heat of passion in order to survive?

Or was it something altogether different? Was I seeing the white coyote again, after all these years. Have I finally caught it, only to see it shape-shift its form from trickster to woman? Or had it merely changed the color of its hair, as Pima shaman Virsak Vai-I dreamed when he sang the Coyote medicine song, "*Pan Nyni?*"

A-ye'eh a-ho, a-ye'eh a-ho, a-ye'eh a-ho, a-ye'eh a-ho . . .
Coyote commences singing;
Coyote commences singing.
The young woman hurries forth
to hear the Coyote songs.
A hat of eagle feathers;
A hat of eagle feathers,
A headdress was made for me
That made my heart grow stronger.
Coyote ran around it;
Coyote ran around it,
Ran into the blue water,
Changed the color of its hair.
A-ye'eh a-ho, a-ye'eh a-ho, a-ye'eh a-ho, a-ye'eh a-ho . . .

I turn away, not knowing how to respond to the Trickster's words, "with me," and start running again; as soon as I do, the spell is broken, and I try to regain the momentum I'd lost during the interlude. But I'm in such a hurry to get away that I trip over a backpack. "Sorry," I say to no one in particular. But once the rest of the group sees that I'm a runner, out here, on the edge of civilization, they give me a collective where-on-earth-is-he-going look. I'm not sure either. I turn back to try and catch sight of the

Coyote Trickster's grinning snout; instead I see the purple fire of twilight burning in her eyes when mine longingly meet hers, but I keep running—feeling her eyes trace my movement across the Tonto as night drops like a trapdoor across this inner Canyon frontier.

Running, my footsteps probing the rocky surface like feelers twitching in the dark, the words of something I read, by Haniel Long, I think, float around me: "The body of man, the body of earth, they may be part of the same reality." Suddenly the canyon interlude is a distant dream, and I return to the alpha state of "picking 'em up and putting 'em down." In moments I am no longer separate from the Tonto. It's taken hold of me, and I'm physically a part of it as I continue heading on an endless bearing west, my footsteps but fleeting tracks that will be swept clean by the next *remolina* whirling wind and dust through the Canyon's depths.

Her supple breasts are molded by a white T-shirt. . . . I want to hold her in my arms, and be held fast in her passionate embrace by all the worldly security she represents. . . . Was I seeing the white coyote again?

Out here, running in the footsteps of the Anasazi, shadowed by the cool blue light of a moon, covered by a nebulous canopy of stars and constellations, as far removed from everything in the outside world as I could ever hope to be, I feel I can run all night—I'm so at peace with myself. There is no torment or pain, there is no exhaustion or fatigue, there is no thirst or hunger. They are fleeting dreams from the distant past. There is only running, and I wonder if I've stumbled upon a territorial song line that once linked the Coyote Tail band of Havasupai at Indian Gardens with the *havåsú*, the Cataract Canyon band of Havasupai to the west? If I had, did their dream tracks have the same power to carry runners along, as the Chemehuevi believed, while crossing the vast deserts of the Mojave to the west? Is that what I had been following throughout the day that made this leg of the journey so mystical and effortless? Maybe I would discover that answer in the

I feel I can run all night—I'm so at peace with myself.

Canyon; or, if I survived the end of this journey, perhaps I'd have to follow the path of the Chemehuevi to know for sure.

Sometime later—I'm not sure how much real time has elapsed—I streak down a dark drainage wriggling off the Tonto formation into what I think is Bass Canyon, and I see what looks like a backpack propped against a rock.

I stop to examine it more closely, but one backpack becomes three. What's stranger is that I don't see any sleeping bags rolled out on the ground. So I reach out to touch one of the packs to find out if it's real. But as soon as I feel the coarse nylon between my fingertips, three shadows spring up from behind a boulder, their heads bobbing and weaving: " . . . Annerino . . . ay hey . . . can't believe it . . . all right . . . you made it . . ." Disconnected snippets of words float out of the bodies dancing around me. Are they real? Or are they fox spirits? Was *she* real? Or was she a white coyote trickster? I look up and see the red glow of a cigarette butt reflected in a pair of blue eyes piercing the darkness. It's Tim, and I'm home. After losing myself in dreamtime for the last forty-five miles, I am suddenly mauled with warm physical affection. Ginny, Tim, and Margie. I break down. I couldn't ask for a better journey home.

IV.

In 1898, John L. Stoddard wrote: "A monstrous cloud wall, like a huge gray veil, came traveling up the cañon, and we could watch the lightning strike the buttes and domes ten or twelve miles away, while the loud peals of thunder, broken by crags and multiplied by echoes, rolled toward us through the darkening gulf at steadily decreasing intervals." What was an omen for early Canyon tourists proved a blessing for Havasupai *giøiye'*, "weather shamans." Using a gourd rattle throughout a four-night ceremony, the *giøiye'* dreamed of "clouds, thunder, lightning, and of great rain and hailstorms" that would nourish their small fields of corn, beans, and squash in the depths of *wigåsiyávå*, "Cataract Canyon." Seen in either light nearly a century later, the impending storm did not bode well for the final leg of my own Canyon dream.

The following morning breaks cool, damp, and windy; the buildup of clouds charges the air with electricity, and I can hear the sizzling hum of Saint Elmo's fire as it flitters my hair on end. That's when Tim tells me the South Bass Trail between the Tonto and Esplanade formations is too steep and rocky to run safely. Having little idea of the kind of terrain I've run, thus far, I don't dispute the matter; in fact, the opportunity to visit with Tim during the leisurely four or five miles we climb out of the Upper Sonoran Desert into the Canyon's piñon and juniper woodland is too good to pass up. He, Craig, and the others have expended so much energy supporting me that I feel compelled to share the adventure with him—what I can put into words. I try explaining the trance I'd run myself into. But he asks me about the broken bota bag. That seems like a week ago, I tell him. I mention the Canyon mistress, but he assures me she was real, that he had bumped into her group coming down the South Bass the day before. But I don't pursue the matter of what was said to me—"You can stay in mine . . . with me"—because I long to remember that mystical interlude as I perceived it at the time, not through someone else's eyes.

Known to the Havasupai as *huethåwålí*, "white rock mountain," the 6,275-foot Coconino sandstone butte was an important landmark on my journey. Climbed by prospector William Wallace Bass during the 1890s, Mount Huethawali sat at the junction of the South Bass and Apache Trails. When we reach this junction in the drizzly early afternoon, I know I've linked another ancient milepost along my pathway. Originally called the Mystic Springs Trail in 1887, Bass's namesake trail reportedly followed an Indian trail (probably Anasazi or Havasupai) down off the South Rim to Mystic Springs hidden below Mount Huethawali on the outer reaches of Spencer Terrace. Bass forged the lower section of that path into the Inner Gorge, where he built a cable crossing to ferry tourists across the Colorado River to his orchard in Shinumo Creek. The

> Giddy with food, companionship, and the taste of success so near, the group consensus is that I should finish the run by the light of the moon.

upper end of the Mystic Springs Trail, however, linked my pathway with the Apache Trail; situated fifteen hundred vertical feet below the South Rim of the Coconino Plateau, the Apache Trail interlocked with the rim-top Topocoba Trail that led to Havasupai in Cataract Canyon. Why it was named the Apache Trail is not known for certain. It either had to do with the fact that fear-struck settlers commonly used the term "Apache" for a number of Native American groups they encountered while traveling throughout territorial Arizona, or, perhaps there was some truth to historic speculation that the Tonto band of Western Apache joined the Yavapai during their raid on Havasupai during the 1860s, and so the name was applied to a long-forgotten Anasazi or Havasupai trail. But before I can pursue this line of thought further or muse on Bass's own journey along the Tonto formation when he reportedly followed it east of here all the way back to Boucher Creek in 1887 to visit the Hermit, firebrands of lightning begin drilling the Esplanade formation encircling this ancient trail junction. Towering cumulonimbus in the form of mastadons march in over the edge of the Canyon rim. And hail the size of double-O buckshot pelts us. So the four of us dash through the downpour for a large overhang, where we hole up and wait for the rest of the support crew.

I drift off as the storm continues to lash the water-streaked escarpments surrounding our stone shelter. But sometime later, Tim wakes me up. Chris Keith is standing just inside the overhang; dripping wet and wearing a glistening Shiva smile, she has cameras dangling around her neck as though she's just returned from covering a guerrilla war. Standing behind her is Chris May, a med student and computer whiz with a mind like a steel trap. Behind him stands lanky Brian Gardner; a cigarette permanently dangling from his mouth, Brian only takes it out to stab the air when discussing existentialism, or Taoism, or climbing, which are always on his mind. Except for Craig and Dick, who've returned home, our eclectic group is now gathered. We are on the verge of finishing what I thought was impossible before Tim and Craig led the rest of the support crew through this Canyon dream. Giddy with food, companionship, and the taste of success so near, the group consensus is that I should finish the run by the light of the moon.

But the weather is not in the good humor we are. Curtains of snow drift ghostlike across the storm-locked North Rim. A bone-chilling rain hammers the mile-high Darwin Plateau. A fierce wind whips and lashes the sprawling red-rock escarpment around us, recharging hundreds of shallow *tinajas*, "rock tanks," with glimmering pools of water. Reluctantly, the seven of us leave the cozy warmth of our lair and slog through the wind, rain, and ankle-deep red mud to a series of ledges beneath sixty-four-hundred-foot Chemehuevi Point. Swaddled in damp sleeping bags beneath a stone overhang, we camp for the night so that I'll be in position to start running this ancient track at first light.

It's still raining when Tim nudges me awake with a cup of hot black coffee the next morning. The ground has turned to mush, and heavy fog limits visibility to a few feet. In fact, had I been headed to the North Rim in the footsteps of Capt. Hance, the fog would be definitely "about right to cross." But I'm not, nor is this the break in weather I'd been hoping for to run the unknown stretch beyond. But it's now half past six of day 6, and we can't wait any longer. Much of day 3 was spent waiting for the Hermit food drop, and most of yesterday was spent sitting out the weather. Nearly everyone has other pressing commitments to tend to in the "real world," and for most it will be their last day in the Canyon. So if I'm going to finish what I've begun, it has to be now—abysmal weather or not. I depart. Ginny and Margie follow close behind. The rain does not abate.

Although I had been able to trace my pathway across the Tonto formation with the relative ease of a sign cutter, the seldom-if-ever-used Apache Trail is more difficult to follow across the greasy red sandstone of the Esplanade formation. Where visible, this incipient foot-wide track slithers through snakeweed, rabbit brush, and banana yucca and climbs through steep talus and boulders covered with 285-million-year-old reptile tracks. But for each yard I gain through this fossil wonderland, my left leg is forced to take a sidehill bite out of the soggy talus while my right leg pushes from behind. I struggle with this strange, reptilian lurch, my hot breath condensing into steamy puffs in the cool morning air. But as hard as I try, I can't even out my strides enough to attain a self-perpetuating rhythm. Worse, the Paleozoic mud clings to the bottoms of my shoes like dog shit, and I have to fling it off with a kick every other step.

The bright side to the stormy weather is that the temperature is the coolest it's been throughout my journey—in the mid-fifties, I'm guessing. The woodland vegetation is more lush; the fog- and rain-glistened piñon and juniper trees seem to rove through the coral-red landscape like fat green bears. And the trail's position below the very rim of the Canyon, a full thousand vertical feet higher than the Tonto formation, doesn't weigh on me with that swallowed-up-whole feeling I frequently had while running through the treacherous, escape-proof corridor of the Tonto, where one misstep often would have meant a deadly plunge into the Inner Gorge.

Barely an hour out of camp, however, it suddenly comes back to me that I've run this maze before—a year ago, with a companion, in the warm winds blowing through the Mojave Desert. We crossed the threshold between sunset and twilight by running through the ancient Mojave's "mystic maze," a relic spirit track of furrows etched by hand and stone in the desert pavement. Renowned photographer Edward S. Curtis first described this intaglio in 1908 in *The North American Indian*:

> Whatever Tim had seen in my eyes this morning, whether it was . . . fear of dying, or fear of success, he didn't want to risk having me run this final leg alone, not when we were this close.

In southeastern California along the Colorado River south of Needles are many mesas, the loose surface stones on the summits of which, covered hundreds of acres, have been gathered by prehistoric people into long parallel rows. . . . The Mojave Indians nearby have utilized the area, so marked, in recent years, as a maze into which to lure and escape evil spirits, for it is believed that by running in and out of this immense labyrinth one haunted with dread may bewilder the spirits occasioning it, and thus elude them.

. . . as I'm now trying to do in this immense labyrinth, running through the endless maze of fog-shrouded drainages that cleave the Esplanade formation between Chemehuevi, Toltec, and Montezuma Points in hopes of shaking off the two runners accompanying me. Not that I don't enjoy their companionship; it's just that I am being pulled in two opposite directions. In the misty horizon of the west, I can finally envision the end of this journey; barring a broken ankle or accident, I'm on the verge of reaching it. Yet, from behind, Margie is tugging me in the other direction: "Come on, wait. What's the hurry?" But I didn't come to the Grand Canyon to walk; Fletcher had already done that here, below the South Rim, and Ginny and Wuerhman had already done that across the river below the North Rim. I came here to run wild along an ancient pathway through the Grand Canyon of the Colorado River, and now that I'm about to complete that journey I'm inexplicably torn in opposite directions. Whatever Tim had seen

> The weather deteriorates; an unforgiving downpour soaks us to the bone . . . but this isn't as unnerving as the cacophonous thunder and lightning that threaten to blow us apart if we remain on this exposed ground much longer.

in my eyes this morning, whether it was fatigue, uncertainty, or just plain fear—fear of dying, or fear of success—he didn't want to risk having me run this final leg alone, not when we were *this* close. So I agreed to let Ginny and Margie accompany me, in his words, "in case something goes wrong." We were peeling back the layers, trying to discover what was feasible for us within the specter of the Grand Canyon and ancient Native American running. So I went along with Tim's decision, but only because he and Craig had spearheaded such unflagging support on a journey I knew would be impossible to embark on, or finish, without them.

But as I pick up the tempo to blast across these slick ledges of raw stone, I still feel I'm running through my own maze in hopes of eluding the spirits occasioning me. Whether they were real or imagined I did not know.

At the edge of the flat land
Here I come out and run.
On top of the mountain.
Here I come out and run.
I come forth running,
I come forth running,
Bearing a cloud on my head,
I come forth running.

What bears the name of the Apache, and carried the ancient tracks of the Anasazi and the footprints of the Havasupai, was also the war trail of the Yavapai. Numbering close to two-hundred fleet-footed warriors, whom the Havasupai described as good runners, the Yavapai used this ancient track to raid the Havasupai in Cataract Canyon sometime between 1860 and 1863. Caught off guard by forces nearly superior in number to their entire tribe, the Havasupai regrouped and held off the Yavapai attack on their Canyon paradise, killing two Yavapai in the running battle. One Yavapai was shot by Captain Burro, and another fell in the sights of Captain Navajo. As a grisly warning to the others, the normally peaceful Havasupai cut off the heads of both Yavapai, their bloody faces still adorned with black-and-red-striped paint; the Havasupai scalped them both, hung them on a pole, held a scalp dance, and the Yavapai retreated. Sinyella, the seventy-one-year-old Havasupai elder who told this story to ethnographer Leslie Spier in 1918, said: "That is what I saw; that is the way they did it in the old days. They kept the two scalps, so they could have a dance whenever they wanted." But two years after this raid, the Yavapai returned, not to seek retribution but to offer peace: "It is not right for us to kill each other," said one of the Yavapai leaders. "Our language is nearly the same. It is not right; we ought to stop and be friends." And so peace returned to the Havasupai's canyon Eden of blue water and red stone.

What originally looked like twelve to fourteen miles on my Havasupai Point topographic map feels more like twenty. And by the time the three of us muck through the red mud and cheek-stinging wind from Points Huitzil, Centeotl, and Quetzal to the base of 6,296-foot Apache Point, the weather deteriorates; an unforgiving downpour soaks us to the bone, as we struggle up a series a sandstone chutes running with rainwater. But the prospect of being swept away by a flash flood or buried under an avalanche of boulders and mud isn't as unnerving to me as the cacophonous thunder and lightning that threaten to blow us apart if we remain on this exposed ground much longer.

But if there is a trail leading up to Apache Point—and both the map and the oral history of the Havasupai indicate there was one—it's escaped our notice; so we stop during our grueling ascent to catch our breath. When we do, we notice five small horses grazing in the stony basin of Apache Terrace far below. They look like remnants of the mythical pigmy ponies once believed to have roamed the western Grand Canyon long ago. In 1938, the National Park Service conducted a field investigation into the matter and concluded that these hornless unicorns, which stood forty-eight inches high and weighed three-hundred pounds, "were simply [Havasupai] Indian ponies, stunted from poor desert grazing." Captivated by this rare sighting, I wonder what it would be like to mount up and ride out of here in comfort? Was that the temptation the great Native American runners found so difficult to resist when Spanish padres, explorers, and conquistadors reintroduced horses to North America during the 1500s? Horses were the very reason the Yavapai raided the Havasupai—and what produced the great equestrian cultures of the Comanche, Apache, and Navajo, among others.

"I learned to ride a horse bareback and go as fast as the wind."

We turn, face the rain-slickened talus, and continue struggling on all fours toward a natural shelter high above.

Once inside this airy, wind-lashed grotto, the three of us clinging like bats beneath a slippery sandstone belfry, I realize it offers little more than psychological protection, since lightning can conduct its deadly currents down the rain-moistened fissures of the rock wall. That fear, along with the image of a mud slide burying us alive, sends me reeling out from beneath this overhang toward the exposed summit of Apache Point. But Ginny is hesitant; if she's one of the premier canyoneers of the day, her Achilles' heel, ironically, is rock climbing. This is where Margie's buoyant fearlessness and experience as an outdoor instructor come to the fore; she patiently works with Ginny, coaxing and spotting her from below, until both of them surmount the exposed slab of wet rock to the ledge I'm standing on.

It's twilight when the three of us reach the crest of 6,296-foot Apache Point. It's still raining. The wind is building, gusting more often than not. And my left knee feels like it's blown out. To make matters worse, there is no cover between us and Pasture Wash, where we are scheduled to camp for the night. Nevertheless, Margie wants to push on, and I go along with her decision in hopes we can maintain a rapid enough pace to stay warm. But Ginny and Margie are fatigued by the strain of having already hiked in and out of the Canyon twice to support me; given that, combined with my own locked-knee efforts, we can't go fast enough. That's when I start hedging my bets. I don't know whether either of my companions has bivouacked in the open before or not, and with the pace we're maintaining we're not going to reach Pasture Wash any time tonight, especially in light of the fact that we'll have to shoot a compass bearing in the stormy darkness to reach it.

Cold, clammy, and shivering, I use their wretched appearance as a mirror for my own. I tell them I'm headed back to Apache Point to look for the cave we saw when we first topped out on the Canyon rim. Margie hesitates, but I keep moving; if she has something to prove to somebody, I'm not playing. If the two of them want to keep stumbling in the dark and shiver like dogs all night, I can't stop them, but I'm headed back. Reluctantly, they turn and join me, and we quickly find the cave overlooking the headdress of storm clouds boiling over 6,421-foot Great Thumb Mesa to the west.

I stare out through the mouth of the cave, but it's too dark to trace the line Fletcher followed around Great Thumb Mesa two decades earlier; so I turn my attention to the dark interior of our shelter. Standing on the floor of the cave is a stone shrine two foot high; a sun-bleached deer antler sticks out of the top, and a fetish bound with wood and eagle feathers sits at its base. I've never seen a prayer bundle before—what the Navajo call *jish,* the Hopi call *paho,* and the Pima call *ʔoˑmini.* But when I look to the west and see silver-blue lightning drilling Great Thumb Mesa with a firestorm of ground strikes, I can't help but wonder whether this cave was once used by *giøiye,* "weather shamans," to communicate with *Pagiyógå,* the Havasupai god "who draws spirits into the sky." I'm not sure. One by one the three of us lie down on the damp floor of the cave to sleep, careful not to touch the ceremonial bundle or disturb the soil around the shrine. But there has been so much strain today that we each shiver independently, too proud to admit to one another that we'd be much warmer if we spooned our bodies together.

Dreams of my journey, the future, and these companions hurtle through my subconscious as I struggle to stay warm, but the mundane images I conjure up fail to provide even fleeting comfort. The one picture that repeatedly emerges is that of Margie and the strange chemistry between us; I can't explain it, but maybe it has something to do with her expectations. Then again, maybe Alan Sillitoe had it right when he titled his classic short story "The Loneliness of the Long-Distance Runner": running truly is a private affair, that can only be intimately shared with runners and friends who know your strengths and weaknesses not with someone who may be trying to analyze your motives. Then, maybe it's just the stress of trying to survive long enough to finish the journey. I don't know, other than I'm shaking uncontrollably, and so are they. It's so cold it feels like the earth is trembling beneath us.

Something has to be done; if Ginny and Margie are too proud, or if they misread my actions, I can't help it. "Ginny," I whisper, "I'm cold." I curl up behind her. Fortunately, Margie takes that as a cue to snuggle up behind me. But the body heat emanating from the three of us is not enough. According to the odd-looking timepiece still wrapped around my wrist, it is a quarter past midnight, and I'm shivering like a dog passing a peach pit.

With my teeth clacking and my feet stuck on the end of my rigid legs like cold stones, I roll to my knees and draw my knife and flint. I'm not sure who, but Margie or Ginny gets up and holds the small flashlight as I try desperately to get a fire going before we succumb to hypothermia. But the tinder I'd hastily gathered in the dark before bedding down is too damp; so Margie and I grope in the back of the cave and gather small chunks of fiber from a pack-rat midden. I strike the flint again and again against these strange clusters, until the tiny flame ignites the matted clump of twigs, cactus spines, rabbit hair, and gum wrappers. In three other Grand Canyon caves not unlike this one, archaeologists dug up prehistoric California condor bones, along with split-twig figurines carbon-dated to 2145 B.C. $\pm$ 100 years. What mystical relation the majestic condor had with the split-twig figurines, which were thought to be effigies of antelope and desert bighorn sheep for a successful hunt, is not known. But the fragile talismans were linked to the mysterious Pinto Basin Desert Culture that predated the Anasazi. Our intention is not to disturb what may have been a prehistoric ceremonial chamber still used by Native Americans, only to survive. Still shivering, Margie and I begin slowly adding twigs, first small ones, then larger and larger ones, while Ginny's narrow beam of light shines on the meticulous movement of damp, cold fingers stoking what ancient man knew was the miracle of life; when the fire takes, I finally admit to myself we're going to survive and I'm going to reach the end of my quest.

> Running truly is a private affair, that can only be intimately shared with runners and friends who know your strengths and weaknesses.

Huddled like paleo-hunters around this life-sustaining fire, shadows dance off our bodies and flicker against the walls of the cave. Havasupai *giøiye* believed an individual's *witagosa'*, "shadow," was the spirit that traveled with him by night and day; our shadows, too, have traveled with us through the Canyon's burning sun and freezing rain, through joy and pain. Now we are warm, I am happy, but we are silent. Whatever our worldly concerns had been earlier in the day, we have since traveled eons together between a sun that never rose and one that never set, and nothing needs to be said, because we are surviving the night together, and nothing is

Whatever our worldly concerns had been earlier in the day, we have since traveled eons together between a sun that never rose and one that never set, and nothing needs to be said

more elemental than that. One by one, we lie down on the floor of the cave to doze in the warm communal glow of our fire; occasionally one of us is silently summoned from our reverie-filled half sleep to restoke the fire when the cold breath of night exhales through the smoky mouth of the cave. A ceaseless procession of raindrops seeps down along the roof of the cave; I watch them fall and hiss on the burning red coals, each drop sending up a little puff of steam and ash.

During one of these somnolent fire stokings, I notice petroglyphs adorning the moist walls of the cave. Was this the last ancient link along my pathway? Have I finally felt the day-to-day, dawn-to-dusk struggle of ancient Native American runners singing a spirit path? I lie back down, too tired to answer my own query, but my closed eyes open a doorway to the past: I watch fleet-footed shadows running through the desert, singing the spirit song of the Southern Fox as they cross *Kunayiwaavi*, "Fire Valley" (Death Valley), to reach their ancestral hunting grounds:

At Fire Valley,
burn't off by fire
burn't off by fire
At Fire Valley,
burn't off by fire

burn't off by fire
At Fire Valley,
burn't off by fire
burn't off by fire . . .

Whether or not I was able to relive a modern vision quest along my own pathway, I can now see a lone man following in the footsteps of the ancient Chemehuevi runners across the great Mojave Desert to the west: a hot wind blows across that fearsome land, inflating a brown wall of dust that envelops the horizon in four directions. Running head-on into the storm, the tiny silhouette is swallowed by the dreamy cloud of dust and disappears. The only sensation in this monstrous cloud is feeling: parched lips, a throat choked with dust and thirst, a face streaked with white salt, eyes whipped and lashed by sand, legs slick with sweat . . . . When the silhouette finally emerges from the billowing sandstorm, it burns across the desert pavement into eternity where there is no ego, only running.

When I peer through the mouth of the cave early the next morning, the Canyon is still shrouded in a foggy mist. But that's all I can see: white clouds, rimmed by the dark orifice of the cave entrance. And I'm reminded of a passage from Lama Govinda's *The Way of the White Clouds*: "There are mysteries which a man is called upon to unveil, and there are others which are meant to be felt but not to be touched, whose secrecy must be respected." And now, as far as I have followed my inner Canyon pathway through both reality and my dreams, other voices are asking me to respect the secret: finally, it dawns on me I can't follow my pathway into Havasupai as I dreamed of doing for so long.

That's what Tim had told me the night I floated into the South Bass drop. But I was so dorphed out, confused, and excited that I shrugged it off when he said, "John, you can't run to Supai." In fact, I ignored it all the next day and the day after that, because I knew it would take whatever concentration I had left just to reach Apache Point, where I could practically fall into Havasupai. What a way to finish the journey, floating down *wigásiyává*, "Cataract Canyon," along the route of the Desert

Culture, the Anasazi, the Havasupai, Hopi traders, Yavapai warriors, Navajos on the run, Spanish missionaries, and explorers.

So I really hadn't given it much thought until now, as Ginny, Margie, and I crawl out of the cave into the swirling white clouds, wondering which way to go from here—east to Pasture Wash or west to Havasupai? Once again, I am pulled in opposite directions, because Havasupai is the only place to end this quest, at the very village Hopi traders traveled to from the east and Mojave traders traveled to from the west. But I'd have to run those last fourteen miles as an outlaw because the *Tovokyóva*, "precipice trail," (commonly known as the Topocoba Trail), used by Francisco Tomás Garcés as early as June 25, 1776, is now part of the Havasupai's traditional use area. Not even Colin Fletcher had had to face that obstacle when he followed his magic line around Great Thumb Mesa through the heart of the Havasupai's ancestral land.

At one time, the Havasupai's vast homelands on the Coconino Plateau extended from the Little Colorado River in the east to the territorial lands of the Hualapai near Aubrey Cliffs ninety miles west, and from the brink of the Grand Canyon in the north to the foot of 12,633-foot San Francisco Peaks seventy-five miles south. In 1880, however, President Rutherford B. Hayes opened the Havasupai's ancestral domain to mining by reducing their lands from an estimated 6,750 square miles to a paltry sixty square miles; two years later, this criminally small tract of the Havasupai Reservation was further reduced to 518.6 acres by President Chester A. Arthur. Culturally, the Havasupai were devastated, and it wasn't until 1974 that Congress passed legislation returning 160,000 acres of the Havasupai's ancestral lands to them, including permanent cultural rights to use 95,000 acres of the western Grand Canyon encompassing Great Thumb Mesa, which comprised their traditional use area.

Whether or not I thought there was any historic or spiritual insight to be gleaned by crossing a small part of this restricted area, it was, in light of the Havasupai's disastrous relations with the U.S. government, off-limits without a special permit to non-Indians. Had we known, we would have talked with the Havasupai beforehand and applied for a special-use permit, but we did not know of such requirements. And even if I was tempted to run to Havasupai anyway—and I was—there had been too much boldface ink and too many glowing radio reports to sneak in the foosteps of the Coyote Trickster. Rangers at the Grand Canyon Backcountry Reservation Office had told Tim there was nothing they could do to stop me from running to Havasupai, but if I did it might harm the delicate relations between the Park Service and the Havasupai tribe, so that this traditional use area might remain permanently off-limits to backpackers and canyoneers. And I wasn't the one to close that door.

Reluctantly, I turn east-southeast at Apache Point and begin stumbling through the heavy mud, sagebrush, Apache plume, piñon, and juniper toward Pasture Wash Ranger Station, fifteen miles cross-country by compass bearing. But this running back from the end of the run has the most difficult footing of the entire journey. And I try not to cave in to the thought of how much easier, and spiritually fulfilling, it would be to run to Havasupai—that's where ancient traders went, not to an abandoned government way station.

> I feel more like an old man who's been chasing windmills than the conqueror the headlines are already making me out to be.

I continue flailing through the sagebrush, which covers this burned-out, over-grazed tract of the Coconino Plateau so densely it tears at my legs from the knees down. Margie and Ginny cheer me tirelessly from behind. But I feel more like an old man who's been chasing windmills than the conqueror the headlines are already making me out to be.

But the dream is behind me now, and I'm not certain whether or not it ever evolved into reality, because the threshold between the dream of running through the heart of the Grand Canyon and the reality of it was so permeable that I couldn't grasp it anymore than I could hold quicksilver in my fist. What yawns before me as I struggle toward Pasture Wash is a feeling of emptiness, that my life force has been so completely consumed by the Canyon that I have nothing more to give to it—or anybody else. And I feel as though I'm running through a spiritual void as vast and awesome as the Canyon itself.

But if I should forsake this Canyon, as I promised myself I would if I didn't perish during my quest, I know this feeling of emptiness—what the great Chemehuevi runner George Laird described as being "wind-broke"—will stay with me forever, as cold and lonely as any bivouac. And the journey will remain not something tangible that I can hold on to, take pride in, or even point to and say, "Yes, one day I followed that path," but a long-forgotten dream of one man's attempt to master his fears and emotions by running in the footsteps of the Anasazi through the Grand Canyon of the Colorado River. All because the Canyon—the beautiful, marvelous, godforsaken Grand Canyon—remains unmarked by my passage, my tears, my struggles, and my dreams. And because it would remain out there on the edge of my day-to-day existence, beckoning me, teasing me, luring me like the quintessential Canyon dreamstress, and taunting me that I'd left the frontier of my spirit and visions unexplored.

If I am ever to fill the stark void I now feel as the three of us lunge toward a parking-lot press conference and South Rim celebration, I know, as I taste the tears streaming down my weathered cheeks, that I will have to embark on the shadow legs of my inner Canyon pathway: the rim-bound path of the ancient Hopi-Havasupai trail and the savage arena of the North Rim. Then I will have to contemplate the possibilities of both journeys, train my heart out, and finally abandon each journey as impossible for me to survive or complete—until I can no longer stand the taunting, and, trembling once more with dread and awe, I'll wrap my scarlet bandanna around my head and try running for a few eternal moments in the spirit tracks of those who ran before me.

5

LESSONS FROM THE ANCIENT PATH

No more moccasined feet tread

silently upon hard-packed trails

whispering tcawa, tcawa, tcawa . . .

a whole mode of tranportation is

lost, never to be regained.

Carobeth Laird
The Chemehuevis

IN THE COLD, BLUE LIGHT OF DAWN, A WHISTLING SIROCCO LASHES US WITH THE bitter winds of March as the two of us run for daylight across the Mojave Sink. But for every step we take, this merciless *norte*, "northwind," chills us to the bone as we struggle across the horizonless salt pan toward the Devil's Playground. We've been following the pulse of the Mojave River, which flows through a subterranean aquifer beneath the sere crust of this dry lake, for more than a day; and now that the "upside-down river" has spilled its lifeblood in the white heart of the Mojave Desert, these tempestuous winds threaten to slam us back two steps for every step we punch forward. But we feign, bounce, and weave, shadowboxing with a force we can neither see nor reckon with; it hammers us relentlessly, and I wonder how soon this cold, furious beating will leave us sprawled facedown on the salt-caked floor of Soda Lake. It's not the idyllic conditions we'd envisioned when we set out to cross the Mojave Desert before summer turned it into the killing ground that once left thirst-ravaged emigrants digging for water in the hot sand, but conditions are seldom ideal for man in an environment that has existed for eons without him.

The ageless path we're tracing once connected the Mojave settlements on the lower Colorado River with those of the native Gabrieliños, Fernandeños, Ventureños, and Barbareños near the cool Pacific Ocean three to four suns west. Traversing more than three hundred miles of blowing sand, dry lakes, desert pavement, lava flows, cinder cones, creosote flats, Joshua tree forests, boulder-strewn washes, alluvial fans, and soaring ridges of stone that erupt out of the Spirit Land of the Mojave and the Storied Land of the Chemehuevi, the Mojave Indian trail links a series of springs and water holes westward across the Mojave Desert until it reaches Soda Lake, or the Mojave Sink, which drains the very heart of this ancestral desert. Moving, as venerated anthropologist Alfred L. Kroeber wrote, "across the country in a trot that carries them over long distances rapidly," the Mojave ran west from Soda Lake, along

> . . . three hundred miles of blowing sand, dry lakes, desert pavement, lava flows, cinder cones, creosote flats, Joshua tree forests, boulder-strewn washes, alluvial fans, and soaring ridges of stone . . .

the course of their namesake river, called *ayatapagah*, a hundred miles to Cajón Pass; this great divide separated the 10,004-foot San Gabriel Mountains from the 11,485 foot San Bernardino Mountains to the east. It was through this four-thousand-foot-high mountain passageway that the Mojave ran, carrying little more than a gourd of ground wheat and a gourd of water each for sustenance, in order to barter with coastal tribes for precious haliotis and olivella shells in the heyday of ancient traders.

For Spanish explorers, American mountain men, gold seekers, and emigrants who later followed in the Mojave's footsteps along this desolate leg of what became known as the Old Spanish Trail, North America's smallest desert proved to be everything but the promised land they'd envisioned on the west end of it. But for indigenous people like the *makhá·v* or *ʔahàmakná·v*, "people who live along the river" (commonly known as the Mojave), who reportedly ran a hundred miles a day along this prehistoric track, it was mythical running country; as it was for their symbiotic neighbors, the *ʔaci·mu·é·v*, "always moving around people" (commonly known as the Chemehuevi), whose own running prowess knew only the limits of their territorial hunting songs.

As we run through desert winds that buffet us around like tumbleweed, the Mojave Desert still is as mythical running country as I can imagine. The timeless path now guiding us across the *ayatanaugutivipi*, Mojave Spirit Land, lures us toward a holocaust of pink light mushrooming out of the eastern edge of our cold planet. But soon, I know, the Mojave Trail will cross the song tracks of the Chemehuevi, who sang and ran across their own mythological landscape guided only by their ancient songs, which created a sacred link between them, this desert, their spiritual landmarks, and the desert bighorn sheep they hunted and revered. In her eloquent book *The Chemehuevis*, linguist Carobeth Laird wrote:

> . . . Even in the closing decades of the nineteenth century, there were still some groups of as many as twenty-five or thirty men inheriting the same song and hunting range. When a Chemehuevi asked, "How does that song go?" he did not refer exclusively to its words and tune; primarily he meant, "What is the route it travels?" Each landmark and watering place was mentioned in order, by recognizable allusion or description if not by name, so that a man's song constituted an oral map of his territory.

Songs like the "Route of the Southern Fox" originated in the heartland of the Chemehuevi and guided them more than two hundred miles north to Death Valley, called *Kunayiwaavi*, "Fire Valley," where the body of the mythical Fox "was consumed by fire until only his head remained." The free-roaming "Salt Song" flew in around the desert and mountains bordering *pagah*, the Colorado River, like the mythic wing beats of the Chemehuevi birds it carried.

Beyond the Chemehuevi's own songs and trails, however, the Mojave trail was only one leg of a much longer trade route that wound its way eastward from the Pacific Ocean, across the Mojave Desert and Grand Canyon region, to the Zuni pueblos in what would become the territory of New Mexico. It was along this desolate eleven-hundred-mile-long track that the Mojave, Hualapai, Havasupai, Navajo, and Hopi traveled to one another's distant villages to trade seashells, deerskins, desert bighorn sheepskins, woven goods, pottery, baskets ceremonial paint, and other precious, easily transportable goods. Some tribes acted as middle-men, and tribes like the Mojave reportedly ran as much for the adventure of visiting distant territories as for the benefit of trade. What was it like to follow a leg of this great trade route? Could the land still be seen as the Mojave and Chemehuevi envisioned it if one ran in their footsteps? I'd dreamed of finding out.

After staggering away from the South Rim a year earlier, I knew it was feasible for the Anasazi and other ancient traders to have run through the heart of the Grand Canyon, but I couldn't know how practical it was for them unless I compared my inner Canyon journey with the rim-bound trade route that linked the Hopi village of Oraibi with Havasupai. And the best place to start, I first thought, was not with the Hopi-Havasupai leg but out here at the beginning—or near the end—of this trade route, where the ancient path could still be followed. But I was beginning to stack the deck against myself, because I was intent on leaving Oraibi some-time in April, before summer scorched the white caprock of the Coconino Plateau and the black sand and red-rock mesas of the

> As we crunch across the broken-eggshell surface of Soda Lake . . . I suddenly feel hungry enough to eat a horse . . . what mountain man Kit Carson and his party of trappers were forced to do.

Desierto Pintado, "Painted Desert;" that meant I'd have to run the Mojave Trail in March, and I simply did not know if I'd recover soon enough to embark on the Hopi-Havasupai trade route. Dick Yetman realized that much sooner than I and earnestly went about making plans to run the Mojave Trail while I was still researching it; and if, in a moment of weak-ness, I was miffed that the Mojave Trail might be run by someone else, I had doubts about being able to run the Mojave and Hopi-Havasupai trails back-to-back. So I eagerly fell into support position in hopes that I could help Dick on his own quest, as he had done for me. Besides, the Hopi-Havasupai trade route closely paralleled the South Rim of the Grand Canyon, and I thought running it would come closer to proving or disproving my inner Canyon hypothesis than would running the Mojave Trail.

That's where the two of us are now—almost 40 miles into a 130-mile-long track that, during the summer, zigzags across the Mojave Desert like a molted, sun-bleached rattlesnake skin. But this March wind, blowing out of the depths of the Grand Canyon two-hundred miles northeast, threatens to snuff out Dick's burning desire to reach the Colorado River ninety miles away, even as he continues to bob and weave his way across the Mojave Sink into the sunrise of day 2; in the amber light of dawn, Dick is jabbing at forces most travelers contended with more than a century earlier. The first non-Indian to travel the entire trade route from the Pacific coast east to the Hopi villages, and to persevere on this dangerous leg, was Spanish missionary Francisco Tomás Garcés. Like Padre Kino, Garcés also crossed the Sonoran Desert's deadly Camino del Diablo, but Garcés was the first non-Indian to do so mid-summer—only to be beaten to death by Yuma Indians shortly after that grueling journey. Garcés crossed the Mojave Desert in February 1776. Somewhere in the vicinity of the Providence Mountains, what the Chemehuevi called the *timpisag-wagatsitci*, Green Stone, he met a group of Mojave, most likely runners. In his diary, Garcés wrote:

> Here I met four Indians who had come from Santa Clara to traffic in shell beads. They were carrying no food supply, nor even bows for hunting. Noticing my astonishment at this, where there is nothing to eat, they said, "We Jamajabs can withstand hunger and thirst for as long as four days," giving me to understand they were hardy men.

So is Dick. As we crunch across the broken-eggshell surface of Soda Lake, which Garcés's historian Elliot Coues crossed a hundred years before us, the singing winds finally subside with the rising sun, and I suddenly feel hungry enough to eat a horse—or at least part of one. That's exactly what mountain man Kit Carson and his party of trappers were forced to do when they crossed the Mojave Desert in the winter of 1829. Wrote Carson: "We met a party of Mohave Indians and purchased from

Running the Mojave Indian trail. Blasted by bitter March winds, the author and Dick Yetman are seen running across the Mojave Sink on the second day of Yetman's unprecedented journey.

them a mare, heavy with foal. The mare was killed and eaten by the party with great gusto; even the foal was devoured." But Dick is running so strongly now, he seems impervious to hunger and fatigue. And it's only with tremendous effort that I'm able to dart far enough ahead to frame him with my telephoto lens before he runs by me.

Established on April 19, 1860, as a military base camp to hunt down the Mojave, Camp Cady is now a historic outpost; photojournalist Chris Keith and I have been alternately shadowing Dick since leaving Camp Cady the dawn before. We figured the best way to document this journey was by running every other stretch of it with him. Covering only half the distance he ran was the easy part. The difficult part was following this ancient path across a forty-thousand-square-mile desert; without a

Chemehuevi or Mojave elder, or the intimate knowledge of their spirit songs to guide us, tracing the trail would have been nearly impossible without the help of Mojave Road historian Dennis Casebier. The trail was first described in Garcés's own diary, translated and annotated by Elliot Coues in *On the Trail of a Spanish Pioneer*, but no modern man knew exactly where the Mojave trail lay until Casebier sauntered into the perplexing badlands of the Mojave Desert. It was an ethnogeographical puzzle that took the physicist twenty years of gumshoeing through the National Archives and other records—and innumerable exploratory trips to the eastern Mojave—before he pieced the Mojave Trail together, on foot.

In *The Desert*, John C. Van Dyke wrote: "The weird solitude, the great silence, the grim desolation, are the very things with which every desert wanderer falls in love." Casebier was one such wanderer who fell in love with the Mojave Desert, and he wanted to see the Mojave Trail preserved, possibly as a National Historic Site. And If Dick were successful, it might add another page of favorable ink to Casebier's tireless efforts to preserve the trail. So Casebier sent along a cassette tape describing in exacting detail how to stay on the trail and where to look for it if Dick wandered astray. Before each leg of the journey, Dick would play this tape for Geary Redmond and Jim Gaston, his support crew, so they'd know exactly where to pinpoint the midday checkpoints and evening campsites. Wrestling with windblown topographic maps in the middle of a boundless desert that was bordered by the Colorado River far to the east and the San Andreas Fault far to the west, I found

> As frustrating as this run is, however, it's difficult to hold back the laughter every time one of us misreads this crater-pocked footing.

it strange yet comforting to listen to the distant voice of this master puzzle solver: "Here we are at what I suppose is the most dangerous part of the trail . . . so take out your Cave Mountain quadrangle." The Chemehuevi called such gatherings *haikuuyiwitci*, "white men sitting down," and we squatted around the tape recorder hanging onto Casebier's every word— as if fate itself hinged on them.

But even with Casebier's tape and our topographic maps lined with felt-tip tracks guiding us from waterhole to water hole, some relic stretches of the Mojave Trail couldn't be followed *in situ* because they'd been engulfed by sand or recklessly destroyed by off-road-vehicles and motor-cross races. So once Dick and I emerge from the salt flats of the Mojave Sink, we strike out cross-country for Seventeen Mile Point. Fortunately, the wind has turned back on itself, and it's now chasing us through the desert like ghost bands of Mojave, who, wearing frightening striped face paint, once preyed on emigrants for their cattle in order to supplement their meager rations of lizards, screwbeans, and maize. This blustery run ends, however, as soon as we enter a field of kangaroo-rat holes that Casebier had warned us about. Every few minutes, one of us plunges into a knee-wrenching explosion of sand and saliva and struggles out only to drop like a fallen horseback rider another fifty to seventy-five yards downwind. As frustrating as this run is, however, it's difficult to hold back the laughter every time one of us misreads this crater-pocked footing.

I'm still wondering if the Mojave runners didn't somehow teleport themselves over this field of sinkholes when we finally reach Seventeen Mile Point. It's 9:00 A.M., the Mojave wind is now breathing down our backs, and my knees and ankles feel hammered. Dick, on the other hand, is a picture of stalwart determination, conjuring up images of a tireless frontier scout leading the great California migration of wagon trains west along this thirty-fifth-parallel route in pursuit of Manifest Destiny. Suddenly, however, I'm confronted with two vehicles from Dick's support crew; and while I eagerly greet Jim and Geary's hearty welcome, their fossil-fueled wagons temporarily whisk me away from a path that once only whispered of footsteps dancing in sacred communion with the desert, long before it was churned to dust by the ceaseless grind of wagon wheels.

POZOS DE SAN JUAN DE DIOS

On March 8, 1776, Fr. Francis Garcés, OFM,

On his most famous journey of

Over 2,000 miles from Mission San Xavier

Del Bac, Tucson, Arizona to

Mission San Gabriel, California, rested

here and named these waterholes

"St. John of God Springs" (Marl Springs),

and on the return journey

Passed through here, May 22, same year.

At sixty-six miles out, Pozos de San Juan de Dios marks the halfway point on Dick's journey to the Colorado River. And by the time his silhouette floats out of the steamy horizon of lava and cinder cones lapping at the flanks of the 4,508-foot Marl Mountains, he says he "can hear wagon wheels on rocks and the snorting of horses." The voices Dick hears echoing from the past may be ghosts of the Whipple expedition, whose Pacific Railroad survey churned through Marl Springs on March 9, 1854. Expedition quartermaster Lieutenant David S. Stanley wrote that he thought the Mojave Trail was "unfit for wagon road or for pack mule trains . . . . Had we no Indian guides, well acquainted with the country, we would have certainly lost all our animals, if not men." Whomever Dick hears, it is becoming more apparent that, like the Chemehuevi, he is finding his own connection with the land.

But there are other forces at work out here besides the phantom wagon trains. Winter light refracting off the shimmering *bajadas*, "lowlands," and desert pavement magnifies the distant mountains, and, in the clear desert air, they seem larger and closer than they really are. Eighty miles to the north, the 11,049-foot Panamint Mountains form the west wall of Death Valley; to the Chemehuevi, this range was *nariwiinativipi*, "sacred land, the Storied Land, where the great myths were said to begin and end." A hundred miles to the south, however, the snow-dusted San Jacinto Mountains pierce the blue heavens; naturalist John Muir remarked that the view from the 10,804-foot summit of that range was "the most sublime spectacle to be found anywhere on this earth."

As day 2 draws to a close at this historic water hole, the four of us watch Dick streak into camp. The sight of a lone man running this path through a desert marked by the Storied Land to the north and the most sublime spectacle on earth to the south stirs such deep, atavistic impulses, I can't help but believe that, before the reintroduction of horses, running was simply the most practical way to cross this mythological region.

In *The Chemehuevis*, Laird also wrote: "In the last two decades, they [the Chemehuevi] ran simply for the joy of running in each other's company, taking the old trails well back from the [Colorado] River." As I cradle a metal cup of hot coffee next to a small fire on the crisp dawn of day 3, it's easy to imagine the scenario Laird described. Chris and Dick are sticklike silhouettes floating through the gray mirage of the Mud Hills and 7,049-foot Providence Mountains. These ranges were traversed not only by the free-roaming Mojave but also by the Chemehuevi, whose running paths crisscrossed those of the Mojave near here while following their ancient path of the Southern Fox north to Death

> Before the reintroduction of horses, running was simply the most practical way to cross this mythological region.

Valley and the "Salt Song" south to the Colorado River. In moments, the tiny figures of Dick and Chris disappear into the shimmering mountain wall, and through my telephoto lens they seem to have transcended the physical act of running on a pathway and moved back through the ages of man, when a mile was determined not by distance but by the living features of the Storied Land.

To the Chemehuevi runners, according to Laird, a mile was "the land from the top of one mountain range, through the intervening valley, to the top of the next mountain . . . literally, one desert." It takes Dick and Chris most of the morning to run one and a half *cuukutiiravi*, "Chemehuevi miles," from Pozos de San Juan de Dios, through the spring desert wild-flowers, around the northern flanks of the snow-flecked Providence Mountains, to Government Holes. Jim, Geary, and I rendezvous with them at this historic water hole, named for freighter Phineas Banning who dug the well in the summer of 1859 when he found nearby Camp Rock Spring dry. But the cold Mojave wind cuts them to the quick; so Dick runs one last "white mans's mile" alone to the shelter of Camp Rock Spring. Seen through the long lens of my camera, he is still running as if yester-day never occurred and tomorrow will never come. But the loose footing has torqued and wrenched his tendons and joints, and Dick begins favor-ing his left leg; and each step that nibbles at a tiny piece of the horizon mirrors the pain of my own inner Canyon journey.

By the time his silhouette dances with the petroglyphs at Camp Rock Spring, however, he's going to do whatever it takes to reach the end of his pathway at river's edge. Known to the Chemehuevi as *Tooyagah*, "Center of the Pass," this prehistoric water hole was also important to the moun-tain men, emigrants, prospectors, and explorers who crossed this hard desert in hopes of reaching the Mojave River without dying of thirst. In April 1884, surveyor Lieutenant John C. Frémont painted a vivid picture of how white men viewed travel through this ancestral desert: "Between us and the Colorado River we were aware that the country was extreme-ly poor in grass, and scarce for water, there being many *jornadas* [a day's journey without water], or long stretches of 40 to 60 miles, without water, where the road was marked by bones. . . . "

By noon, I'm anxious to start running the next *jornada* with Dick, but his legs have fatigued since leaving Camp Cady eighty-six miles earlier. He soaks them in a cool mud pack while I pace around waiting to take off. Two hours later, Dick's earthen remedy seems to have done the trick, and we trot down the gravel bed of Watson Wash until we can break out of it and head cross-country; once we do, though, we are confronted by a dense forest of cholla cactus. There is no trail through this menacing stand of "jumping cactus," so we begin hunting for a way through it without getting peppered by clusters of cactus needles. Only then will we be able to concentrate on relocating the Mojave Trail.

It's at this point in the journey that I begin to realize Dick's pathway is as much a geographical puzzle as it is a trans-temporal adventure. Ancient paths that tracked the Southwest had one of two distinct characteristics. Either they were so well trod, and so well preserved in the dry soils of the desert, that you could still follow the exact path of the ancients from one trail shrine, or water hole, to the next, as was generally the case with the Mojave Trail and the Hohokam shell trails that crossed El Gran Desierto; or, like the Hopi-Havasupai trade route, because of its wetter climate, higher elevation, corresponding life zone, soil composition, and topography, only the basic route of travel could be followed from one geographical point or sacred landmark—a mountain, cliff, canyon, monument, cave, river, or springs—to the next.

Having somehow slipped through this savage cholla forest unscathed, we put our noses to the ground and zigzag back and forth trying to cut sign of the trail where Casebier said we might: "When you get over there about where the map says 4660, you're gonna have to find the trail there or you probably won't find it most of the way across Lanfair Valley. It's not really a trail, it's a ditch." We hop down into this ancient path, which has been worn so deep by the heavy iron-rimmed wheels of eight-mule-team wagons that it now acts as a storm drain for monsoon runoff, and start running below the level of the ground. Our eyes peering a few feet over the edge of the desert floor gliding past, we beat cheeks for Lanfair Valley seven miles distant.

But sitting in the middle of this desolate valley is the strangest sight I've ever seen in this desert or any other: a telephone booth! There's not a building for miles around; there are no signs, survey stakes, or other clues that some eastern developer had a hallucination about building a casino or resort community in the midst of this hidden quarter, just sage, Joshua trees, a few zebra-tailed lizards trying to stir up a little excitement with an afternoon regimen of push ups—and a telephone booth. Dick and I rendezvous with his support crew in this zone of mystery, otherwise know as

Lanfair #1, then push on toward Paiute Springs. We're not a half hour out from this ancient water hole, what the Chemehuevi knew as *paasa*, how-ever, when I realize we're running through the desert's mythic time, when its natural forces shape your movement, your per-ceptions, your vision. Shadowing each other side by side, we ham-

> Sitting in the middle of this desolate valley is the strangest sight I've ever seen in this desert or any other; a tele-phone booth!

mer our pace, but we can't run fast enough now. We gulp double drafts of air, blow in and out: *hih-hih/huhhh, hih-hih/huhhh, hih-hih/huhhh, hih-hih/huhhh, hih-hih/huhhh.* Our feet tap a staccato beat, whispering *tcawa-tcawa, tcawa-tcawa, tcawa-tcawa, tcawa-tcawa.* We are no longer running; we are gliding across the ground, and we can't go fast enough: *hih-hih/huhhh, hih-hih/huhhh, hih-hih/huhhh, hih-hih/huhhh.* . . . And the faster we glide toward the 4,076-foot Paiute Mountains, bristling in the distance like the mythic Chemehuevi *huna,* "badger," crawling across the landscape, the more I feel like a shadow slipping through the orange luster now blanketing the desert. There is no identity. Inner dialogue is still. Desires and emotions no longer exist. There is only the feeling of flight. Shadows streaking through the palpitating orange specter of after-noon light until it dissipates in the rufous glow of sundown, only to be swallowed by the luminescent blues of twilight. Gray fades to black, and the incipient path is lost in a maze of braided washes.

In the distance, a full moon climbs over the Paiute Mountains, what the Chemehuevi knew as *ʔampanigaiva,* "talking mountain," showering them with a brilliant lunar dust as our shadows continue floating toward the moon. A feeling of bewitchment transcends the physical act of run-ning, breathing, of sensory deprivation, and I feel as though we can run forever. The incandescent glow of the moon distorting the unworldly shadows of Joshua trees swaying back and forth over us only enhances that feeling—of movement within the specter of time standing still. I wonder if this is what the late Chemehuevi runner George Laird meant when he quietly spoke of "the secret way of traveling, which is the old way." A runner by the name of *Kaawɨʔa*, Rat Penis, was the only Chemehuevi known to travel this way; according to Laird, when Rat Penis ran "with his companions, he ran as they did, but when he went alone, he used his secret method. This was possibly a way of teleportation, but of it only this is known for certain: that it enabled him to arrive at his destination with no lapse of time." One day, a group of Chemehuevi runners followed Rat Penis to see just how he did this, but his tracks, Laird wrote, "became further and further apart and lighter and lighter on the sand" until they

> A runner by the name of Rat Penis . . . used his secret method . . . that enabled him to arrive at his destination with no lapse of time.

reached the distant village they had pointed to. Wrote Laird: "When at length they reached the village at the mouth of the Gila [River] they inquired 'Did *Kaawɨʔa* come Here?' 'Yes,' the people answered, 'he arrived on the day that he had left them [the other runners] just as the sun was rising.'"

But any insight into this ancient knowledge of running escapes me when Dick and I are forced to grapple with the reality of struggling over the gnarly spine of the Paiute Mountains into Paiute Canyon. It is tomb-black in the depths of this rugged canyon, the moondust now lost behind the towering black walls. The footing is too treacherous to consider running. And my lips are cracked and bleeding. The flimsy plastic bladder of my bota bag broke an hour ago, but I'm reluctant to ask Dick for any of his water. The Chemehuevi runners carried their water in the rumen of a desert bighorn sheep, which could be cooked and eaten as a survival ration if needed. That's when the Chemehuevi still sang the "Mountain Sheep Song":

My mountain canteen
will go swinging like a pendulum
swing like a pendulum
my mountain canteen
will go bouncing up and down
will go bouncing up and down . . .

No such luck with my broken bag, which hangs still and lifeless at my side like a dead rabbit. And the drier my lips become, the wetter and colder I imagine Paiute Springs to be, 150,000 gallons of artesian water gurgling magically from the sand each day.

Voices yelp like coyotes in the distance as Dick and I swat and flail our way out of a thicket of trees and brush toward a roaring fire. We're late—whatever that means in a desert whose only timepiece is the circadian rhythms of the sun, moon, stars, and what the Chemehuevi called *Naugupoh* for the Ghost Trail of the Milky Way—and Dick's support crew has been worried. But we're happy; in fact, we're giddy, and, for no reason, we break out laughing. The taste of adventure ignites our communal merriment, which we toast late into the evening.

Herman Grey was a Mojave, of the *shul-ya*, or "beaver," clan, when he wrote in *Tales from the Mohaves*: "A test of endurance for men was a trip into southern California, the whole distance covered at a jogging trot, to trade for abalone shells." Jim Gaston surprises us at daybreak the next morning with a fragment of abalone shell he'd found lying next to the crumbling rock walls of old Fort Pah-Ute. Like Camp Cady, Fort Pah-Ute was a military outpost strategically positioned along this leg of the Old Spanish Trail to protect wagon trains of emigrants as

By the time he struggles around the northern end of the Dead Mountains, however, he is physically and emotionally spent.

they drove their teams westward along the Mojave trade route. And evidence of their ancient commerce is now gingerly cupped in the palm of Jim's hand! Who was the runner? What song did he sing? What vision did he have? What did he endure while carrying that precious shell more than two hundred miles east from the Pacific Ocean before it was dropped here in the sands ages ago? Was he Mojave? Or was he Hualapai, or Havasupai, trading red ocher paint from the river's edge in the western Grand Canyon for the shell that journeyed here from the Pacific?

Maybe I'd have better insight into this trade route once I started down the Hopi-Havasupai leg a month from now, but for now these questions are left for Dick to answer. As among the Chemehuevi, who passed their territorial songs from one generation to the next, in my eyes this fleeting pathway momentarily belongs to Dick, not me, and he still has a *cuuku-tɨɨravɨ*, "Chemehuevi mile," of sand and rock to go before he reaches the Colorado River. But he's weary. The hundred-odd miles almost did him in during the night, and he's now on the verge of either physical collapse or self-discovery—I can't be certain. But he needs to run the final leg of his pathway alone to find out for himself.

The 3,598-foot Dead Mountains, which the Chemehuevi knew as *tuuhavitcɨ*, "black lying," is the last range of desert peaks standing between Dick and the end of his pathway at river's edge. By the time he struggles around the northern end of the Dead Mountains, however, he is physically and emotionally spent; tears are snaking down his salt-caked cheeks, trailing their own pathways. Yet the Colorado River is so close now he can literally feel it pulsating on the horizon, but his Achilles' tendon is on fire. Worse, the desert pavement has turned into a frying pan, and his bota bags were both sucked dry an hour ago.

It's strange, then, that Dick sees a rare, and endangered, desert tortoise engaged in its own life-and-death struggle for survival. To the Chemehuevi, the *ʔaya* is sacred, "its tough-heartedness equated with the will and ability to endure and survive." On this last day, it becomes Dick's own *tutuguuvɨ*, or "spirit-animal," because seeing it reinvigorates his painful run. One footstep, then another, it feels as though he could walk faster, but he keeps running.

The Colorado River is getting closer, s-l-o-w-l-y, only two miles now; the previous 128 miles rewind in front of him with the precision of Casebier's words: "Paiute Springs, Rock Springs, Marl Springs, the Mojave Sink . . . " They're fleeting images of moments that no longer exist. They may be what Carobeth Laird meant when she wrote:

> No more moccasined feet tread silently upon hard-packed trails, whispering tcawa, tcawa, tcawa . . . that a whole mode of transportation is lost, never to be regained. Even if the remaining people increased and prospered their thought has so departed from the old ways, that there would be no eyes to see [the] desert, mountains, and River as they were once seen.

Off in the distance, the Needles can be seen towering over the Colorado River. To the Mojave, these jagged desert peaks were known as *huequeamp avi*, "where the battle took place," where their god Mastamhó killed the mythical sea serpent. The sacred peaks of *huequeamp avi* also marked the passageway Mojave spirits traveled through en route to the Shadow Land after cremation. When Dick finally stumbles into the cool embrace of the Colorado River, where it drifts south toward this passageway, voices of joy cry out. He doesn't say much though. In fact, Dick is so weary he wonders just what it is he's accomplished, if anything. His eyes, streaked with blood-gorged pathways, tell their own story—that on this final, grueling, stifling-hot and dusty day, he may have glimpsed, if only for a moment, the desert, mountains, and river as they once were seen by the ancients who ran before him. And I can only hope for as much if I survive in the Shadow Land of the Hopi-Havasupai trail.

II.

It's almost sundown when the three of us enter the east arm of Moqui Trail Canyon on the western edge of the Grand Canyon. We are weary. Our flimsy clothes are tattered. My bare limbs have been repeatedly slashed, leaving a maze of strawberry-red scratches. And, for me, the prospect for survival has never seemed more desperate. It has taken me nearly five days to reach this point, retracing the aboriginal Hopi-Havasupai trail 174 miles across the searing Painted Desert and stark Coconino Plateau to what the Havasupai called *itcahuá'gawáwawaguwa*, "enemy scalp place." And what I'd originally envisioned as an enchanting journey along the prehistoric trade route from Oraibi to Havasupai has been crisscrossed by a labyrinth of historic wagon trails and pickup tracks. Worse, unseasonably hot, dry weather dragged me to my knees, almost killing me, the second day out.

> We are weary. Our flimsy clothes are tattered. My bare limbs have been repeatedly slashed . . . the prospect for survival has never seemed more desperate.

So the final leg from Moqui Tank to Havasupai is supposed to be the pay-off, the opportunity to step completely into this trans-temporal adventure by running wild through the untrammeled depths of Cataract and Havasu Canyons, along a pathway first used by ancient traders long before

The author "camels up" at Moqui Tanks, the only water hole in Moqui Trail Canyon.

Fray Francisco Tomás Garcés first traveled it in 1776. But if the last four miles of running from that stinking, slime-covered water hole are any indication of what lies beyond, it will be a finish as desperate as that faced by forty-niners crossing territorial Arizona's merciless *Camino del Diablo*, "Road of the Devil."

Grim-faced, the three of us scan the ground and quickly root out two bathtub-sized *tinajas* brimming with cool water and teeming with insect larvae. This is the last known water source between us and Havasu Springs, eighteen miles or more downstream. So we "camel up," fill our half-empty bota bags, and debate whether or not to push on.

Dave Ganci has joined me for this daunting leg. Having spent the better part of his life skulking around the lower Sonoran Desert, he has the convictions of a desert rat, and he votes to bivouac near these precious *tinajas*. But he's carrying an "elephant's foot," a half sleeping bag used for mountaineering bivouacs, and I'm only carrying a wool blanket; so I vote for the balmier depths

> The trail is no more than a desert bighorn sheep path mashed into a forty-five-degree slope, and it's the most exposed and dangerous trail any of us has ever been on.

of Moqui Trail Canyon almost a thousand vertical feet below. Chris Keith is just carrying a Nikon F, and she doesn't care where we bivouac, so long as she's able to photograph the ensuing journey; she is the expedition shooter.

According to my fifteen-minute topographic map, we have two and a half to three miles to run by dark before we can hunker down in the depths of Cataract Canyon, confident that we'll reach Havasu Springs by midmorning tomorrow. But Dave hesitates, explaining that running thirty-four miles in a day is enough for an old gila monster like himself. I agree, but the opportunity to sleep in the warm bed of the *wigásiyává*,

Cataract Canyon, below is irresistible; I've spent the last four nights curled up around the fire, shivering in a flimsy wool blanket, and I'm as weary and brain-dead from those near-sleepless bivouacs as I am from the long hot miles I've run.

I decide to keep going, but Dave lingers—until I remind him that I'm carrying what remains of the food: a small bag of Hopi piki bread, a few strands of sand-covered beef jerky, dried apricots, chia seeds, dates, and piñon nuts, also covered with sand and dirt. He decides to continue.

The three of us scurry along a narrow trail toward 5,660-foot Antelope Point. The trail is no more than a desert bighorn sheep path mashed into a forty-five-degree slope, and it's the most exposed and dangerous trail any of us has ever been on—worse than any trail I encountered along my inner Canyon route the year before. By twilight, we still can't find the break through the rimrock indicated on our Supai, AZ, quadrangle, so we continue contouring the edge of the brink, ever

Author retracing the Hopi-Havasupai trade route across the Painted Desert.

mindful of the consequences of one misplaced step. Two to five feet of steep, loose talus is all that stands between us and a deadly plunge over

Rimrocked on the Hopi-Havasupai trade route. the author and Dave Ganci look for a way into Moqui Trail Canyon.

a headwall of Coconino sandstone into the shadowy depths of Moqui Trail Canyon.

By nightfall, I know I've been outfoxed, either by the large, undefinable scale of our fifteen-minute map or by the combination of sleep deprivation, physical exhaustion, dehydration, and mental fatigue. "Distance running kills brain cells," I tell Chris and Dave, but they are not amused. It's too dark to continue and too dangerous to backtrack, even with Dave's small flashlight. A haunting precipice looms above us, and a gaping abyss yawns below. We can go neither up nor down. We are, as locals say of cattle stranded in Utah's slickrock canyon country, "rimrocked"—only we are rimrocked on the very edge of northern Arizona's six-thousand-foot-high Coconino Plateau, a land that, tonight, appears as lonely and sublime as it did when anthropologist Frank H. Cushing followed Garcés's century-old trail from the ancient Hopi village of Oraibi to Havasupai in 1882.

> We will have to spend the entire night perched on this slippery ledge without sliding into the brink or dying of exposure.

And now, finally, I'm about to complete my own *entrada*, "entrance," to that same village on a pathway I've been tracing along Garcés's and Cushing's route across the Painted Desert and Coconino Plateau. But whereas Garcés and Cushing rode horseback along this trade route, I run, as I've theorized ancient traders did before Spaniards reintroduced horses to this primeval land, running as the Mojave did along their own leg of the trade route seven sleeps west of here. But the only guides I have to keep me oriented on this pathway are the vague, personal accounts of Garcés and Cushing, and several scientific papers that attempted to pinpoint the route from one geographical feature, sacred landmark, and water hole to the next. Unfortunately, Casebier had not yet retraced this regionwide trade route eastward beyond Kingman, Arizona, after linking the historic Beale's Wagon Road to it from the east end of the Mojave Trail. Standing on the edge of the black precipice of Moqui Trail Canyon, I longed for the same methodical guidance Casebier had provided Dick only a month earlier.

Wherever the hidden entrance to Moqui Trail Canyon is, our only option is to bivouac where we stand. But there is nothing to anchor our bodies to in the mushy cryptogamic soil of the Toroweap formation that erodes back from its tenuous contact with the Coconino wall. So we carefully paw our way through the dark on all fours down a short, steep sandstone chute toward camp. Camp is a sloping, park-bench-sized ledge covered with dirt, loose rocks, and, no doubt, slender scorpions; fortunately, it is too dark to see for sure. Standing there, hanging on to the dagger-tipped,

> It is cold. The wind is whipping sand into our eyes and ears, but Dave and I cannot control our sudden laughter; it is the nervous laughter of the condemned.

thorn-fringed palm of a century plant, we begin sweeping the rock shelf clear of debris with our feet. A noisy avalanche of stony rubble cascades over the rim into the chasm below, covering our faces with swirling dust.

It is cold. The wind is whipping sand into our eyes and ears, but Dave and I cannot control our sudden laughter; it is the nervous laughter of the condemned. Meanwhile, Chris wonders aloud why she actually thanked Tim and me for allowing her to photograph this last perilous marathon.

The laughter stops abruptly when the three of us realize we will have to spend the entire night perched on this slippery ledge without sliding into the brink or dying of exposure. The temperature at our Anita Station camp the night before had been in the twenties. Even if there were any piñon or juniper to set ablaze with my knife and flint, there is no room for a fire. So we carefully spread out what passes for my Indian blanket, sit on it, then pull it over our shoulders like a shawl, while Dave lays the elephant foot across our legs. But he keeps most of it for himself, until I bring out the food bag. "He who has the sharpest tooth has the finest coat," I tell him, reminding him of his own wolf-pack philosophy. And so the bartering of food and shelter begins. A trade route indeed.

Our gnawing hunger temporarily sated by our scant rations, the three of us spoon our bodies together and reluctantly face the long, dark journey we'll have to make together in order to survive the night. But our airy lair is not the cozy sleeping circles once used by the Southern Diegueño of the Mojave Desert; they reportedly scraped away the hard desert pavement so that roving tribal members could sleep together beneath rabbit-skin blankets for warmth. Our perch is more the smooth divots of one or two desert bighorn sheep, what Havasupai hunters called *amudjuwóviga*. Stalked along precipitous canyon benches such as this, mountain sheep were either driven over cliffs or shot with arrows by Havasupai hunters camouflaged in ewe's head robes. According to Havasupai elder Sinyella, it was dangerous hunting that claimed the life of one hunter when others shouted, "One man has fallen down the white cliff [Coconino] and has been killed."

Perched on our dangerous ledge, without the benefit of the juniper bark mats the Havasupai used for sleeping, the next hour or so becomes a restless tug-of-war to make a cold slab of rock more comfortable than it could be. Since Chris is hunkered down between us, Dave and I toss and turn at her command.

When the rubescent moments of twilight fade to black, we are greeted by what the Chemehuevi called the Ghost Trail of the Milky Way; and it looks like it's been airbrushed across the dark heavens, crossed by shooting stars trailing phosphorous light, and tiny white satellites whirling at distant corners of our universe. For the next eight hours, our dreams will play out against these celestial skies; tenuously perched as we are, we don't dare close our eyes for more than a few minutes at a time. But there, I see, is Orion's Belt twinkling above. The Havasupai were said to view this constellation as *amu'u'*, a herd of bighorn sheep that were ambushed by *hatakwila*, the "wolf man."

By midnight the biting cold has seized our bones like the fangs of the mythological *hatakwila*, and we're on the verge of shivering off the edge of our perch. My whimpers are echoed by the clacking of Chris's and Dave's teeth. Desperately, we reach out for better handholds. Mine is the slick, waxy base of a dagger-tipped century plant, its withered roots loosely anchored to a shallow crack. Chris's is the strap of my bota bag, now choking my shoulder and neck while Dave has his bony right hip painfully smeared across the cold rock. Thus set, the three of us resume our reverie-filled journey through the night, back along the Hopi-Havasupai trail.

Old Oraibi is perched atop windswept 5,996-foot Third Mesa eighty miles east of the Grand Canyon in the heart of the Painted Desert. Now a secluded, modern Hopi settlement, Oraibi first appeared as Moqui on Padre Kino's 1701 map *Paso por Tierra a la California*, and today it vies with the spectacular New Mexico village of Ácoma as the oldest continuously inhabited pueblo in the contiguous United States. Like the Eastern Pueblo peoples of New Mexico, traditional Hopi have

> I realize that I'll have to burn my bridges with my support crew if I'm to experience similar hardships and risks ancient traders encountered.

steadfastly clung to their sacred beliefs and ancestral values in the face of extraordinary pressure to adopt non-Indian ways, though many drive pickups where their ancestors once ran and rode horses.

Nonetheless, I was not sure what the *hópi*, "wise, knowing," would think of a *bahanna*, "non-Indian," running along an ancient path that once linked their village with that of the Havasupai. So several weeks prior to my departure date, I sought out the sage advice of Don Decker, a Native American college counselor; I was troubled by the thought that the Hopi might somehow associate what I was doing with what the controversial Smoki Dancers do. The Smoki's story began around 1911; that's when the Boy Scouts of America started offering Indian lore merit badges. By 1915, the idea took hold, the Order of the Arrow was formed, and Scouts were performing sacred Native American ceremonies such as the Sioux Buffalo Dance, the Eagle Dance, and, of all dances to be adopted by non-Indians, the haunting Ghost Dance. Seen in a vision by the great Paiute shaman Wovoka in 1887, and adopted by many tribes throughout the Great Plains and the West, including the Havasupai, the Ghost Dance was used to call back the spirits of deceased kin and to drive out the White Eyes. The Smoki Dancers were a spin-off of the popular Indian hobbyist movement that attempted to perform ceremonies that Native Americans themselves were banned from performing by the government until the 1930s. The Smoki adopted the Hopi's sacred Snake Dance, which they performed for money at their annual Smoki ceremonials. Hopi priests and traditionalists were justifiably disturbed that a ceremony inextricably linked to Hopi religion, culture, and lifeways had been adopted by a group of white Prescott businessmen. It was a serious matter. Even when the neighboring Zuni asked the Hopi to teach them the Snake-Antelope ceremony, the Hopi refused, lest the sacred knowledge be compromised. On August 7, 1893, Alexander M. Stephen, a Scotsman and one of only a handful of non-Indians known to be initiated by the Hopi into the Snake-Antelope society, wrote of the Zuni meeting in his *Hopi Journal:* "Some years ago about fifteen *Zuñi* came here [to First Mesa] begging the Hopi to initiate them into the mysteries of the Snake and the Antelope. The Zuñi offered these people two large oxen, ten or more sheep, much wheat, rawhide, moccasins and other wealth. But Wiki, Nasyuñ', and Ha'hawi were opposed to permitting the Zuñi to acquire the desired knowledge, lest the medicine lose its virtue." Decker knew I wore no sacred eagle, hawk, or turkey feathers, that I claimed no Native American ancestry, and that I carried no homemade prayer bundles in mock reverence to Southwest Indian ceremonialism. Nor did I have any interest in visiting or photographing the Hopi's *chu'aki,* "Snake Shrine;" *tawápa,* "Sun Springs;" *Sha'pukpu,* "Scalp House" [of slain Apache]; or other sacred shrines described in "scientific" papers and books. In further deference to Hopi religious beliefs, when I trekked sixty miles down the length of the Little Colorado River Gorge earlier, I even refused to look at *sipápuni*—though it's become a popular day hike for rafters walking up from the Colorado River—because it was the opening through which Hopi ancestors emerged from the Underwold. Decker knew I was interested in running the Hopi-Havasupai trade route primarily from an ethnogeographer's perspective and to learn what ancient traders—be they from the Desert Culture, Anasazi, Hopi, Navajo, Havasupai, Hualapai, Paiute, or Mojave— might have endured physically and mentally

> For the first time in sixty miles, I have doubts about my ability to reach the Little Colorado River alive.

to cross it. Religion, sacred rites, and ceremony I strongly felt were the Native American's sacrosanct domain. Period.

Decker lowered his glasses, looked me in the eye, and said, "John, if you ask enough people up there, you'll find someone to say *no*. Just go do it."

So that's what I did. I slipped out of a small campground next to Oraibi at 4:30 A.M. under cover of darkness and ran through the black sand of Oraibi Wash, along the route of the ancient traders, ten miles south to Burro Springs.

I haven't run two hours west of Burro Springs across the red sands of sixty-three-hundred-foot Padilla Mesa, however, before I realize that my rim-bound pathway to Havasupai isn't going to be the near-pristine journey my inner Canyon route had been. A nearly indecipherable system of dirt roads, wagon paths, and horse trails threads the Navajo-Hopi Joint Use Area of the Painted Desert, and it's a far cry from the "well-beaten trail into the Desierto Pintado" Cushing had followed west from Oraibi a hundred years earlier. It's along this sand-whipped maze that the twentieth century comes hurtling back through my aerobic time warp. A young Navajo, driving a beefed-up, gunmetal gray Dodge Charger slides into a hurricane of red dust and stops to ask where I'm going.

"Grand Canyon," I yell over the rumbling engine without breaking stride.

"Want a ride?" he asks, apparently thinking I'm too stoic to stick out my thumb and hitchhike.

"Thanks, no," I tell him. "I'm *running* to the Grand Canyon."

The Navajo shakes his head, throttles the engine until it rumbles and shakes, then punches it; spitting up fifteen-foot rooster tails of red sand in his wake, he careens down the ancient path, plunging deeper into his own cross-cultural adventure.

By the time I stride into Sand Springs at the thirty-mile mark another hour or so west, I'm wondering if this reaction will be the norm. Three kids and a hairless mutt come running out of a traditional Navajo hogan and stand at the edge of the sandy track. Their mouths agape, they point at the apparition of a *belegonna*, "non-Indian," running toward them and laugh. The dog barks, and suddenly I'm mumbling to myself, "You can run, but you can't hide."

Once a key geographical feature for early travelers crossing the badlands of the Painted Desert, Dinnebito Wash drains the western flanks of Garcés Mesa before reaching its confluence with the Little Colorado River at Black Falls. It's late afternoon when I finally rendezvous with Tim and Craig at what the Navajo called *Dinnebito*, "people springs," eight miles south of Sand Springs. The driving force behind my inner Canyon journey the year before, Tim and Craig have joined me on this new pathway to pursue a similar end: to help me survive an ancient journey that was commonplace for those who knew as second nature the nuances of survival in this austere, mile-high desert, and the mode of fleet-footed long-distance travel. When Tim and Craig greet me, the motor drive of Chris Keith's camera whining in the background, they make me feel as though I've achieved my first step in trying to undergo a primeval metamorphosis.

Our camp in the sagebrush at the foot of a small sand dune is a curious mingling of the old and the new. I build my fire with flint and steel; they build theirs with matches and newspapers bearing the headline RUNNER WILL RELIVE HISTORY IN TRIP ALONG CANYON ROUTE. They eat thick bean burros, chased down with cold beer, and sleep in pillowy down sleeping bags. I long to do the same, but I'm trying to see whether I can cross the threshold between the present and the past; so I munch on native fare of jerky and piñon nuts and curl around my fire in a thin wool Mexican blanket; I'm substituting it for an expensive Navajo blanket. Such blankets were so prized during the 1860s that the Havasupai traded a burden basket of shelled corn for each Navajo blanket.

Shivering all night around a small fire to the peaceful snoring of Tim, Craig, and Chris, I know by first light I won't be able to journey back through time if I'm continually forced to confront our two different worlds. It's then I realize that I'll have to burn my bridges with my support crew if I'm to experience similar hardships and risks ancient traders encountered. Without those elements, this journey will lack substance and authenticity for me. But Tim and Craig give me such selfless logistical support, I know they're intent on doing whatever it takes to make this journey a safe one. So I tell them I need the risk of running from water hole to water hole alone, as the ancient traders had. They point out the day is unseasonably hot and that ancient traders ran together from village to village, hunting ground to hunting ground, or one food-storage cave to the next. That is true; today, however, at least north of the Sierra Madre's "cave-dwelling Tarahumara," that lifeway has disappeared. So we strike a compromise: we'll rendezvous at Black Falls, at the sixty-eight-mile mark, on the Little Colorado River, what Havasupai traders called *Hagaøeíla*, at high noon.

By 8:00 A.M. I realize I've burned my bridges. Horse Water Tanks and other springs and stock tanks I run by are bone dry; I'd counted on them to help me reach Black Falls, what the Havasupai called *Hářny átovakóvá*, "black water precipice." The two liters in my bota bag won't be enough. It's the driest I've seen northern Arizona in years; worse, the temperature is pushing ninety degrees in the shade. And my mind and body feel like they're undergoing some sort of metamorphosis.

For a moment, I falter and my running seems less graceful. I can feel the moisture being sucked out of my body and lungs with each footfall. For the first time in sixty miles, I have doubts about my ability to reach the Little Colorado River alive. It's too hot. Without extra water, my brain

Flint and Steel. The author used flint and steel to make many of the bivouac fires he relied on to keep warm—and alive—during his long runs, as seen here in Cataract Canyon on the the Hopi-Havasupai trade route.

will fry, and I'll drop in my tracks. I've got to slow down and walk; it's the only way to get the most out of what little fluid reserves may be left in my body. But walking takes too much time. I'm having trouble enough running through this cerebral wildland; walking it would be unbearable. So I keep running, knowing I'm treading the fine line between heat stress and heat exhaustion. Of the same desert, Cushing wrote: "Only the beaten trail before us, the bones, sometimes human, the bits of castaway cordage, show that man has ever penetrated its solitudes. Tortured by thirst . . . "

Shimmering in the distance, floating on waves of heat drifting off Tloi Eechii Cliffs, is 4,915-foot Black Point; to the Navajo, it is *tsezhin deez'a'hi,* "traprock spring," the traditional stopping place of the Western Water Clans. To the south, a dreamy field of black-lava flows, cinder cones, and dormant volcanoes ripples toward the lofty, snow-covered flanks of the 12,633-foot San Francisco Mountains. To northern Arizona's indigenous people, they are the most sacred peaks in the world, the dwelling place of deities. To the Navajo, they are known as *Dook'o'oosliid,* "Never Thaws on Top"; it was fastened to the earth by a sunbeam, and it is the sacred mountain of the west—one of four cardinal mountains that embody the legends and define the four directions of the Navajo's spiritual universe. Traditional Navajo believe "these peaks are our father and mother.

We come from them; we depend on them . . . each mountain is a person. The water courses are their veins and arteries. The water in them is to their life as our blood is to our bod-

As I float toward this most sacred mountain through a stifling wall of heat, I revere it the only way I know how—by running.

ies." To the Havasupai, the San Francisco Mountains are *Huchassahpatch,* "Big Rock Mountains;" together with *wigadawi'sa,* 7,326-foot Red Butte, and *Huegawoola,* 9,264-foot Bear Mountain, they form the supernal heights that feed the sacred blue springs of Cataract Canyon. To the Hopi, the San Francisco Mountains are *Nuva teekia ovi*, the "Place of Snow on the Very Top," the home of their *katcinas*, who bless their corn and parched homelands with rain. And as I float toward this most sacred mountain through a stifling wall of heat, I revere it the only way I know how—by running. For a moment, maybe an hour, it draws me toward it, and I feel as though I'm running back through time:

Li-i hi-la
Listen, my mothers.
You have prayed
That it would rain on your plants.
Li-i hi-la
Listen, my fathers.
You have prayed
That it would rain on your plants.
Li-i hi-la
When you look after the rain
You shall see what you have prayed for.
Li-i hi-la
When the rain falls among your plants
You shall see the pools of water,
My fathers.
This is what you prayed for.
Li-i hi-la

The pool of water I have prayed for is still nowhere in sight. But it wasn't far from here that Garcés stopped at a *ranchería* of thirty Yavapai and wrote: "There arrived later two Indians from Moqui, dressed in leather jackets . . . and they came to trade with these Yavapais, and the word was sent to a neighboring *ranchería*." Running in the footsteps of those ancient traders, I am alone out here, as alone as anyone could hope to be in our troubled global village, and that fills me with contentment. Although the burnished red escarpments, sand dunes, and Triassic badlands of shale, siltstone, and Chinle sandstone do not appear, in passing, as spectacular as the Grand Canyon, this land is inhabited by spirits and deities the Navajo have revered since they dispersed throughout the Four Corners region between A.D. 1200 and 1500. What appears simply as a scorched stretch of the Painted Desert is a small tract of what traditional Navajo still know, and revere, as *Dinetah*, "the land," a twenty-five-thousand-square-mile region of the six-thousand-foot-high Colorado Plateau. Yet, scattered throughout their ancestral domain are untold majestic landforms, caves, springs, rocks, and canyons made by the hands of their gods and the Holy Ones, and the Navajo continue to revere them through ceremonial sings, or chantways. Running through their sacred landscape, I am awed by their perception of what I first viewed merely as a desert to cross. I achieve a sense of isolation and vulnerability where this land, the endless running, begins to strip away my ego, the societal mask and costume I wear in what the Navajo view as the Fifth World of modern man, where they pray to Talking God for help:

Now I walk with Talking God.
It is with his feet I go;
It is with his legs I go;
It is with his body I go;
It is with his mind I go;
It is with his voice I go;
I go with twelve feathers of the white eagle.
With goodness and beauty in all things around me I go;
Thus being I, I go.

My feet pad softly across the sandy desert floor. Mushrooms of red sand erupt beneath each footfall. My arms flap in stark rhythm to the ghost-beat of a sun-bleached hawk skeleton lying by the side of the track. I suck hot air in through my cracked lips. There is no pain, no effort. The only feeling I have is that of dry feathers being blown across the red sand as far as I can see.

Author recovering from heat exhaustion on the Hopi-Havasupai trade route. Salt stains his bandanna.

Heat waves shimmer on the western horizon below Black Point, filtering out all perceptible color; the only hint of color that exists in the haze-shrouded distance is gray and grayer. Yet, through this diffused, somber light, I see a man on horseback. Is it Dehydration, my own Fifth Horseman of the Apocalypse, merely a Navajo sheepherder, or, worse, a Skinwalker, carrying corpse powder and death? These supernatural Navajo *Ye·na·lo·si*, or "Were-Animals," were believed to wear the skins of wolves, coyotes, foxes, and other animals, and at night they ran after their victims at inhuman speeds. But it was day, he rode a pale horse, and he simply wore the look of death. What was it? I'm not sure. My arms and legs are no longer glistening with sweat, a sure sign that without water or help death rides the horizon. My perception seems stultified, and I wonder if I've already begun an irreversible slide toward heat exhaustion, hallucination, and death in the desert.

I continue running but not consciously. I feel more like the wax figure of a runner, and that my movement is triggered by the most atavistic of instincts: to get to water and survive. Even if I could sit down and wait for my road warrior friend to come screaming over the horizon to rescue me, I wouldn't make it. There is no shade in the middle of this holy land, no water, no aid station, no pueblos, no villagers cheering me on. Nothing. Worse, the only finish line is some nebulous point on the distant horizon five sleeps west of here. Yet my body keeps racing the sun toward the fleeing horseman. Is he real? Or have I already reached that point where I'll get down on all fours and, in a deranged effort to quench my thirst, start lapping up the hot sand as if it were snowmelt tumbling down the sacred heights of the San Francisco Mountains?

> There is no pain, no effort. The only feeling I have is that of dry tumbleweed being blown across the red sand as far as I can see.

The deadly treadmill I'm locked into, the vast sweep of mesas, buttes, and sand dunes of the Painted Desert, is also sacred ground to the Hopi. They ran across it in ceremonial prayer to beckon the Cloud spirits to flood their dry arroyos with fresh water; they ran through it at sunrise to wash their bodies in sacred springs where they prayed for health and vigor; they even ran back and forth across the breadth of it from Old Oraibi to Flagstaff to deliver urgent messages. That's what Charlie Talawepi did as a young man at the turn of the century; in nearly twenty hours of nonstop running he ran 156 miles round-trip across the Painted Desert to hand deliver a wire that needed to be sent to Washington, D.C.

I have no such urgent message to deliver, and I wonder if the horseman I'm still chasing isn't a hologram of the horseback Hopi elder we met the day before we left Oraibi. Wrestling with our maps in the windblown

A Hopi sheepherder elder shares some firsthand knowledge of his homeland with the author, outside Oraibi on the Hopi Reservation. "It's a long way to Supai," he advises Annerino, before he begins his run.

sand, Tim, Craig, and I were staring into the western horizon when a Hopi man rode up and asked us, "Going the Hopi way to Supai?"

"Yes," we told him, awestruck by his knowing our intentions without our having explained them.

"*L-o-o-n-n-ng way*," he said, his hands clasped on his saddle horn, as blue clouds drifted over the red mesas behind him.

By the time *l-o-o-n-n-ng way, l-o-o-n-n-ng way* is resonating through my bones like a Native American chant, I'm beginning to wonder if the Hopi didn't have their own version of the *cuukuti-iravi*, Chemehuevi mile. But my support crew hears its own strange voices when I finally reach Black Falls in the white heat of noon. "As you came around the

Have I already reached that point where I'll get down on all fours and, in a deranged effort to quench my thirst, start lapping up the hot sand as if it were snowmelt?

bend," Craig told me later, "we heard this gasping—a death chant. You stumbled over to the water and fell in." I remember collapsing face down in the water, my overheated body hitting the water with what I imagined was a perceptible hiss. I remember lying there a l-o-o-n-n-ng time, trying to cool down my inner core, wondering what happened to the horseman, wondering if ancient traders suffered the same way, or if they all ran like Charlie Talawepi, or used the "secret way of traveling . . . which is the old way" the Chemehuevi used? How else did they run a hundred miles a day, day in and day out? I still didn't have a clue. I was only trying to run forty.

In the 1860s, Captain Navajo, known to his people as *Wasakwívama*, became a big Havasupai chief when he rode alone into a Navajo camp and, in a daring midnight raid, stole back the herd of horses the Navajo had stolen from the Havasupai while they were trading with the Hopi at Oraibi. Once I recover, I follow Captain Navajo's route north from Black Falls through the deep wet sand of the Litle Colorado River, beneath the

Author face down in a mudhole near Black Falls on the Hopi-Havasupai trade route. "As you came around the bend, we heard this gasping—a death chant. You stumbled over to the water and fell in." Craig Hudson, support crew.

towering red cliff of Tse Lichii Point to the foot of Baah Lokaa Ridge. Here, I cross the ancient migration route the Navajo Water Clan followed 120 miles north to 10,416-foot *Naatsis'áán*, Head of Earth Woman (commonly known as Navajo Mountain). I arrive at Wupatki National Monument just as the afternoon sun has painted the walls of Crack in the Rock ruin a brilliant sheen of gold. In the mesmerizing light, it's easy to see how, in 1539, Spanish padre Marcos de Niza

> "As you came around the bend we heard this gasping—a death chant. You stumbled over to the water and fell in."

mistook the Zuni pueblo of Hawikku for the seven cities of gold he later reported to conquistador Francisco Vásquez de Coronado. The golden ruins of Wupatki, however, lay 150 miles west of Coronado's fabled Seven Cities of Cibola. A trade crossroads for the prehistoric Cohonino, Sinagua, and Anasazi, Wupatki was also believed to be the ancient settlement of the Hopi's Snake and Parrot clans, and the great pueblos here take their names from them: *wukoki*, "tall house," *nalakihu*, "lone house," *lomaki*, "beautiful house," and *wupatki*, "long house." It's here I settle in for the night with Craig, Tim, and Chris at the end of day 2.

By the end of day 3, I think I've accidentally discovered what the Chemehuevi's old way of running is: to dissociate from the physical act of running, so that my mind can from float west across the Painted Desert from one geographical feature to the next. Fortunately, my pituitary gland is releasing enough dreamy endorphins to delude me into thinking I'm running the thirty-eight miles from the ancient dwellings at Wupatki, across the plains of the Spider Web Ranch to Moqui Stage Station atop the Coconino Plateau in the tracks of *Kaawiʔa* himself. Throughout the day, as I float across the landscape, the running takes on a certain mystical quality. It's as though I've made a spiritual rite of passage by coming so close to death the day before. Not that I was having hallucinations of long-haired masked Kachinas shaking buffalo rattles as they danced across Black Mesa or that Navajo Mud Dancers embodied every rock and tree I passed; it's just that an unspoken, unseen energy started gelling between me and my support crew, as we traveled independently of one another across the white caprock mesas of the Coconino Plateau. There was no other explanation we could come up with for reaching each obscure rendezvous point simultaneously. Had we glimpsed a power that Navajo medicine men sang for during the fifth morning of the Coyoteway ceremony, when they sent their gods home to the west?

Beneath the Two Setting, he ran.
With Yellow Twilight Girl, he ran.
With Corn Pollen for feet, he ran.
With the Yellow Prayerstick for his hand, he ran.
With the Evening Twilight for his feather, he ran.
With Yellow Air breathing from his mouth, he ran.
With Happiness behind him, he ran.
With Happiness before him, he ran.
With Evening Twilight, he ran.

And into evening twilight I ran, touched by unseen forces still moving through this holy land. I knew I had to maintain a right-brained grasp of physical reality in order to know which spur road to take, so I tried to think of those interminably long hours of running as if I were simply going to work, dutifully punching my mental time card into sunrise and sunset. But there were always too many sandy roads spiraling off in too many directions and too many miles to cover. And it became difficult not to dissociate myself from the physical act of running, the dreary midday sun, and pass the day running through my dreams and Native American myths and legends. And each time I'd lapse into that spirit world, time, space, and geography served only as a backdrop to my running. Yet, somehow, out in the middle of the parched white caprock of the Coconino Plateau, we'd meet: Tim, Craig, Chris, and I. Dead on! And

Craig would say, "We just got here. How'd you get here so fast?" "The *old way*," I'd tell him. We'd shake our heads and laugh, wondering if we didn't have our own ally guiding us down this ancient path.

None of us could forget the Hopi man we'd met in Flagstaff a week earlier who told us he "taught the old way to young people." Like the horseback Hopi elder we met the day before leaving Oraibi, this man seemed to know what we were up to without our having explained our plans. We were in the parking lot of a large shopping center, and we'd just finished loading our supplies into Craig's pickup when the man quietly approached us. He was good-looking, healthy, probably in his early sixties; he had a slight paunch, and he was visibly amused that we were busy duct-taping a plastic tarp over the bed of Craig's pickup. "Maybe it'll keep the rain off," he said. Tim tapped on it with the palm of his hand and said, "This is our drum." The old fellow laughed, then started dancing in place, as if in step to a chantway. We all laughed. "Should work," he said, still laughing at the white man's four-wheel-drive tom-tom. "I'll have to try that." And then, without any warning, he walked away, silently, expressionless, as if he hadn't seen us. "Hey, goodbye . . . bye . . . ," we yelled, trying to get his attention. Suddenly, he wheeled around in his tracks, stared at us with the calm, pleasant demeanor of the knowing, and said, "See you in dreamland." We stood there dumbfounded. And here we were five days later, three of us perched on the very rim of Moqui Trail Canyon, while Tim and Craig beat cheeks down the Hualapai Canyon cutoff to Havasu Springs for a jubilant rendezvous we might not make for at least another day, if we made it at all. We were as isolated and vulnerable to death as anyone who traveled the path before us. Yet, watching

> I tried to think of those interminably long hours of running as if I were simply going to work, dutifully punching my mental time card into sunrise and sunset.

Author running through the ankle-deep muck of the Little Colorado River on the Hopi-Havasupai trade route.

these reveries dance across the cosmos, I realized we had seen the Hopi elder, as he promised, in our journey through "dreamland."

It's time; the three of us know it. There is no postponing it. Daylight will soon be upon us. The sun is already burning across the rim of the Coconino Plateau, and the heat will soon turn everything in its path to vulture carrion, bones, or corpse powder. Slowly, we unlock our human pretzel. Our muscles creak and groan from the cold.

> After five nights of sleeping in the dirt and ashes, and six days of running through sand, wind, and rock, I feel as though I no longer have any connection with the outside world.

Dave and Chris have only been running with me for a day, but their eyes already bear the dazed look that comes from journeying through this forgotten land. Framed in a mop of curly, shoulder-length ringlets, Chris's face is gaunt; her eyes have lost their luster, and she is cold and nervous. Dave's hair sticks up on end like unruly clusters of porcupine quills; his face is flushed, his eyes are almost swollen shut, and his heavy moustache has been tugged down into a weary Fu Manchu. I'm not sure what I look like, but after five nights of sleeping in the dirt and ashes, and six days of running through sand, wind, and rock, I feel as though I no longer have any connection with the outside world.

What I do know is that together we've survived the night without sliding into the brink or dying of exposure. But the prevailing mood is that we've been condemned to serve out our remaining days running through a canyon gulag unless we can miraculously find a way to escape.

"Boy, that was fun . . . wouldn't have missed that for anything." Snippets of dialogue whirl around us as we claw our way back along the deadly rim of Moqui Trail Canyon in an attempt to locate the hidden passage into its depths. Somewhere very near here, what the Havasupai called *itcahuá'qawáwawaquwa*, "enemy scalp place," Sinyella recalled the desperate escape of twenty Yavapai warriors after their raid on Havasupai in 1855: "In the morning . . . they were gone. They carried off the one [Yavapai] who had died on the hill. They took the body up on the cliff and hid it before they ran off. Two Yavapai had been badly wounded; they went with the others but both died on the road. Later their bones were found on the plateau just beyond Moki Trail, with their arrows, blankets and a little water jug near a little fire that had been made for them."

Nothing remains of their deadly passage along the rim of Moqui Trail Canyon, but the canyon walls now roar with dawn's fiery light. When Cushing reached this point a century earlier, he aptly described our own struggle to reach the canyon floor alive:

> Who would have imagined that between the terraced plains which we saw ahead and the one we were passing through was a canyon, which, though narrow, was so deep that no one could cross it for miles up or down its length? Even the entrance to that tremendous chasm can scarcely be pictured . . . [a] descent of twelve-hundred feet, almost vertical, except to say that we here wound around a great bank of talus, with tons of rock impending above us, there scrambled over great rocks, and crept along a foot-wide trail, where one misstep would have precipitated us hundreds of feet.

Even with Cushing's forewarning, it is going to be a bad day in these red-rock canyons, I know. After hours of terror-fraught backtracking in the stifling heat and another hour of debating the merits of Dave's suggestion that we head thirty miles back across the Coconino Plateau to Grand Canyon Village instead of running fifteen miles to Havasu Springs, we finally reach Jwa Qwaw Gwa Spring on the floor of Moqui Trail Canyon. The spring is dry. And just to drive home the point, some clever Havasupai cowboy has hung the splintered white skull of a steer above the water tank as an omen of what lies beyond.

We sniff around the dry water hole like mangy lobos and find what looks like six bags of horse feed. "At least we'll have oats," Dave says.

"Open it," I tell him. Peering through the 35 mm lens of her camera, Chris frames the scene of two men about to gorge themselves on a Havasupai food cache. But she breaks out laughing when powdered cement pours out of the small slit in the top bag. "The final fuck you," Dave says, staring at six ninety-pound bags of Ready Mix. And there's not a drop of water in sight. I lick the imaginary granola from my lips, and the three of us start back down Moqui Trail Canyon.

When Cushing traveled down Cataract Canyon to Havasupai in 1882, he counted "forty-three abrupt turns . . . each one deeper, each turn narrowing the vision . . . [until] only a narrow strip of sky could be seen from our pathway." Cushing had counted and knotted those turns on the fringe of his buckskin shirt. By the time I knot nine turns on a string dangling from my blanket, the immense walls of Cataract Canyon are swaying back and forth above me and I realize the day is going to be a rerun of Black Falls.

The heat is appalling. We are dangerously low on water, and we have entered what Cushing called the Kuhni Desert, a stranglehold of impenetrable canyon walls, hot glaring sand, and lifeless forage. There will be no four-wheel-drive pickups waiting for us around the next bend, only horseback Havasupai cowboys savvy enough to venture into this heat. But the only horses we see are skinny, paranoid nags that look like they've been strung out on fluid deprivation for so long they don't know whether they're up canyon or down. They're pale, ashen apparitions of the bleached skeletons that litter the floor of the canyon, and they remind me of the Havasupai Coyote legend, "Havasu Canyon Walls Closing Up": "Coyote said that long ago the walls of Havasu Canyon used to open and close so no one could come down this canyon. Many people were crushed between them."

As I feel these canyon walls will to do to us. Jwa Qwaw Gwa failed us, and somehow we have to make it to Havasu Springs on the water we have left. But I wonder if we won't suffer the same fate as the Coyote people or those horses swaying back and forth in front of us on legs that are about to buckle. Walls erupt out of the barren floor of this canyon, hem-

Struggling through the Kuhni Desert. Dangerously low on water, the author struggles through the depths of Moqui Trail Canyon near the end of the Hopi-Havasupai trade route, what Cushing called the Kuhni Desert a century earlier.

ming us in a hell that offers two ways out: death or Havasu Springs, whichever comes first. So running these last few miles no longer seems to matter. The only thing that does is survival, and if surviving means having to walk the last "Indian mile" to Havasu Springs, so be it. I don't think I could survive another hot, dry run like the one to Black Falls; my body is too worn-out and I'm now responsible for the lives of two of my friends.

But even walking, I feel so listless, light-headed, and nauseous I don't think we're going to make it unless we can find water somewhere along the way. The prickly pear cactus, hedgehog, and other succulents we'd normally rely on in such a perilous situation are withered and dry. If worse comes to worst, I tell myself, we can always corner one of those horses and stone it to death. I try this thought out on Dave, and he agrees—if that's what it takes to survive. Chris is shocked by such talk, but we are rapidly being reduced to cave dwellers or mountain men—if we haven't already stepped over that line. "Come on," I yell out, "it's right around the next bend." And the next. And the next. Down this twisting defile, the three of us float through the stony walls of the Wescogame, Manakacha, and Watahomigi sandstone toward the vanishing point of the 285-million-year-old Supai formation.

I drift back out of this canyon, not to ancient traders journeying in and out of it but to a year ago, near the end of my inner Canyon journey, when Tim told me, "John, you can't run to Supai." I'd thought about that the entire year I'd trained for the Hopi-Havasupai trade route in the mountains and plains surrounding Prescott, and had placed numerous long distance calls to Havasupai tribal headquarters in hopes of speaking to the chairman to get permission to cross this traditional use area. But I never got past the secretary. She always gave me the same answer: "He's not in. You have to hike down from Hualapai Hilltop and get a permit." The Havasupai were justifiably big on selling hiking and camping permits to the *hay gú*, "white men," because tourist revenue formed the backbone of their fragile economy. But I wasn't a hiker, and I had no intention of going to 5,441-foot Mount Sinyella or the edge of Great Thumb Mesa, the two known sacred areas the Havasupai visited in the western Grand Canyon during *itckayúga*, "mythical times," to make rain before the death of their last weather shaman in 1963. I only wanted to run in the footsteps of ancient traders, and if they crossed those of Sinyella, then it was said:

When I was six years old, my father said, "Do not sleep after sunrise; wake as soon as daylight appears. Run toward dawn. You should do this every day. Run out as far as you can. Do not walk, run. Do this always when you are a young man too; then you will be able to run fast, and when you race someone you will win. If you do not, you will be beaten.

As the Havasupai receptionist had beaten me, over the phone, without running. She had no idea what I was talking about when I tried to explain I was running from Oraibi to Havasupai. Trade route, what's that? So I decided that when, and if, I reached Moqui Trail Canyon, I would follow Don Decker's advice, and "Just go do it, John." If the mystical greetings of the two Hopi elders we'd met were any indication, I was looking forward to meeting the Havasupai on this canyon passage.

"Where's Dave?" Chris yells, and suddenly I'm jerked back into the physical reality of this dream track.

"I don't know," I yell back, wondering what my eyes had been focusing on while I was dreaming. "Check for footprints," I tell her.

We zigzag back and forth across the main stem of Cataract Canyon, wearily dragging our feet in the dry sand, until we find Dave squatting on all fours, digging for water with his bare hands. "What's it look like?" I ask him.

"Dry, the whole place is dry." The three of us look at one another, wondering if we'll share a common grave. "The final fuck you," Dave says.

We turn and plod on toward impending doom, wondering how close to death we'll travel before we're forced to slit the throat of one of those scrawny nags and drink its blood. But this isn't the Mojave Desert, and we're not traveling with Kit Carson; this isn't the Chiricahua trail to the Sierra Madre, and we're not running with Geronimo's *Bedonkohe*, "Fast Friends," band of Apache; this isn't the Galiuros, and we're not trapping beaver with mountain man James Ohio Pattie. This is the twentieth century, and people in America no longer kill horses and antelope to drink their blood to survive the ravages of thirst. So Dave and I make a pact to hold out a little longer; those horses have to be getting water somewhere, we figure. Chris, however, has since resolved to accept her fate, now revering those horses no less than Hindus revere sacred cows. As she well should.

> We turn and plod on toward impending doom, wondering how close to death we'll travel before we're forced to slit the throat of one of those scrawny nags and drink its blood.

During the 1850s, famished Yavapai raiders hobbled a Havasupai horse near here, but they were caught by the Havasupai before they could roast and eat horse flesh. A battle ensued, and arrows flew till nightfall. By morning, the Yavapai were cornered by the Havasupai and fled down Cataract Canyon on the very path we were now following; Sinyella recalled: "They [the Havasupai] gave them some food to eat. Then they killed them one at a time. They cut around their heads just above the eyes and ears, and pulled off their scalps, throwing their bodies aside . . . . Everybody, men and women, came to see the scalps hanging up there [on a pole]. Everybody felt glad and wanted to dance. Everybody danced around and hollered, clapping their mouths."

> There's only one way out, death or Havasu Springs, whichever comes first.

We pull out all the stops that afternoon in our desperate search for water, but the lush green maidenhair ferns, a good indicator in the Grand Canyon of perennial water and intermittent springs, are brown and brittle. Even the trickling seeps that we could normally rely on to provide water from the horizontal cracks of the Supai sandstone are dry. There's only one way out, death or Havasu Springs, whichever comes first.

When twilight finally seeps into the canyon like a cool, dark rivulet of water, a chorus of crickets echoes through this defile like the willowy legs of what I imagine to be the sound of ancient split-twig figurines dancing across old deer hide. Then comes darkness, and mindless chatter about where we are. It doesn't matter. We stop. We're not sure where, only that we're downstream from where we bivouacked last night at "enemy scalp place." I gather tinder and ignite a brilliant yellow flame with the first strike of my flint, while Dave and Chris shuffle around in the darkness and gather firewood. Even without a handheld mirror, we know our wretched appearance reflects those of the living sawhorses peering at us from across the wash. They obviously haven't found water either. "You can lead a runner to water, but you can't make him drink it," I say, giddy from fatigue and dehydration. Dave and Chris do not laugh.

When Navajo refugees fled the scorched-earth campaign of Kit Carson in 1863, some ventured as far west as Cataract Canyon to trade with the Havasupai. Sinyella recalled one such trading party not far from our own camp:

> After a few sleeps the Navaho men began to drift in, but none of their women. The Navaho said they brought blankets to trade for food. We gave corn for blankets, about one tray full of shelled corn for a saddle blanket; if the blanket was big, we gave the shelled corn to the amount of a good-sized small burden basket (gaøokke'dja) full. Two bundles of dried squash, about two feet long, were traded for a big blanket. Beans were valued high; only one small basket full, just level, was given for a goodsized blanket. The biggest burden basket of shelled corn was traded for a horse. When we traded buckskin, the skins of two big bucks with a little corn in the sack to boot were given for a horse. Those Navaho came from the country around Grand Canyon and Red Butte to trade for corn.

We, too, are traders, and we haggle and barter around the fire that night for our own precious commodities. Dave offers a cup of his water, which he carried from Moqui Tank, for eight of my jojoba beans. I count them out on my blanket. one, two, three, four, five, six, seven, eight. But my beans have traveled further than Moqui Tank, more than two hundred miles

We wake long before dawn and breakfast on two aspirin and a dusty mug of warm water each.

north from the McDowell Mountains, the ancestral lands of the Salado and Hohokam people. To me they are more precious than cashews, and I demand two cups. Dave hesitates; Chris smiles. "Throw in four aspirin, and you've got a deal," Dave says. Agreed.

With short, crude strokes, Daves mashes these beans with a makeshift mano and metate and sets his metal cup in the coals of our fire to brew

Bivouac Fire. The author rolls up his blanket after a night spent without food in Cataract Canyon on the Hopi-Havasupai trade route. (Running Wild)

up a hot cup of waxy, bitter-tasting jojoba bean "coffee." I give Chris a half cup of my water, before using the other half to chase down the bitter white powder of a three-aspirin dinner. "Don't get any ideas," I warn them both, "I'm saving the other cup for morning." I curl up around the fire and try sleeping with one eye open, while Chris frames the scene and Dave expounds on another version of his oft-repeated "days of wooden ships and iron men" campfire tale.

We wake long before dawn the following morning and breakfast on two aspirin and a dusty mug of warm water each. It is a light breakfast, to be sure, but we start loping toward dawn with renewed vigor, red dust whooshing up and down our bare legs with each footfall. We are trying desperately to go fast, now, in hopes of beating the merciless sun into the depths of Cataract Canyon. But the miles peel off slowly, with the writhing tedium of a Mojave rattlesnake molting its scaly, parchment-thin skin. And as we journey into one turn and around and out through the next, we soon return to the dreamy trance of the day before. And I drift off again, out of this endless gorge, to day 4 of this journey, and I wonder if today could possibly be any worse.

The year before, day 3 had almost been my ruin on my inner Canyon odyssey, and day 4 along the Hopi-Havasupai trade route was no different. Not long after rolling up my blanket and dousing my fire at Moqui Stage Station, I wanted to quit; physically and spiritually I did not want to continue running across the Coconino Plateau. The whole idea of running—anywhere, for any reason—repulsed me. "Why would anybody want to do that," I wondered.

But there were others tracing the ancient route of the Hopi-Havasupai trail with me, and I would not let them down, so long as I could take another step. Tim Ganey was the expedition point man. For him, "the adventure began in that crowded Safeway parking lot, when that Hopi elder came up and greeted us as if he knew what we were up to. All your life you could have waited for him, but it could have happened only on that one day, because the chemistry was right." Craig Hudson was Tim's counterweight and the most levelheaded among us. At first Craig wondered what he was "doing out there in the middle of the Painted Desert . . . [but] soon I realized I was being ripped out of society and stuck in a magical place." Christine Keith was the tireless photojournalist, who ran every grueling step of the way with me the thirty miles from Moqui Stage Station to Anita Station on day 4. While Tim and Craig shadowed us, she was the one who picked me up every time I sat down to quit, prodding me on as I sobbed and whimpered: "Come on, Annerino! Not much farther." My ankle burned with pain every time my left foot kissed the red earth as I ran beneath the hallowed flanks of 7,326-foot Red Butte, what traditional Havasupai know as *wigadawi'sa*, "The Landmark," and what Navajo medicine men singing the hunting tradition of the Blessingway ceremony revere as *Tse zhin e'ahi*, "Black Rock Standing Up." I couldn't let Tim, Craig, or Chris down, any more than I could let Dave down. On less than thirty miles of training a week, he ran forty-one miles with me on day 5. Physically and emotionally, it had been my best day; I woke up feeling I was born to do nothing but run wild along the Hopi-Havasupai trail—the two of us chewing up the piñon and juniper woodland from Anita Station to Moqui Tank because our "legs were like horses."

These friends and others were reason enough to continue yesterday and the day before that. But how would it end now? I wasn't sure; it could go either way. I only knew I should have run Moqui Trail Canyon and Cataract Canyon alone. They were too stark dry and desperate to bring anyone else. And, if my inner Canyon journey was any indication, I feared I might lose my focus running in the company of others. I had. But Tim and Craig thought it would be safer if Dave and Chris accompanied me through the depths of Cataract Canyon. Not even the Havasupai, Hopi traders, Yavapai warriors, or Navajo refugees traveled alone through Cataract Canyon. But Dave and Chris wanted to share in the excitement of the summit push. So I didn't argue with any of them, because I knew the Hopi-Havasupai trail was beyond my grasp without Tim and Craig's support. I only wondered if after suffering with me, Dave and Chris would find the same meaning that the oasis of Havasu Springs held for me in completing the Hopi-Havasupai trail. Or, if we actually reached it alive, would they only remember the thirst and desperation of the desert path leading to the blue waters bubbling out of the red sand?

A shadow looms before me, and I stop dead in my tracks. A Havasupai cowboy is staring down at me. Was it an *amíye,* a "ghost" of the dead men once believed to dwell in Cataract Canyon? I didn't think so. He's sitting on a short, healthy horse that, in another time, looked good enough to eat. He's wearing a sweat-stained cowboy hat, his hands are resting on a rope worn saddle horn, and his round belly hangs over them. His tan cheeks puff out, and a glint stirs in his eyes.

"Where'd you come from?" he asks. But he already knows. The echo of strangers travels far and fast in this timeless land.

"Oraibi, six days ago," I say proudly. He stares down at me dressed in the rags of a desert runner. I stare back at him dressed as a cowpuncher. A bond has been struck; we stare at each other smiling. And I wonder if this is the lesson I'm to learn from this journey: that each of us has explored the other's past in order to go forward, or perhaps that survival isn't something you learn once but something you live with as closely as your own heartbeat—as the Havasupai had, inhabiting the canyons near the red rocks of *Wigailaila* (the point of the Grand Canyon and Cataract Canyon) since A.D. 1050; as the ancient traders had, the ones who traveled to Havasupai and *back* from the Mojave Trail seven sleeps west of here and from the Hopi villages six sleeps east. I'm not sure. Maybe the lesson I've learned can't be verbalized. It may be the unknowing, the unspoken, carried on canyon winds from the eastern mesas by a Navajo *Hatáál*, "singer," or medicine man:

> With my Mind I walk in the presence of the Sun,
> with my Mind I walk, with my Mind I walk,
> with my Mind I walk, with my Mind I walk.
> Beneath the Two Rising, with my mind I walk.
> Where White Coyote Medicine is, with my Mind I walk.
> Where White Air is, with my Mind I walk.

With distant memories of chasing the white coyote through the land of the Pima, I have now been forced to walk. I mumble something to the cowboy about having to push on. He turns and resumes riding up *Wigasiváva*, Cataract Canyon, past the ancient dwellings of the Cohonina, ancestors of the Havasupai who dwelled here since A.D. 600, along the war trail of the Yavapai, the trade route of the Hopi and Navajo, the path of Spanish missionaries, through his own dreamscape that leads back to *itckayúga*, "mythical times," when the Havasupai still ran through this stony domain toward sunrise as far as they could. I turn and start for Havasu Springs, wondering why I hadn't asked the Havasupai cowboy for a long pull of water from his canteen? Was I trying to prove I could be as stoic as the Mojave traders Garcés had met who told him, "We *Jamajabs* can withstand hunger and thirst for as long as four days"? Answers elude me. I only know that Chris and Dave are somewhere behind me, I'm not exactly sure where. But we've made it, because, as I come around the "forty-third abrupt turn" knotted in Cushing's buckskin fringe, I find soda

But we've made it, because . . . I find soda cans strewn along the sandy floor of the canyon. It's a sure sign civilization is not far off—anybody who carries an aluminum can instead of a pine-pitch-covered water basket into the burning depths of Cataract Canyon does not stray far from creature comforts. All I have to do is run another mile to the cool, soothing waters of Havasu Springs to reach the end of this pathway, and it will all be over—at least for another year. Only when the last crescent moon of spring appears, what the Havsuapai called *mawaiat'úviaga*, for the snow melting off the Canyon's icy rims and warmth returning to their Eden, will Tim, Craig, and I know if we'll follow the path of the coyote into the unknown together again.

I turn, wait for the shadows of Dave and Chris floating through the distant heat waves, then press on, running wild through Cataract Canyon:

From out of Canyons, Happiness will come to me.
From all red Canyons, Happiness will come to me.
From all black Canyons, Happiness will come to me.
From under the Rocks, Happiness will come to me.
From the Echoes of Canyon Walls, Happiness will come to me.

From Cataract Canyon, Happiness has come to me. From Havasu Springs, Happiness has come to me.

6

SAVAGE ARENA

As the departure date grew nearer,

the full consequences of going to

the Himalaya made their impact. I

seriously doubted I was going to

come back.

Peter Boardman
The Shining Mountain

It is dawn. A cold wind is howling through the ponderosas, and a late winter storm threatens to engulf northern Arizona's eight-thousand-foot-high Kaibab Plateau. I am shivering, not only from the cold that cuts me to the bone but also from fear. I am standing on the eastern escarpment of this densely wooded plateau, staring down the dark corridor of Nankoweap Canyon, and I am about to embark on the most dangerous journey in my life. I haven't been marched to this brink at gunpoint; I have come here willingly, along a spiritual path that's been as winding and elusive as the physical one I'm about to descend. It is a journey that, if I'm very lucky, will finally prove, at least to me, that ancient traders could have run through this glorious chasm long before horseback Spaniards first viewed it from the distant South Rim. But if I fail, and I assume I will, I hope to escape from this mythic canyon alive.

That's why I've dreaded this moment for an entire year; the twelve months I've trained for this pathway have dogged me with such trepidation that for the first time in my life I'm seriously questioning the dangerous path I'm about to descend; it leads through the fearsome depths of the greatest canyon on earth, and trying to cross that haunting ground has shadowed me since reaching Havasu Springs the year before. I knew all along that the succession of ancient paths I'd been following only pointed in one direction—the North Rim. Like a climber who's been protected by the hands of fate up the highest mountain in the world by two previous routes, I was inexplicably drawn to attempt this last dangerous and elegant line through the heart of the Grand Canyon.

However, if Tim, Craig, and I had originally thought the South Rim was impossible and the Hopi-Havasupai trail incomprehensible, the North Rim was truly both. Of the estimated 250-mile-long route that courses east to west through the seldom-explored, inner Canyon frontier below the North Rim, less than 50 miles of it followed any kind of trail.

> I am about to embark on the most dangerous journey in my life. . . . If I fail, and I assume I will, I hope to escape from this mythic canyon alive.

And, in spite of studying Ginny Taylor's detailed maps of her own North Rim route, I still did not know how much of my route was actually runnable, what cliffs needed to be climbed, and what flood-swollen creeks might need to be forded. I could die trying to run such treacherous terrain. Bolstered by our back-to-back successes with the South Rim and Hopi-Havasupai trail, however, and Ginny's unwavering voice of confidence, Tim and Craig thought otherwise. "Look at Messner," we'd mused. But there was no comparing myself to the Himalayan superstar; Reinhold Messner was the first man in history to climb the world's fourteen eight-thousand-meter peaks without oxygen. And the second time he climbed Everest without oxygen, he did it solo! Yet, owing to my own image of the man, I at least had a way of gauging the impossible scale of the virtually trackless North Rim; I could envision someone else running it solo but not me. Yet, the further I explored the concept of a lone man confronting the North Rim, the more I took to examining the impossible challenge two Britons had overcome on October 15, 1976. Joe Tasker and Peter Boardman were drawn together to attempt what the world climbing community considered impossible: an ascent of the imposing, ice-plastered mile-high West Wall of 22,520-foot Changabang in India's Garwahl Himalayas. Tasker and Boardman sought out the sage advice of fellow Brit and Himalayan giant Doug Scott. Tasker wrote, "He had seen the west face himself and told me it was beyond the bounds of possibility." Undeterred, Tasker and Boardman took leaves of absence to go have a look at this impossible wall; in the true spirit of mountaineering, they just wanted to see how far up they could get before storms, avalanches, altitude, or the inhuman scale of the wall forced them to retreat. Once on the West Wall, however, Tasker and Boardman kept climbing and climbing, until, as Tasker wrote in his diary, "without stopping to talk about it, by some imperceptible transition of thought, it was clear we could climb the West Wall, provided we could stick it out." They did.

Knowing of their remarkable success, I still thought the North Rim was too big, too dangerous, and too remote for me to run. Unlike my South Rim route and the Hopi-Havasupai trail, where my resupply crew was able to reach me nearly every day, below the North Rim I would be virtually cut off from all logistical support and emergency help. It was then I realized the North Rim might be the ultimate pathway—not for me but for someone else. I just wanted to go have a look, to see how far I could get before I'd have to turn back. Then, that's why I feared this very moment. I know once I step off the white rim of the eighty-eight-hundred-foot-high Kaibab Plateau, there will be no turning back. Throughout history, the

> Unlike [my previous runs] where my resupply crew was able to reach me nearly every day, below the North Rim I would be virtually cut off from all logistical support and emergency help.

Grand Canyon of the Colorado River has lured ancient traders, Spaniards, mountain men, explorers, miners, scientists, artists, and tourists into its timeless embrace, and many simply vanished.

A primal fear surges through me as I start running down the icy Nankoweap Trail. It is here, only moments out, that the world suddenly avalanches beneath my tumbling legs and feet as I trace the faint line of this Anasazi trail through the Kaibab limestone, Coconino sandstone, Supai sandstone, and Redwall limestone through a rainbow of geologic history back 1.7 billion inconceivable years, until my eyes reach the silver strand of Nankoweap Creek far below. It is here, free falling into the abyss, that I want to turn back—should turn back—before it's too late.

But *it is* too late. Once called *kaivavic*, "mountain lying down," I have stepped off the Kaibab Plateau and entered the ancestral canyon domain of the Kaibab band of Southern Paiute who also took their name *Kaivavituniwi*, the "Mountain Lying Down People," from the great plateau that rims the eastern end of the Grand Canyon. And I keep running, endlessly down, down, down this ancient route; it was first used by the Anasazi circa A.D. 1050 to reach their dwellings scattered throughout Nankoweap Canyon between the North Rim and the Colorado River, what the Kaibab Paiute who later roamed the area called *paga*, "big water." Following their ancient steps, I knew why I had shuddered with such fear when I said goodbye to Chris May and Chris Keith only minutes before—because once I reach the terminus of the faint Nankoweap Trail, I will be completely cut off from the rest of the world. Success and survival will rest solely on my ability to adapt to the extremes of weather, terrain, loneliness, and fatigue. Every move I've made in my life, every judgment I've ever made, right and wrong, will decide my fate. Out here, there is no room for error. One seemingly inconsequential mistake, like not knotting my shoes properly, could cause me to slip and fall; and if I got hurt or knocked unconscious, I might as well have stepped off the face of the earth. Below the North Rim, there's little chance anyone

> No matter how we broke the route down into sections, each scheduled resupply point was a minimum two day's journey apart for me, and two of them necessitate dangerous river crossings in forty-five-degree water.

would actually find me alive. And perhaps it was for that reason more than any other that just ten days earlier—after a difficult year of training— I still did not know whether or not I was going to attempt the North Rim. I was torn. The odds of running the North Rim and surviving were too frightening to dwell on.

Much of my fear had to do with marginal access; access from the North Rim for my resupply crew is, in fact, out of the question. Besides the non-maintained trail I am running down, there are only two other practical routes descending the 720-square-mile area of the North Rim between here and Thunder River, the end of this pathway: the North Kaibab Trail, which intersects my route near the midway point, and the non-maintained Shinumo Trail an estimated three days west of the North Kaibab. But as far as the National Park Service is concerned, the North Rim is closed until the snow melts. Consequently, all support will have to come from the South Rim, which presents a logistical dilemma. No matter how we broke the route down into sections, each scheduled resupply point was a minimum two day's journey apart for me, and two of them necessitate dangerous river crossings in forty-five-degree water. The trick would be not just to reach them, but to reach them at the same time my small support crew did, leapfrogging as they'll be from one trail to the next, without the benefit of portable communication between us.

There was also the question of emergency evacuation to consider. But after a year of analyzing my options and escape routes, I considered helicopter rescue by the Park Service out of the question. It was my journey, and I believed it was my personal responsibility to assume whatever risks were involved in trying to complete it. It wasn't right to put someone else's life on the line if my plans went awry. Ancient traders didn't have air support. They adapted or died, based on their own judgment and experience. And if I was to learn those same lessons, lessons long forgotten by the modern world, I was going to have to risk running the brink alone. And that made me tremble whenever I thought about the possibility of making a mistake.

Still running on the wings of fear, the sun strains to break through the ominous layer of gray clouds drifting over the vast sweep of Blue Moon Bench and the edge of the Desert Facade. I have only one thought: I must reach the Colorado River at Lava Canyon tonight. Tim, Craig, and I originally thought I should take two days to attempt this first leg, but I am now so dwarfed by the imposing scale of the North Rim and so unnerved by the fact that I've actually embarked on a pathway I know is beyond the bounds of possibility that the only way I can put the rest of the North Rim route into mortal perspective is by somehow reaching the Colorado River tonight. If I can do that, the route will at least make theoretical sense. But I really couldn't think in terms of reaching Thunder River, which I won't see, if I see it at all, for seven to ten days. Nor can I really think of reaching the Colorado River, except as the completion of a tentative first step. I'm so awed by the North Rim—perhaps because of what I had experienced below the South Rim—that I simply will have to focus on putting together enough footsteps until the vibrant history and Native American myths and legends of this inner Canyon frontier shape the rhythm and mood of this impossible quest.

Haunted by the specter of time and distance, I'm forced to stop a half hour out. Anglicized from the Kaibab Paiute description of this point, *ninkoipi*, "people killed," the Nankoweap Trail plummets into the void near the southern end of 8,824-foot Saddle Mountain. In the summer of 1932, Kaibab Paiute elder Captain George recounted a tragic incident in the oral history of his people at Saddle Mountain for ethnographer Isabel T. Kelly: "Just for fun, and because they wanted Kaibab Plateau, Apache forded the Colorado [River] and at night came upon Kaibab camp. With handled-stone weapons, hit each sleeping Kaibab on the head, killing all but one woman who escaped to Moccasin. Kaibab never got even with them." The Kaibab Paiute called the Apache *Muwinakac*, "Nose Earring," for the nose ornaments they reportedly wore, but whether the Apache truly had extended their raids this far north and this deep into Kaibab Paiute territory is not known for certain; nor is it known if the marauders used the dangerous Anasazi route that descended Eminence Break to cross the Colorado River before climbing above the precarious Anasazi footbridge to reach 4,484-foot Point Hansbrough in order to launch their deadly attack on the sleeping Kaibab Paiute; or whether they followed the route of the horse thieves from Tanner Canyon along the Butte fault to reach this point. It was a mystery I hoped to unveil if I succeeded in running the Butte Fault to the Colorado River, but first I had to cross the dangerous passage ahead.

I take a deep breath and stare up at swirling black clouds spitting pellets of icy snow down on me. There is little time to waste. Another few minutes and my route will be covered with ice. Tentatively, I start across a sloping cinder ledge of Hermit shale, kicking the toes of my running shoes into the mushy soil like the front points of crampons and using my bare fingers on the cold, brittle rock to keep myself from being sucked into the gaping maw of Nankoweap Creek. I try not to think of the consequences; I can only move tentatively, in the hopes of completing this icy traverse without slipping.

Of the four named trails that slide off the North Rim, the Nankoweap Trail has perhaps the most peculiar history. Following the faint paths of the Anasazi and Kaibab Paiute, Major John Wesley Powell and geologist Charles Doolittle Walcott constructed the Nankoweap Trail during the winter of 1882 so that Walcott could study the Grand Canyon series of rock layers, which he discovered "were much older than had been thought." How much older? Without the passage of man through this geological marvel, the age of 1,200 million years held little meaning for me. That Powell and his men were "encamped in snow, often concealed for days in driving frozen mist and whirling snow" so Walcott could spend the remainder of that winter on the floor of Nankoweap Canyon, completely cut off from the outside world, was more comprehensible to me than discovering whether the Precambrian strata were 545 million or 1,200 mil-

> There is little time to waste. Another few minutes and my route will be covered with ice.

lion years old. But what concerns me most now is that this hand-forged trail, which Walcott called "perfectly frightful," offers me little more than a route to run along its dangerously exposed and crumbly sandstone ledges after I complete the traverse.

Once I do, I take a deep breath and start running again, still twitching with fear, until I establish a rhythm of melding footsteps into switchbacks and begin careening down one switchback after another through the Supai sandstone toward Tilted Mesa. It's then I recall Uncle Jim Owens. A one-time cowboy from the Good Night Ranch in Texas's panhandle country, Owens was appointed Forest Service warden on the North Rim at the turn of the century. But that was akin to hiring the fox to guard the hen-house, because during his twelve years of "game management," Owens reportedly killed 532 mountain lions! By 1930, however, the offi-cial North Rim death toll for predators stood

Jim Owens was appointed Forest Service warden on the North Rim at the turn of the century. But that was akin to hiring the fox to guard the henhouse, because during his twelve years of "game management," Owens reportedly killed 532 mountain lions.

at a staggering "781 lions, 554 bobcats, 4,889 coyotes, and 20 wolves." As a result of such drastic conservation measures, the Kaibab deer population soared unchecked, and estimates ranged wildly from 10,000 to 100,000 mule deer. The Kaibab Paiute believed the Kaibab deer herd was owned by *Tukumumuc*, "Big Lion," before it became the property of the spirit *kai?nasavi*, who was revered and appeased throughout the Kaibab Paiute's hunting season. Non-Indians had no such beliefs, and, incredibly, they concocted a plan to herd a thousand deer down the Nankoweap Trail, across the rugged Butte Fault, where it was further supposed the herd would obediently swim the Colorado River and walk single file up the Tanner Trail to the South Rim and disperse throughout the Coconino Plateau. What nobody apparently bothered to consider was that mule deer could not be driven in herds like Texas longhorn were by cowboys, who drove them north along the Chisholm Trail to the railhead at Kansas City during the 1850s; nor could deer be driven like Mexican horses were by Geronimo who pushed them north from the Sierra Madre along the Chiricahua Trail to San Carlos during the 1880s. When the *Tatanka Oyate*, "Buffalo Nation," of the Oglala Sioux drove bison on horseback during the 1830s, ungulates known to move in vast herds sometimes six miles wide and fifty miles long, they often used wildfire to stampede them over buffalo jumps. Even when Havasupai hunters managed to drive small, skittish bands of desert bighorn sheep along the narrow benches of the Tovokyóva Trail, they sometimes used fire to drive them over the rimrock; yet, the canyon trails were so precipitous that Sinyella recalled it was sometimes deadly work: "The ram stood at the abrupt end of the ledge. My father and Jess' grandfather followed the ledge. The ram turned toward the men and ran fast at them; he held his head down sideways. My father stood right against the wall; the other stood right on the edge. There was not enough room; it was very narrow there. The ram butted Jess' grandfather off the cliff to the bottom. The ram stood right there, until all the others came and killed it [with bows and arrows], and then it too fell down the cliff at the same place." But Kaibab mule deer were not bighorn sheep, bison, horses, or cattle, and what was billed as "The most original roundup . . . in the history of the Southwest" included filmmaker W.H. Griffith, novelist Zane Grey, 105 Navajo trackers, and 20 pistol-packing cowboys. But even with a 125 horseback men riding nearly arm in arm, some of them firing .45-caliber pistols in the air, wild, half-starved mule deer would have none of it; the snowstorm did not help. That fact was headlined on page one of the Thursday, December 18, 1924, edition of *The Arizona Republican*:

KAIBAB DEER DRIVE IS CALLED OFF
Snowstorm Ends Plans of McCormick. Motion Picture Men Return to Flagstaff in Blinding Snowstorm: Deer Scatter Wildly.

Before this dream finishes, I've descended the Redwall break below Tilted Mesa and reached the floor of Nankoweap Canyon. Reaching this point is a success, I tell myself, but I am more overcome with fear than elation. I am on the bottom of the Grand Canyon, six-thousand vertical feet, and more than a dozen miles, below the Kaibab Plateau, but any thoughts I have of turning back are futile. Even if I were now capable of running nonstop back up so steep and precarious a trail, Chris May and Chris Keith won't be there to take me out. At this very moment, they are making their own frantic dash back to their vehicle at the edge of Houserock Valley before this late winter storm lays in for good.

I look back up at the snow-covered rim. Dwarfed by the soaring canyon walls of the Kaibab Plateau and its southern extension, the Walhalla Plateau, I realize I've severed my one known link with the outside world. Is this what Walcott felt like in here during the winter of 1882? No doubt. And like Walcott, I am on my own now. My only way out of the Canyon lies southward along the Butte Fault to Lava Canyon, where I'll have to swim the icy river. How far? In miles, I really don't know. It would only be a guess in this trailless terrain. Time and visual distance are my only mileposts with larger symbolic goals like the Colorado River and the Tanner Trail constantly present on the periphery of my consciousness. In that light, it's easy to understand why Native Americans once talked in terms of suns, sleeps, and moons when they traveled, as the Chemehuevi had with their own practical interpretation of a mile. As far as reaching the Colorado River at Lava Canyon, I estimate the distance to be two sleeps. But I'm still overcome with such fear, that I know in my bones I am going to try to make it in one.

I boulder-hop across the mossy-wet stones of Nankoweap Creek, turn south, and reach the foot of the Butte Fault. Formed by tectonic forces that fractured and dislocated the storybook sequence of the Grand Canyon rock strata, the Butte Fault is a hogback spine that cuts across the labyrinth of canyons and creeks that drain the eastern escarpment of the 8,579-foot Walhalla Plateau. According to an unconfirmed National Park Service report dated March 27, 1945, the route I've been following since leaving Saddle Mountain, and will attempt to follow all the way to the foot of the Tanner Trail, was the northern leg of the same horse-thief trail I followed into the Canyon two years earlier. Of it, onetime Colorado miner Peter D. Berry "claimed that after the [horse thief] gang shot it out with the sheriff, one wounded man reached his place at Grand Canyon. Before he died, he confided that a copper kettle at the foot of the Tanner Trail contained the gold collected for [stolen] horses."

I think about that as I struggle up the Butte Fault to the pass between 6,242-foot Nankoweap Mesa and 5,430-foot Nankoweap Butte and descend into the hidden valley formed by Kwagunt Creek. Was riding horseback across this corrugated terrain driving a band of stolen horses any easier than trying to run it? The Kaibab Paiute had no such horses when they followed the Butte Fault into Kwagunt Valley. or descended directly into it from the Walhalla Plateau.

I have reached the floor of Nanokweap Canyon—6,000 vertical feet and more than a dozen miles below the Kaibab Plateau. Though a success, I am more overcome with fear than elation. But any thoughts I have of turning back are futile.

According to Captain George, another Kaibab Paiute named Kwagunt and his brother and sister discovered this narrow valley before the turn of the century and claimed it as their own when they fled the Apache. And in spite of the horse thieves' depending on the water here, Kwagunt discouraged others from learning about it because the sage seeds he wanted for himself were so abundant.

Beyond Kwagunt Creek, the Butte Fault continues south to the Colorado River, and I wonder if the horse thief trail was also the trail of the Apache, as well as the salt trail of the Kaibab Paiute. While there was a salt mine at the confluence of Kwagunt Creek and the Colorado River two miles east of here, artifacts unearthed at Beamer's Cabin near the confluence of the Little Colorado River and the Colorado River above the Hopi and Navajo salt mines—as well as recent reports—indicate the Kaibab Paiute also visited the area. Was the rugged Butte Fault a more practical approach to those salt mines than Salt Trail Canyon? Traditionally, the Hopi called Salt Trail Canyon *Owngtupka*, and the Navajo called it *Bekihatso*, when they journeyed across the Painted Desert to reach it from the east. The Kaibab Paiute were coming from the northwest, and, while it was more rugged, the Butte Fault appeared to be the shortest and most direct approach to those salt mines, what several bands of Southern Paiute revered as the ceremonial site of *oavaxa*, "salt water."

During my South Rim run, I was forced to skirt the rim of every tributary canyon and sub-canyon in order to proceed west along the Tonto formation; in order to proceed south along the Butte Fault, however, I'm forced to travel against the natural lay of the canyons and climb over the high ridgeline of each intersecting canyon before

> Was riding horseback across this corrugated terrain driving a band of stolen horses any easier than trying to run it?

descending it. It is grueling work to cross Malgosa Crest and descend into Malgosa Canyon, before struggling over the flanks of 6,377-foot Kwagunt Butte and dropping into Awatubi Creek.

By the time I climb over Awatubi Crest and descend into Sixtymile Canyon, four parallel canyons south of Nankoweap Canyon, hunger and fatigue sack me. I peel off my two bota bags and unshoulder my twelve-pound rucksack; from it I remove a warm pile jacket and two foil-wrapped bean burros. But as slowly as I try to eat the morning's rations, I swallow them and pass out where I sit. The tinkling music of Sixtymile Creek soothes me, and, for a moment, perhaps an hour, my battle with the Butte Fault is over. Tucked into the cocoon of my warm jacket, pleasant images whisk me far away from this dangerous journey, images of home, family, and friends.

The clock is running, though, and before I'm ready I'm back in the middle of the eastern Grand Canyon, rubbing the trail of saliva off my mouth and chin, the sand and sleep out of my eyes. My legs are stiff. I feel as though I've aged ten years. And what lies beyond is the dog work of trying to run the Butte Fault the rest of the way to the Colorado River.

[Unlike the South Rim run,] I'm forced to travel against the natural lay of the canyons and climb over the high ridgeline of each intersecting canyon before descendng it.

I swallow three aspirin and gather the contents of my pack, which lay scattered across the ground. I refill my two bota bags, drop in some iodine tablets, and set off again, striding on cramped legs up the steep saddle dividing Sixtymile Creek from the East Fork of Carbon Creek. The nap has given me a much needed respite, but it has also provided the fundamental transition between morning and afternoon. Consequently, I'm able to divide the day psychologically into two shorter runs versus one interminably long one.

I am choking back a harsh, throat-burning cough when I finally top out on an unnamed five-thousand-foot saddle. My legs are knotted with fatigue, and the storm front that's been haunting me all morning finally hammers me. I continue running anyway. Snow and hail pelt the bare slopes around me as I make a wild dash for the floor of the East Fork of Carbon Creek. I am breaking my own rule of thumb—"Never run so fast or carelessly that you'll break an ankle"—but reaching the Colorado River tonight is everything to me. And I continue flying out of control, leaping over one rock then another, flapping my arms like wings, using my heels like the metal edges of skis to glide and break, to slow each skidding landing, until I'm dropping so rapidly that I can no longer control the speed and precision of my descent and I'm rolling. Dust

> My legs are knotted with fatigue, and the storm front that's been haunting me all morning finally hammers me.

and rocks spew everywhere as I try to count the somersaults before I can dig my heels into the steep cinder slope and stop. When I finally do, I continue to lie there, snow stinging my face and arms. I take a deep breath and wonder how badly I am hurt. Miraculously, except for some scratches and bruises, I am all right. So I begin looking for a cave to hole up in and lick my wounds.

I find a large boulder fifty yards upslope from my fall. I crawl inside to shiver and worry away the hour it takes the storm to abate. Fortunately, the hail and snow don't stick for long, but when I crawl away from the steep talus, gloom overtakes me, not just because of my wreck but because 6,394-foot Chuar Butte looming high above me is a grim landmark of what miscalculations can mean to life out here.

On September 19, 1870, Major John Wesley Powell held council around a roaring fire with his Kaibab Paiute guide Chief Chuarumpeak on the North Rim's Uinkaret Plateau. Powell wanted to learn the fate of William Dunn, Seneca, and O. G. Howland, three boatmen who abandoned his first Colorado River expedition at Separation Canyon in 1869. Speaking through Powell's interpreter, Mormon missionary and guide Jacob Hamblin, Chuarumpeak admitted that members of the Kaibab and Shivwits bands of Paiute had killed Powell's men the year before because they mistook them for the drunken miners who had killed one of their women.

Shortened from Chuarumpeak, the respected Kaibab Paiute chief's name was given to a magnificent temple that, 114 years after the Dunn-Howland killings, was the site of the worst airline disaster in the history of the Grand Canyon. On June 30, 1956, a United Airlines DC-7 carrying fifty-eight passengers and a Trans World Airlines Super Constellation carrying seventy passengers collided at twenty-one thousand feet over the eastern Grand Canyon, scattering charred bodies and burning wreckage over Chuar Butte. The terrible collision foreshadowed the grisly deaths of ninety-nine other victims who perished in Grand Canyon air disasters in the next thirty-six years. If reporters described two commercial airliners as mere "smudges" in the Grand Canyon, what could possibly be said of a lone runner who'd flown out of control? All the more reason to keep running in the fading light, I tell myself, wondering how the Navajo who still dwell on Blue Moon Bench to the east of here, continue to see beauty where the *belegonna* encounters tragedy.

Aye na-ya-ya-ya, aye na-ya-ya-ya, aye na-ya-ya-ya, aye na-ya-ya-ya . . .
Beneath Where the Stars Turn, he ran.
With the Darkness Girl, he ran.
With Corn pollen for his feet, he ran.
With the Black Prayerstick for his hand, he ran.
With Darkness for his feather, he ran.
With Night-air breathing from his mouth, he ran.
With Happiness behind him, he ran.
With Happiness before him, he ran.
With Darkness, he ran.
Aye na-ya-ya-ya, aye na-ya-ya-ya, aye na-ya-ya-ya, aye, na-ya-ya-ya . . .

When I reach the base of 3,945-foot Chuar Lava Hill, it is beginning to drizzle. My eyelids are heavy with fatigue, and exhaustion is about to bring me to my knees. It is time to bed down for the night, but I keep stumbling until I find what looks like a suitable overhang somewhere along the sandy floor of the West Fork of Carbon Creek. In the growing darkness, I drop my pack and gather what seems like half a cord of firewood. It's going to be a long, drizzly night. So I drag crooked limbs of dead mesquite toward my lair and begin breaking them over a boulder into neat two-foot lengths, finally stacking each piece next to my pack for easy reach.

Unless it's an emergency, building a fire in the Grand Canyon is illegal; so I reevaluate the necessity of it. Without a fire, I'll get hypothermia; with a fire, the bivouac will be tolerable—provided I keep the flames stoked throughout the night. The choice is obvious, as is the location of the fire. I build it beneath the overhang, on the edge of the creek bed, so that summer flash floods will scour away all traces of my passing. Otherwise, charcoal from my fire, like charcoal from the ancient hearths of the Anasazi, could remain for hundreds of years.

I drift off to the ghost images of shadows dancing against the Canyon walls. An hour later, however, I'm awakened by a cold draft on my back. I turn over, curl up with my back to the fire, and nod off again. A half hour later, I wake up again, turn back over, and add more fuel to the burning embers. I check my watch, nine hours till sunup. At this rate, I won't get any sleep. I look at my watch again, and, in the flickering light, it tells me of another journey. For numbers it has letters that spell out MILLIONMILER. On its lower half is printed J. ANNERINO, and below that the name of a trucking company. Looking through the plastic crystal of this cheap retirement watch, I feel a strong kinship and power. MILLIONMILER represents the distance my father has driven an eighteen-wheel tractor-trailer rig without jackknifing on a rain-slickened highway in the middle of the night, or slamming into a concrete abutment, or succumbing to a thousand other heinous accidents far from home. And as I struggle to stay warm, rain ceaselessly dripping from the roof of the overhang, I know that somewhere out there in the real world thousands of other long-haul drivers like my father are "fighting the white line," trying desperately to stay awake, as they move freight through the dark American night. "A million miles," I whisper to myself, "all I've got to do is two-fifty." I nod off.

II.

My fire doused and buried, I am up and running long before sunup the next morning, striding beneath the black walls of Lava Canyon. But I am still groggy from the damp, restless night, and, and without thinking, I run up a smooth ridgeline of gray cinders to look for a shortcut. But there's no way down the other side; I'm cliffed out. So I backtrack, pick up the creek bottom again, and follow it all the way to the Colorado River.

The wind is blowing, a light drizzle is sprinkling the glassine surface of the river, and the air temperature is in the upper fifties. It's not the bright sunny day I hoped for to swim the icy river, but I must cross it to reach a food drop I hope is cached at the mouth of Tanner Canyon. From my rucksack I take out an inflatable life vest, a small inner tube, and a beach ball. Even without putting my hand in it, I know the water is cold; spilling from the depths of Lake Powell, it ranges from the mid-forties to fifty-five degrees. So I'll use the inner tube to stay afloat and hang my pack from the beach ball while I paddle across the slick current below Lava Canyon Rapid (not to be confused with Lava Falls 114 river miles downstream). With increasing fear, I don a U.S. Diver's life vest and blow up the small inner tube and sit on it. But it doesn't have enough volume to keep me out of the water, so I pull it on like a swim belt and start paddling across the river at Mile 65.

It's less flotation than John Daggett and Bill Beer used when they "swam" 279 miles down the Colorado River from Lee's Ferry to Pierce Ferry in 1955. That was the year before the Colorado River Storage Project began construction on Glen Canyon Dam, an engineering marvel that would drown the two-hundred-mile-long labyrinth of spectacular, wind-sculpted canyons called Glen Canyon and turn the once wild Colorado River into one of the most regulated and over-allocated rivers in the world. Some veteran river runners mused of blowing up the dam and renaming it Dominy Falls in honor of reclamation commissioner Floyd Elgin Dominy, who slapped their faces when he titled his book *Lake Powell: Jewel of the Colorado.* Nonetheless, Daggett and Beer slipped into the Colorado River on April 10; and even though completion of Glen Canyon Dam wouldn't drastically alter the river environment for another eight years, it was still too early in the season for an ultra marathon white water journey in what amounted to spring snowmelt roaring down from the Colorado Rockies. Daggett and Beer each wore partial wet suits and wool underwear to protect themselves from the cold; for flotation, they wore Mae West life preservers and clung to large army-surplus river bags they guided with swim fins. Yet, barely two days into their epic adventure, they wrecked on the midstream rock at President Harding Rapids, which left Daggett with "four or five deep cuts in his scalp and face—one a fraction of an inch from his eye—and a badly ripped knuckle on his right hand." But their main problem was not negotiating the river's legendary pool-drop rapids but enduring the fifty-three-degree water. In the August 5, 1955, issue of *Collier's Magazine,* Beer recounted: "Overexposure had chapped our hands so badly they bled, and our feet were painful from cuts and bruises . . . . Water leaking in through the rip in my shirt was making me unbearably cold." Throughout the twenty-six days the insurance salesmen spent navigating the wild river, they were repeatedly forced to get out and build fires to rewarm themselves in order to complete their treacherous journey.

But I am not trying to float 279 miles of the Colorado River in the wake of Daggett and Beer; I am only trying to cross a hundred yards of it. Even with three seasons of river running under my belt, however, I am still operating off the right side of my brain. And I am so groggy from sleep deprivation, physical fatigue, and endorphins, I am unable to foresee the consequences of my actions until I'm halfway across the frigid river. Still swimming as hard as I can, I realize that the inner tube around my waist is preventing me from ferrying across the current; instead, I am being swept helplessly downstream, my arms, legs, and chest growing numb with cold. The image comes to mind that my body will be found floating facedown in an eddy somewhere between here and Phantom Ranch, if I didn't simply disappear like Boyd Moore did when he and Harvey Butchart crossed the river two miles upstream from here on May 26 of the same year Daggett and Beer survived their adventure. I am too cold and enervated to continue. Fear seizes me: all the thought, training, and planning that went into this journey, and I am going to die because I wasn't cognizant enough to make a simple left-brain decision to float my pack on the inner tube and push it ahead of me.

> I am so groggy from sleep deprivation, physical fatigue, and endorphins, I am unable to foresee the consequences of my actions until I'm halfway across the frigid river . . . the inner tube around my waist is preventing me from ferrying across the current; instead, I am being swept helplessly downstream.

Helpless, I turn and look at my pack. ANNERINO is stenciled on the back of it; eerily, it looks like my headstone bobbing down the current behind me. If they don't find my body, maybe they'll find my pack, the same way they found Moore's below Unkar Rapid. I take one last deep breath, lean back in my life vest, and paddle faintly before death sweeps over me. But something catches my eye: my knife! For some reason—I'd never done it before—I have my knife strapped to the outside of my pack. I grab it, unsheathe it, and slash the vinyl tube writhing around my waist. A gush of air bubbles breaks the surface of the gray river.

Not knowing why, I lift my arm out of the water to toss my knife into the river. But I stop mid-toss and abruptly resheathe the knife. It is then I realize I am determined to survive. Never a master freestyler on any day, I breaststroke as hard as I can, hyperventilating as I try to sprint to the other side. With the inner tube deflated, I'm actually ferrying downstream across the deadly current, and I don't stop breaststroking until I reach the wall of green tammies hanging over the sandy riverbank. I clamber out of the bone-numbing water, put on my pack, and try running as hard as I can. If I stop to build a fire or to take off the life vest and inner tube—if I attempt anything less than all out effort—I will succumb to hypothermia.

But my steps are stumbles, s-l-o-w groggy motion, as though I'm running in a chain-mail shark suit, but the direction is correct: west. So that's the direction I keep stumbling, fearing death if I falter and stop. One sloshy, leaden step slides wearily into the next, and the next, until, slowly, I can feel my inner core rewarm from the forced effort.

Used by the Navajo on their sacred journeys to reach 'Ashiih, "the cave of Salt Woman," as well as by the Hopi, who also used Tanner Canyon as the western approach to reach their salt mines when the Little Colorado River flooded the Salt Trail Canyon route, I don't remember much about the four miles I stumble and lurch along this ancient salt trail toward the mouth of Tanner Canyon; nor do I notice the Anasazi ruins at Palisades Creek or the remains of George McCormick's 1904 Copper Grant Mine. I am stone cold, weary, and beaten. And by the time I reach the mouth of Tanner Canyon, where it spills its alluvial detritus into the Colorado River, I am crying. I had been sucked into the river's icy specter of death, what the Kaibab Paiute called paan?pic, "water babies," for the spirits that have wings, long hair, live in the river, and "drag people into the water and drown them." Yet, for some reason, the river gods have smiled on me. But that's as far as I want to follow this pathway. No more. I knew I could die trying to run the South Rim, and twice I'd almost died of thirst on the Hopi-Havasupai trail. But I am not now willing to pay the ultimate toll to run this desperate pathway. As far as I'm concerned, it's over. I'm out of this godforsaken canyon. End of story.

Still shivering uncontrollably, I find my food cache in the middle of

By the time I reach the mouth of Tanner Canyon, where it spills its alluvial detritus into the Colorado River, I am crying. I had been sucked into the river's icy specter of death . . . yet, for some reason, the river gods have smiled on me.

Tanner Wash fifteen minutes later; when I do, I see Chris May and Chris Keith staring at me with the same disbelief I feel upon seeing them. In the planning stages, the rendezvous were supposed to work this way, as they had on the South Rim and Hopi-Havasupai trail. But the reality of three people successfully linking up at a tiny X marked on the three-foot-long Grand Canyon National Park map still surprises me, especially this time out. I really hadn't been sure there was even going to be a food drop at Tanner Wash, since the resupply crew was spread so thin. But *Life* magazine had provided Chris Keith with film and processing to cover this story on spec, and on a wing and a prayer she and Chris May had volunteered to make the Tanner drop, in the hopes she might get another set of pictures or they would be there in case something went wrong. So my news falls on sensitive ears, but she keeps shooting.

"It's over," I tell them both, tears and snot dripping off my chin. "I almost drowned crossing the river." They nod sympathetically, ask me the how and why of it, then stuff me into some dry clothes and a heavy down sleeping bag. I pass the rest of the gray, drizzly morning and afternoon recovering in their care, contemplating the decision I've made to abort this journey. I'd admitted defeat below the North Rim once before, trying to walk this same route west to east as a fat man several years before my fall. It was a difficult decision then, but I'd lived with it. But that was backpacking, I tell myself, when you carried everything you needed; this is running, and there's no margin for error. Still, no matter what I do with my life from here on out, I'll never be in this position again. Part of me desperately wants to see this jour-

Author recovering from his near drowning after swimming the frigid Colorado River. He decides to abort his North Rim run . . . until he's reminded of the difficulties overcome by one-armed explorer Major John Wesley Powell in 1869: "At one time, I almost concluded to leave . . . but for years I have been contemplating this trip. To leave the exploration unfinished, to say that there is a part of the Canyon which I cannot explore, having nearly accomplished it, is more than I am willing to acknowledge and I determine to go on."

ney to the end, what Tim, Craig, and I had once called the completion of the "Grand Canyon trilogy." But another part of me doesn't want to die trying. I'm torn, and I don't know what to do.

Revitalized by hot soup, companionship, and my warm sleeping bag, I wonder if the route beyond could possibly be any worse than what I've already endured trying to run in the footsteps of the Anasazi and Kaibab Paiute down Nankoweap Canyon, across the Butte Fault, all the way to the river in a day. One-armed explorer John Wesley Powell summed up the situation perfectly when he navigated the Colorado River through the Grand Canyon in 1869: "At one time, I almost concluded to leave . . . but for years I have been contemplating this trip. To leave the exploration unfinished, to say that there is a part of the Canyon which I cannot explore, having nearly accomplished it, is more than I am willing to acknowledge and I determine to go on."

With the snowswept, corrugated terrain of Day 1 and the near drowning of Day 2 behind him, the determined author decides that the worst is over and resolves to continue his unprecedented adventure.

It was a good argument for Major Powell then, and it's a fair one for me now. But if I do decide to get out of this sleeping bag, I still have to cross the icy river three more times: once here, and, assuming I managed to run as far as the Shinumo Trail, I still have to cross and recross the river to make use of the South Bass food drop—assuming the *paan?pic* don't drag me under. But I'm not prepared to risk my life trying to swim the river again. Maybe I can find enough driftwood to build the sort of raft James White used. He was the sunburned and emaciated trapper and prospector who drifted up to the banks of Callville, Nevada, on September 7, 1867, claiming to have spent two weeks floating down the Colorado River in a desperate attempt to escape hostile Utes. If White's incredible tale were true, the thirty-year-old Colorado native was the first man in history to have navigated the Colorado River through the Grand Canyon, two years before Major Powell's first successful expedition in 1869. Early admirers, like General William J. Palmer and Thomas F. Dawson, embraced White as a hero, believing he had, indeed, come through the "Big Cañon." But others, like Major Powell and White's most disgruntled detractor, promotor and railroad engineer Robert Brewster Stanton, said it was impossible for a man to negotiate more than five-hundred miles of turbulent river currents and dangerous rapids on a hastily constructed raft in the time White claimed.

Revitalized by hot soup, companionship, and my warm sleeping bag, I wonder if the route beyond could possibly get any worse than what I've already endured.

At the end of his enlightening, June 4, 1917, Senate Resolution No. 79, "First Through the Grand Canyon," Dawson suggested that Major Powell knew months before he embarked on his 1869 Colorado River expedition that James White had already traversed the "Great Unknown," proving to Powell that there weren't any rapids that couldn't be run or portaged. Yet, to this day, no one knows for sure whether White or Powell was the first man through.

Even if White had beaten Powell through the Grand Canyon, (albeit not for scientific reasons), as I had come to believe after working a half dozen seasons as a boatman on the Upper Salt, Green, Yampa, and Colorado Rivers, White may have not been the first. Long before he slipped into the San Juan River with his companion George Strole, who drowned, the Hopi recounted the mythic river journey of *Tí-yo*, known simply as "the youth"; wrote J. Walter Fewkes: "All day he would sit there, gazing down in the deep gorge, and wondering where the ever-flowing water went, and where it finally found rest." Tí-yo had to find out; with the help and counsel of his father, he built a *wi na ci buh*, "timber box," or canoe, from a log they'd hollowed out with stone axes, cured with burning embers, and sealed with pine pitch. Carrying traditional food and sacred offerings for his journey down *Pí sis bai ya*, "Colorado Grande," into the Underworld, Tí-yo "floated over smooth waters and swift-rushing torrents, plunged down cataracts, and for many days spun through wild whirlpools where black rocks protruded their heads like angry bears." A sacred journey to the ocean that has been linked to the Hopi migration and the origin of their Snake Ceremony, the physical rigors Tí-yo encountered echoed those of James White, who wrote: "I wend over falls from 10 to 15 feet hie. My raft Wold tip over three or fore times a day. I see the hardes time that eny man ever did in the World." If White could build a raft to float even partway down this turbulent river, I could build one to float a hundred yards across it.

Before I can advise my friends of my plans to build such a raft, a group of river runners rows four nineteen-foot neoprene rafts into our camp. By

> Before I can advise my friends of my plans to build such a raft, a group of river runners rows four nineteen-foot neoprene rafts into our camp.

a stroke of luck, I know one of the boatmen from having worked on the river the previous summer. After patiently listening to my tale of woe, Wesley Smith offers me passage back across the river. And suddenly the sun shines on my dream again.

But I'm initially troubled by the idea, because the Grand Canyon's indigenous people did not have the benefit of modern rafts to cross the wild river. The Havasupai called the Colorado River *hagataía* for the same reason Juan de Oñate called it the *río colorado*, "red river," in 1604: every time the Little Colorado River floods, or the Paria River spills its red silt into the main stem of the Colorado River sixty miles upstream, the Colorado River turns a muddy red that some early explorers said was "too thick to drink, and too thin too plow."

> Every time the Little Colorado River or the Paria River floods the Colorado River turns a muddy red that some early explorers said was "too thick to drink, and too thin too plow."

The Kaibab Paiute called this same river *Piapaxa*, "Big River," and both the Paiute and Havasupai crossed it on small rafts made of a gridiron of poles, or logs crisscrossed with braces; as the men swam alongside pushing them, they floated their bedding, food, bows and arrows, women, and children on them. Or they simply swam across the river. When the Havasupai and Hualapai sought revenge with the Uinkaret band of Paiute for killing many of their people, they crossed the river on rafts, climbed out the North Rim of the western Grand Canyon, and attacked the Uinkaret Paiute, who they feared for their running prowess. Outnumbered on enemy ground, the Havasupai and Hualapai retreated back to the river; fighting as they went, the Uinkaret Paiute rolled boulders on them as they ran screaming through a narrow canyon passage. Sinyella recalled:

The good runners who got down to the river first, plunged right in and swam across. Some of those who were weak were carried off by the stream and drowned. Nearly all the Hualapai were killed. Those who had taken refuge in the cave were difficult to kill; so the Paiute dragged logs and green trees along the plateau and threw them down by the entrance, where others pushed them into the cave. When the entrance was filled, they set fire to the wood and suffocated all those inside: none escaped.

For trade or warfare, by raft or swimming, the Paiute, Havasupai, and Hualapai repeatedly crossed the Colorado River, as did the Navajo who swam the river far to the east at what the Paiute called *parovu*, "crossing," for the Crossing of the Fathers used by Spanish padres Francisco Silvestre Vélez de Escalante and Francisco Atanasio Domínguez in 1776. But those crossings were usually made in the summer when the water was

Author running near the mouth of Tanner Wash dressed in wool longjohns.

A boatman Wesley Smith ferries the author back across the Colorado River, so he can continue the run of his dreams.

low, relatively calm, and a warm eighty degrees, unlike today's icy river. Weighing all these factors against the possibility of being reported to, and fined by, park rangers for violating backcountry regulation 36 CFR 2.1(a)1, which prohibits disturbing of natural features, such as collecting logs to build a raft, I accept Wesley's offer as being within the legal constraints of a modern national park.

I turn in for the night and start to doze to the peaceful ebb and flow of the river as it caresses the sand and rock before surging through the rapids below. But high above, I see the fiery pink rim near Desert View; two years earlier, I'd first embarked on this impossible quest at that point. Yet, 120 years before me, Navajo medicine men journeyed to that same vista, what they knew as *yah'eh'ahi*, "Standing Tower," to seek their own vision. They called the nine-day curing *dzilk'iji bi'áádji*, Female Mountaintop Ceremony. And from its origin came the story of Elder Brother who wandered far from his family's hogan while hunting deer and got stranded on the south side of the San Juan River: "The clouds hung over the mountain, the showers of rain fell down its sides, and all the country looked beautiful. And he said to the land, 'Aqaláni!' (greeting), and a feeling of lone-liness and homesickness came over him, and he wept and sang this song:

That flowing water! That flowing water!
My mind wanders across it.
That broad water! That flowing water!
My mind wanders across it.
That old age water! That flowing water!
My mind wanders across it.

That age-old river! That flowing river! That icy river! My mind wanders across it as I nod off—caressed by its soothing sounds.

III.

STILL CHILLED FROM THE DAY BEFORE, I'M READY TO RUN BEFORE THE SUN PEERS into the east end of the Canyon the next morning. After two days of cool, damp weather, I would embrace the fiery sun for a few hours, but a tumbling wave of gray storm clouds is frothing down off the North Rim. And I wonder whether I've embarked on this journey a week or two too early. But the known water sources below the North Rim are even fewer and farther apart than those below the South Rim; as a result, Craig, Tim, and I scheduled this attempt to coincide with what we'd discovered was the Canyon's most fickle season: that narrow window between April and May, when temperatures are normally moderate enough to bivouac without a sleeping bag and when the prospect of finding seasonal tinajas between perennial springs and creeks was greatest. Yet, it was a time when Grand Canyon weather systems could vacillate between blinding hail and burning heat within days. I only hoped I wouldn't get strung out between water holes the way I had on the Hopi-Havasupai trail, when the early summer sun turned the inner Canyon into a killing ground for foot travelers.

Except for residual chills, I feel physically recovered from the near drowning; psychologically, though, I'm reluctant to leave my support crew. But once again, they've given me the emotional support I need to venture into the unknown beyond. Chris May and Chris Keith assure me everything will go as planned. "Don't worry," they tell me, "you've got it in the bag." Still plagued with doubts about reaching Phantom Ranch two to three sleeps west of here, I try to muster up a mood of confidence for them as I wave goodbye and Wesley quietly rows me back across the

South Rim Vista Grand Canyon National Park.

calm and deadly river. I don't know whether I'll see them—or anyone else—again.

Between last year's river running and this river crossing, I've only known Wesley a few hours. The Colorado River boatman and Vietnam vet is attuned to the natural forces of the Canyon. And although he views my journey with some bewilderment in a mythic canyon where public perception has been largely shaped by leather boots and wooden oars, a bond has been forged. When we land on the opposite shore, we shake hands and wish each other well.

I step out of the boat and strap on my pack and bota bags as Wesley ferries back across the current. For a moment, self-doubt almost overwhelms me when I realize I've just burned my second bridge with the outside world, but I try to shake it off as I skim along the Hakatai shale toward Unkar Creek. This near ideal footing, however, soon turns into a tangle of tammies, arrow weed, coyote willow, and mesquite, and before long I am clawing my way through this vicious thicket, shaking out mourning doves, vireos, and sandpipers that whirl away in a noisy blur at my approach.

When I finally emerge from this dense thicket, kicking and swearing, my dark-blue long johns are torn, my face is scratched, and any momentum I'd had has been reduced to an irritating lope; I trot along the 1200-million-year-old, rust-red shale and sandstone of the Dox formation until I reach Unkar Delta. Draining the southeast escarpment of 7,994-foot Walhalla Plateau, Unkar Creek

> This near ideal footing, however, soon turns into a tangle of tammies, arrow weed, coyote willow, and mesquite, and before long I am clawing my way through this vicious thicket.

carries the detritus of sand, boulders, and mud down from the North Rim and deposits it in one of the largest deltas along the Colorado River in the Grand Canyon; it also formed one of the largest habitation and archaeological sites along the river corridor, and reaching it is a perplexing crossroads for me.

Settled by the Cohonina people circa A.D. 900, and later occupied by the Anasazi between A.D. 1050 and 1150, fifty-two archaeological sites were excavated on this 125 acre delta during the 1960s, among them multiroom dwellings, ceremonial kivas, fire pits, and agricultural plots that supported a small population of tough canyon dwellers. These ancient canyoneers were dependent on hunting bighorn sheep, mule deer, cottontails, and blacktailed jackrabbits; gathering mesquite beans, wolfberries, prickly pears, and rice grass; and raising marginal crops of corn, beans, and squash. While I had come to admire the work of ethnographers, anthropologists, and linguists who worked side by side with Native American informants to document their lifeways and spiritual beliefs, the fervent passion with which non-Indians embraced the "science" of human archaeology, at least in the Southwest, has always troubled me. I understood the argument for salvage archaeology, to study and record a cultural site before it was destroyed by a highway, flooded by a dam, covered by tract housing, or looted by tourists. But without the informed consent of the Paiute, Navajo, Hopi, Hualapai, and Havasupai who are believed to be the direct descendants of the Anasazi, Cohonina, Cerbat, and others—ancestral people dug up in the name of science—I didn't understand how archaeology could be viewed as anything but grave robbing, especially in light of the fact that the Grand Canyon's indigenous peoples, while largely displaced from their ancestral canyon domain, were still alive and in many cases had maintained their most sacred traditions. As elsewhere in the Southwest, Grand Canyon archaeologists were not only digging up pueblos but ceremonial kivas, as well as sacred burial sites; in the case of Unkar Delta, and the trail of ruins that lead up Unkar Canyon to Walhalla Plateau, four burial sites had also been unearthed. It was this kind of insensible practice, that led to the Smithsonian Institution collecting and warehousing eighteen thousand Native American skeletons in the name of science. As a result, Congress passed the Native American Graves and Protection and Repatriation Act in 1990 to prevent further abuse, and to return human remains, as well as sacred objects and cultural artifacts, which began turning up at esteemed Indian art auctions like those held at Sotheby's and Christie's. Such legislation, however, did not heal the wounds inflicted by a century of scientific plundering of Native American sacred sites by lettered archaeologists, pirating by amateur pot hunters, and destruction by vandals. One of the most devastating recent cases took place in the winter of 1980–81, when two Arizona men stole and

> Without the informed consent of [Native Americans], I didn't understand how archaeology could be viewed as anything but grave robbing.

burned three Hopi deities named taalawtumsi, Corn Maiden, and Dawn Woman from Shungopavi on Second Mesa; it was an evil act that Paul Brinkley-Rogers and Richard Robertson, two investigative reporters who broke the story, said threatened to destroy the ancient Hopi religion and was akin to destroying the sacred Talmud.

In the case of Unkar Delta, I wondered, why wasn't it simply made off-limits to the twenty thousand river runners that raft the Colorado River each year until the Grand Canyon's indigenous people could decide what, if anything, should be done with such an important ancestral area? What ethical license did archaeologists have to dig up ceremonial kivas and human remains here, as well as atop Walhalla Plateau, where four burial sites were also unearthed? And how did this "scientific" knowledge contribute to the well-being

> "If you desecrate a white grave, you wind up in prison. But desecrate an Indian grave and you get a Ph.D."

and future good of Native Americans? Cloaked in cold, scientific terminology, archaeological reports are difficult enough for college-educated Anglo and Native American students to interpret. How would traditional elders who still lived and died by the Navajo or Hopi language interpret the white man's mumbo jumbo? Traditionally, Native Americans were reluctant even to talk about the deceased, and it doesn't take much imagination to understand how they feel about grant-fat teams of white men descending on their mesas and pueblos with shovels and brushes salivating to dig up their grandfathers. Put the shoe on the other foot, and imagine a van load of Native Americans knocking on your front door asking for directions to your mother's cemetery plot so they could exhume her body for the White Eye Cultural Museum they built at tribal headquarters. "And while you're at it, could you throw in some precious family heirlooms we can also put in the display cases?" Indeed, as Pawnee attorney Walter Echo-Hawk was quoted as saying in 1991: "If you desecrate a white grave, you wind up in prison. But desecrate an Indian grave and you get a Ph.D."

Cultural genocide of Native America did not end in 1884, when many of its most sacred ceremonies—including the Ghost Dance and the Sun Dance—were banned until 1935; nor did it end with the unconscionable slaughter of millions of Native Americans who, by 1910, had been "reduced" to a population of 250,000 from the estimated 5 to 10 million Native Americans who inhabited the continent before Columbus "discovered" it. Ethnic cleansing continued with the systematic destruction of Native Americans' sacred sites that removed their most precious connection with their cultural identity—the remains of their ancestors and the ceremonial bundles and pipes that, until the coming of archaeologists, lay quietly buried in the mountains, plains, deserts, and canyons they revered. And that included Unkar Delta, Walhalla Plateau, and numerous ceremonial caves that once contained split-twig figurines that may have been as important to the ancient canyon dwellers' religious beliefs and practices as taalawtumsi, Corn Maiden, and Dawn Woman are to Second Mesa Hopi.

In spite of my own bias against human archaeology in the Southwest, archaeologists dug up olivella shell beads at Unkar Delta that had reached the inner Canyon from the Pacific Ocean; they were no doubt carried along the ancient trade network that was later followed by the Mojave and Hopi-Havasupai trails. Archaeologists also excavated a glycymeris shell bracelet here that was carried north from the Gulf of California by the Hohokam and probably exchanged with the Sinagua and Cohonina. The Cohonina were said to come from the South Rim, probably crossing the river on log rafts. But how the Anasazi reached Unkar Delta from the Kaibab Plateau is less certain. Several direct rim-to-river routes traced out by early canyoneers, including Unkar Canyon and a petroglyph-marked route that descends 7,928-foot Obi Point into Clear Creek, are dangerous, and they may have been less practical for a family to use than descending Bright Angel Canyon and crossing the North Tonto to reach Unkar Delta from the west. Or the Anasazi may have used a prehistoric trade corridor that linked Saddle Mountain with the pueblos in Nankoweap Creek and the small settlement in Kwagunt Valley, then followed the Butte Fault the rest of the way to the river. For the Anasazi or Kaibab Paiute, who recently visited Unkar Delta and described it as a site of the Old People, it would not have been difficult for these ancient traders to use the same route I've followed to reach this point.

Though, the discovery of Hopi and Paiute pottery here by archaeologists posed an altogether different set of questions. Did the Paiute follow their northern trade route from the Kaibab Plateau across the Painted Desert to the Hopi villages to trade bows, arrows, and mountain lion quivers for Hopi pottery? Or did the Hopi journey to this inner Canyon village to trade with the Kaibab Paiute? If the Hopi did so, how did they reach Unkar Delta? For the Kaibab Paiute to reach Unkar Delta, there appeared to be three likely Anasazi routes to use: follow Nankoweap Creek, the Butte Fault, and the river corridor to here; cross the forested Kaibab and Walhalla Plateaus to a precarious pictograph-marked route that descended into Unkar Canyon below 7,865-foot Angel's Window; or descend Bright Angel Canyon and follow the North Tonto to this remote settlement. For the Hopi, there were two logical routes they could have used to reach Unkar Delta from the South Rim: follow Salt Trail Canyon beyond their salt mines to the mouth of Tanner Canyon or follow the Hopi-Havasupai trail across the Coconino Plateau to the head of Tanner Canyon, descend Tanner Canyon, and then swim or raft across the river to reach this point. But if the Hopi did use either route to trade at Unkar Delta, it's not known if they went back the way they came, or if they recrossed the Colorado River and followed the South Tonto formation to their mines on Horseshoe Mesa, and then up their ancient trail to the South Rim, where they could pick up the Hopi-Havasupai trail and follow it back to their villages.

These were questions I hoped to answer, if I succeeded in running the North Tonto all the way to Bright Angel Creek, my next resupply point two to three days to the west. But first I had to gain access to the east end of the North Tonto near a rock formation called The Tabernacle two thousand vertical feet above. To reach it, I start trudging up the steep, loose scree and shale of the Dox formation. It was a journey the Anasazi were thought to have made each spring; but if they followed a regular river-to-rim route to Walhalla Plateau, that route wasn't used enough to leave an indelible path that could be followed 839 years later. Having spent the winter on Unkar Delta, the Anasazi climbed back out to the North Rim to hunt deer, tan hides, and collect and roast agave hearts.

In *The Mountain Lying Down*, anthropologist Robert C. Euler speculated on what it might have been like for the Anasazi to make the same journey up from the river that I was now embarked upon:

> The year was 1143 A.D. It was a raw spring day and a cold southwesterly wind was blowing as . . . two people slowly make their way up a precarious route from the canyon depths to the North Rim. Each carried a large basket supported by a trumpline over their forehead, containing food—dried meat and the cooked and edible portion of the century plant—and skins filled with water. The man and woman were warmly dressed in loosely fitting cotton clothing covered with downy feathered robes. They wore heavy sandals made of yucca fibers.
>
> It had taken them two days to walk out of the canyon. They had camped the previous night under a rock overhang that contained a small spring where they could replenish their water supply [before completing their journey to their summer dwellings atop the North Rim. These people were] thoroughly in tune with the rugged physical environment of the canyon and did not hold it in awe as many people do today.

. . . as I still do when I finally reach the eastern end of the Tonto formation near the 4,802-foot Tabernacle, the halfway point for the Anasazi's seasonal migrations. Unlike the fluted terrain of the Butte Fault, I am more comfortable with the broad terrace of the Tonto; having run its South Rim counterpart, I think I understand the nature of it. Still, this is the North Rim, terra incognita for most people, including myself, so I tread lightly across this uncompromisingly rugged and dangerous pathway, wondering what mysteries the North Rim will unveil for me today.

Two thousand feet below, I can still make out the faint outlines of

Anasazi dwellings scattered across Unkar Delta. And I am still thinking about Euler's conclusions "that human beings were able to adapt to the extreme terrain and to make a very good living in the canyon for about a hundred years . . . more people living in the Grand Canyon during the 12th century than there are today," when I realize that any knowledge I'd gleaned from running the South Tonto two years earlier has little to do with the extreme terrain of the North Tonto. The reason soon becomes apparent: for the most part, the South Rim of the Coconino Plateau drains away from the Grand Canyon, whereas the North Rim of the Kaibab Plateau, including its southern extension of the Walhalla Plateau, is a full thousand-feet higher than the South Rim, and both drain into the Grand Canyon. In the process, the relentless erosional force of water draining off the North Rim created more freestanding monuments like Chuar Temple, The Tabernacle, and Zoroaster Temple, to name a few North Rim temples that rear out of its depths, longer tributary canyons, and terraces far steeper, narrower, and more rugged than those encountered below the South Rim. Thus, the North Tonto is more precipitous, dangerous, and drier, and, like the South Tonto, each dark tributary canyon has to be contoured canyon by sub-canyon in order to proceed west toward Bright Angel Creek.

"[These people were] thoroughly in tune with the rugged physical environment of the canyon and did not hold it in awe as many people do today."

Because of the North Tonto's intimidating exposure and physical relief, my running becomes a taxing mental effort. There is no dissociating from the physical act of running, a practice that had enabled me to dream my way most of the way across the South Tonto and the Hopi-Havasupai trail. The terrain demands my utmost concentration, and the images I'm forced to respond to are both monotonous and life threatening: step; don't knock the boulder down on you here; jump over a rock there; run around that cactus; don't fall to your death there. There is no dream-filled reverie, no further musings about the Anasazi following this treacherous route to Clear Creek and beyond to Bright Angel Creek. And the passage of time drags on and on. Yet, if I lose my concentration, if I make one small mistake in this concerted running, I'll go down. And out here, that means forever.

Guided across the North Tonto from Phantom Ranch by the maintained course of the Clear Creek Trail, a South Yemeni man disappeared in the vast inner Canyon frontier below the North Rim this year. Aided by infrared sensing devices, eight dogs, four helicopters, and a hundred search and rescue personnel, twenty-seven-year old Abdullah M. Balsharas walked off the face of the earth just west of here. I had no trail or cairns to guide me across the North Tonto even to reach the east end of the Clear Creek Trail, where the young man probably vanished, only the hot, dry serpentine terrace of the North Tonto as it coursed beneath the escape-proof cliffs of the Redwall limestone, what prospectors working the South Tonto called the Blue Lime.

As the sun climbs higher and my bota bags are sucked drier, I continue running along this steep, desolate bench of Bright Angel shale and Muav limestone as it slithers its way westward through prickly pear cactus, desert thorn, and black-brush scrub fifteen hundred vertical feet above the Upper Granite Gorge; I loop around 4,990-foot Sheba Temple then drop into the northwest fork of Asbestos Creek to rest and replenish my water supply. In 1894, Captain John Hance

There is no dissociating from the physical act of running, a practice that had enabled me to dream my way most of the way across the South Tonto and the Hopi-Havasupai trail. The terrain demands my utmost concentration.

mined asbestos here; but to reach these prospects from the South Rim, Hance did not use snowshoes to walk across the fog as he was inclined to tell tourists he did. Even before he could lead his pack string down to the Colorado River, he first had to forge the Hance Trail down Red Canyon to Hance Rapid. It was below this legendary rapid that Hance ferried his ore back across the river at low water, but he couldn't pack enough ore out along such a hazardous route to make a go of it. Nonetheless, Hance earned a reputation as a storyteller and raconteur among tourists he continued to guide down his trails and an epitaph from roughrider Bucky O'Neill: "God made the canyon, John Hance the trails. Without the other, neither would be complete."

The tailings of Hance's asbestos mine still spilling into the gorge below, I fill up my bota bags in Asbestos Creek and drink heartily. But the water has a salty, brackish taste that makes me gag and vomit in the hot white sun. My head spins, and my stomach turns. Was this what the Navajo and Hopi dealt with every time they went down Salt Trail Canyon and were forced to drink the mineralized water below Blue Springs? Asbestos Creek water tastes worse, and I contemplate climbing down Asbestos Creek to the river for some fresh water. When Major Powell met with guide and chief Chuarumpeak on September 20, 1870, to investigate the disappearance of William Dunn, Seneca, and O.G. Howland, he also wanted to explore the possibility of resupplying his second Colorado River expedition in 1871 from the North Rim. En route to the Kaibab Paiute trail, which led to Whitmore Canyon below Lava Falls, Chuarumpeak guided Powell and his men to a water pocket that was so rank the horses wouldn't drink from it. So Powell and his men pushed on to the river without water and fell down in the sands when they finally reached the lifesaving Colorado River. For some reason, however, the seasoned Canyon explorer did not order his men to carry enough water for the steep climb back up from the river to the barren Uinkaret Plateau, and when they reached the rank water pocket Powell said the men and horses "were mad with thirst." After watering their horses, Powell wrote, "we carefully strained a kettle for ourselves. . . . We boiled our kettle of water and skimmed it; straining, boiling and skimming made it a little better, and plenty of coffee took away the odor and so modified the taste that most of us could drink it. Our little Indian [chief Chuarumpeak], however, seemed to prefer the original mixture."

My head spinning as I lay staring at the sun, doubled over in a fetal position with nausea; it's too dangerous to venture down to the river in my condition. Yet I have no choice but to force down more water; I hold my stomach and gag down as much of the "original mixture" as I can, stagger to my feet, and run feebly beneath the flanks of Krishna Shrine and Newberry Butte. At one time, Hance planned to build a trail across the North Tonto from Asbestos Creek to Clear Creek. But there is no trace of it I can follow eighty-six years later with my head still reeling. I continue running toward the mouth of Vishnu Creek, my stomach rumbling from the vile water.

> I fill up my bota bags in Asbestos Creek . . . but the water has a salty, brackish taste that makes me gag and vomit in the hot white sun.

The next known water source is at the head of Vishnu Creek; but the sun has set, and I am totally spent by the time I drink that clear, sweet water. I try simple math problems, but I am too dorphed out and exhausted to remember the questions. It is time to eat the last of my food, a warm, damp bean burro, and bivouac—but first, a fire. There is no debate tonight; I simply build one within the confines of Vishnu Amphitheater. I recline in its flickering warmth and stare up at the starry heavens backlighting the stark cathedral of 7,529-foot Vishnu Temple. Named by geologist Clarence E. Dutton in 1880 for the Hindu god, Vishnu Temple forms one of largest and most sublime temples in the Grand Canyon. Of it, Dutton wrote: "It is a gigantic butte, so admirably designed and so exquisitely decorated that the sight of it must call forth an expression of wonder and delight from the most apathetic beholder." As such, it was an alluring temptation for canyoneers M. D. Clubb and his son Roger who first climbed it from the North Rim on July 13, 1945, almost four decades before I managed to reach the foot of it.

Thirty-six years later, George Bain climbed it solo from the Colorado River in one long, punishing day. But he also discovered something far more interesting during his October 23, 1981, ascent than the summit lichens and lizards Clubb reported seeing during his climb. The rare "metallic fossil" Bain found suggests that at least one of the Canyon's stupendous temples proved too tempting a target for U.S. Air Force pilots at about the time Clubb and his son first climbed it. Nearing the needle-tipped summit after twelve continuous hours of climbing, Bain used his small pocket knife to remove a .50-caliber copper-jacketed tracer bullet from the white band of Coconino sandstone crowning Vishnu.

Dawn breaks, and I'm running south along the west side of Vishnu Creek beneath the imposing form of Vishnu Temple, trailing behind campfire images of Vishnu Temple being strafed, John Hance hacking up asbestos, ancient traders burning archaeologists at the stake, James White running Lava Falls on his log raft, and me being drowned by slime-green water babies. Time seems to accelerate. Because I've crossed the threshold of the North Tonto, the point of no return, and I now have only one thing on my mind: to reach Clear Creek, the next perennial water source beyond Eighty-three Mile Canyon far to the west.

Morning dissolves into afternoon, and I am still running beneath Howlands Butte when I finally reach the fault line that fractures Clear Creek. I spend fifteen minutes looking for the cairn that marks the vertical descent into Clear Creek Canyon. Leery of being stung in the hand by a scorpion or struck in the face by a Mojave rattlesnake, I climb down hollow-sounding black ledges of Tapeats sandstone with my pack in front of me, unsure if this dark chimney connects with the talus slope a hundred feet below. Taking one horizontal shelf at a time, I make sure I don't slide down anything I can't climb back up, until I reach the bed of Clear Creek. I stop, fill up my bota bags, and lie under a shade tree with my bare feet soaking in the water.

High above, the misty white plume of Cheyava Falls roars out of a breach in the Redwall limestone; its source began as snowflakes falling on the alpine forests of the Kaibab Plateau. The 250-million-year-old seabed that crowns the 350-square-mile plateau acts as a filter for the twenty-seven inches of precipitation that percolate through the Kaibab limestone each year. In the process, this moisture recharges a subterranean aquifer that feeds the spectacular bridal veils

> . . . images of Vishnu Temple being strafed, John Hance hacking up asbestos, ancient traders burning archaeologists at the stake, James White running Lava Falls on his log raft, and me being drowned by slime-green water babies . . .

that spew out of the Redwall limestone below the North Rim: among them, Vasey's Paradise, Roaring Springs, Tapeats Creek, Thunder River, and Cheyava Falls. At four hundred feet high, Cheyava Falls is the highest of such cataracts; yet, it was one of the last to be discovered when, in 1903, William Beeson studied it through his binoculars from the South Rim. He showed it to newcomers Emery and Ellsworth Kolb who would go on to become renowned for their Grand Canyon explorations and photographs. Five years later, the Kolbs went to explore Cheyava Falls, carrying little more than their cumbersome cameras, provisions, and water for the arduous four-day journey. However, when the Kolbs trekked across the North Tonto from Bright Angel Creek to Clear Creek in 1908, they reported following a deer trail that was undoubtedly the route of the Anasazi. When park rangers, led by Glen Sturdevant, repeated the Kolbs' journey two decades later, they discovered canyon dwellings, kivas, and split-twig figurines in Clear Creek. And it wasn't until 1933 that the Civilian Conservation Corps constructed the Clear Creek Trail across the North Tonto so hikers could visit Cheyava Falls.

Staring at the headwaters of Clear Creek spewing out of stone, I wonder how long the Anasazi might have taken to cross the North Tonto between here and Unkar Delta; the kiva and split-twig figurines discovered here suggest these Anasazi also had a vibrant ceremonial life at the foot of these great falls. Who did they pray and sing to, as the great red stones parted to bathe this inner Canyon oasis with life in the desert?

From the top of great corn
The water splashes,
Down, down.
I hear it.
Around the roots of the great corn
The water foams,
Around, around.
I see it.

Thunder River, I knew, was much like Cheyava Falls. Hypnotized by the leaves fluttering overhead and soothed by water caressing my feet, I dreamed of reaching it.

But if I thought the Clear Creek Trail would provide me with a few easy miles en route to the distant oasis of Thunder River, I was wrong. Once I climb out of Clear Creek, I start running west across the North Tonto again. For the first time since leaving the Nankoweap Trail, I'm running along a modern path; it will lead me eight miles beyond to Phantom Ranch. But if I'd longed to sprint across this trail, it's too late; I'm about to cave in to fatigue and electrolyte imbalance. I am stumbling, whimpering, and sniveling, when I hear the motor drive of Chris Keith's camera sometime later. I've been ambushed, but seeing her lifts my spirits—even though she doesn't have any food. She has crossed the threshold herself to photograph this journey, first by trekking in and out the Tanner Trail, then by hiking down the South Kaibab and across the Clear Creek Trail, more than forty miles thus far. After such a heroic effort, Chris wants to take pictures. But my nerves are so frayed from running the North Tonto

With Zoroaster at his back, the author strides out on the Clear Creek Trail. This was the only maintained park trail Annerino was able to use on his east-west course through the Canyon below the North Rim run.

Author strides out on the Clear Creek Trail. This was the only maintained park trail Annerino was able to use on his east-west course through the Canyon below the North Rim run.

without falling that I fight the bit every step of the way, struggling once again at the foot of the great white horn of Zoroaster Temple. Again and again, I break down from the struggle, but once I reach Bright Angel Creek at Phantom Ranch late that afternoon, I know it's over. I'm through, I tell myself. It's taken everything I had, mentally and physically, to reach this point, and I'm only halfway.

Once again, Dick Yetman is there waiting for me. He has hiked into the Canyon from the South Rim to run the next two days with me. Over a brew at the Phantom Ranch beer hall that evening, I tell him and friend Bob Farrell that the risks are too great. I can't maintain a left-brained focus to run the precipitous North Tonto much longer without making a mistake, and I'm just an accident waiting to happen. They both nod and sip their beers as I stare silently at two groups of hikers who've struggled into this seasonal war zone of wounded canyoneers. Fortified with cold and watery American beer, a group of bright-eyed, blond-haired Germans laugh away the evening. But across the table from them is another group of hikers silently gazing at one another with vacant forty-mile stares; hobbled by blood blisters and swollen knees, they do not look like they've just seen one of the seven natural wonders of the world. They are pasty faced, hollow cheeked, and sunken eyed with heat stress and dehydration, and in spite of the dollar beers they clutch like consolation prizes, they do not look much better than the bleached skull and bones of the prospector the Kolbs photographed near the foot of the Bright Angel Trail at the turn of

> But if I thought the Clear Creek Trail would provide me with a few easy miles en route to the distant oasis of Thunder River, I was wrong. . . . I am stumbling, whimpering, and sniveling, when I hear the motor drive of Chris Keith's camera sometime later.

the century. And I wonder how torturous the journey will be for them to climb out of the Canyon in such wretched shape, how many will quietly cave-in to being "dragged out" by mule skinners or heli-vaced out by Park Service choppers?

I walk back to our camp snuggled between the soaring black gneiss of the Inner Gorge and the banks of Bright Angel Creek, and I wonder about the desolate frontier that awaits me beyond this inter-Canyon crossroads. The Anasazi, circa A.D. 1050, descended Bright Angel Canyon from the North Rim to reach their dwellings at the confluence of Bright Angel Creek and the Colorado River—and no doubt to cross the North Tonto to reach Clear Creek. It wasn't until Major Powell and his men stopped here on August 16, 1869, to look for timber to make new oars that non-Indians ventured up Bright Angel Canyon: Powell wrote: "Early in the afternoon we discovered a stream entering from the north—a clear, beautiful creek, coming down through a gorgeous red canyon. . . . We have named one stream, in honor of the great chief of the 'Bad Angels' [Utah's Dirty Devil River], and as this is in beautiful contrast to that, we concluded to name it 'Bright Angel.'" It would be another 22 years before the first non-Indians trekked from the South Rim to the North Rim via Bright Angel Canyon. That honor was footnoted by Dan Hogan and Henry Ward, yet little else is known of their 1891 canyon crossing. The next recorded descent of Bright Angel Canyon was made by U.S. Geological Survey cartographer Francois Emile Matthes, while surveying the first topographical map of the Grand Canyon in 1902. Eighty years later I was still relying on Matthes's work to guide me across the North Tonto frontier. Matthes

> I'm through, I tell myself. It's taken everything I had, mentally and physically, to reach this point, and I'm only halfway. . . . I'm just an accident waiting to happen.

reported that he had crossed Bright Angel Creek ninety-four times en route to the Colorado River, where he and his men were "startled to see 'two haggard men and a weary burro' emerge from the depths at that point." Who they were is not known. But with construction of Phantom Ranch by the Fred Harvey Company in 1922, this inner Canyon retreat of stone cabins designed by Mary Jane Colter and nestled in among Frémont cottonwood trees became a world-renowned destination for hikers and mule riders. However, while fifty-thousand tourists were using the popular Bright Angel and North Kaibab Trails to reach Phantom Ranch each year, there was little evidence any of them had explored the North Tonto to the west of here. And although I had been able to trace the ancient routes of the Anasazi and Kaibab Paiute from Saddle Mountain, Nankoweap Canyon, and the Butte Fault, along the salt trail and river corridor to Unkar Delta and across the North Tonto to Clear Creek and Bright Angel Creek, what lies beyond to the west was no-man's-land.

When medieval cartographers pointed to the blank spots on their maps and said, "Here be the Dragons," they might as well have been talking about the North Tonto between Bright Angel Creek and Shinumo Creek. The only references I could find of Kaibab Paiute trails that may have probed this region were short, vague descriptions of hunting routes that climbed *kaivavic*, "mountain lying down," or descended into the western Grand Canyon near Kanab Creek—ten river miles west of Thunder River and that was two to four days west of Shinumo Creek. Apparently, prospectors hadn't even crossed the mysterious ground between here and Shinumo Creek, nor had Mormon missionary and explorer Jacob Hamblin ventured into this uncharted realm. Hamblin was believed to be the first non-Indian to journey completely around the Grand Canyon in 1862. Yet, even as seasoned a traveler as Hamblin was, he was forced to eat crow before completing his five-hundred-mile loop atop the Colorado Plateau, a journey that may have been completed years earlier as a vision quest by Captain Navajo of the Havasupai. In his diary, Hamblin recounted: "We were very short on food . . . we lay by one day on the Pahreah [Paria River], and cooked crows to help our rations."

Staring up at the bright stars framed by the black walls of the Inner Gorge, I wonder what I'll be reduced to eating between here and Shinumo Creek?

I try nodding off, but I'm overcome with fear and uncertainty.

IV.

THE NEXT MORNING, I FEEL LIKE I'VE BEEN BUTTED OVER A CLIFF BY A DESERT bighorn. My legs are stiff with cramps, scratched raw from brush, and suppurating with tiny cactus spines called glochids. My feet are weary from the long rough miles and battered from kicking and stumbling over sharp, shoe-ripping Muav limestone. I've got the slight chills and nausea, and my head is throbbing from dehydration and sleep deprivation. The last thing I want to do is get strung out on the North Tonto. A day of rest would do wonders, I tell Bob and Dick. Bob assures me it would. But Dick has to be back at work in three days, and in spite of my sorry condition, I feel compelled to adapt to his schedule for the sacrifice he's made to join me. Work, in the *real* world,—it seemed so strange to me in the depths of the Grand Canyon where the will to run and survive has dominated all my actions.

I rehydrate with a gallon of water, drink four cups of hot mocha, swallow three aspirin, and I'm ready to roll—I think. But it's too late to try beating the deadly pace of the sun as its burns its way through the inner Canyon from the east rim of the Desert Facade. By 9:00 A.M. we are racing a receding shadowline as it slides down the 2000-million-year-old Vishnu Schist; streaked with pink ribbons of Zoroaster granite, this seventeen-hundred-foot high precipice of coarse, obsidian-colored stone forms the nearly unbreachable wall between Bright Angel Creek and the North Tonto.

From our camp on Bright Angel Creek, we scramble along a nameless fault up the steep, craggy talus of the Vishnu Schist toward a notch in the

Bass limestone; this is the passage to Utah Flats, a badlands of Hakatai shale and Tapeats sandstone that fans out from the base of 5,392-foot Cheops Pyramid, and crossing it is the key to regaining the North Tonto in Ninety-one Mile Creek to the west. I reconned this deceptive stretch the winter before; so I know the way. But Dick wants to lead, and he takes the wrong turn, trying to shorten the miles by following the rim of the Inner Gorge through Utah Flats. As a result, we're forced to backtrack through this stony desert, what I call "dead miles," as the sun climbs toward high noon. Having struggled alone for four days, it's odd to run with someone who now feels like both a stranger and a friend. But in spite of my misgivings, and Dick's wrong turn, I realize he is sharing the burden of the journey and our bond is forged.

I rehydrate with a gallon of water, drink four cups of hot mocha, swallow three aspirin, and I'm ready to roll—I think.

Having run what I estimate to be 80 to 85 percent of the first four days—the rest was devoted to scrambling across terrain so steep and rocky it wasn't runnable, or to climbing up and down ledges and chimneys that required both hands and feet, or to route finding, orienteering, survival, and swimming—running now seems impractical for the extreme terrain we're crossing. I know exhaustion may be clouding my perception, and that companionship may be distracting my focus, since this terrain is no more rugged than what I ran the first four days. So I struggle to maintain some semblance of a run, a trot, a jog. But my legs are swollen with edematous, caused by fatigue, or an allergic reaction to brittle bush resin that swaths my calves and thighs every time I brush past the toxic yellow flowers. And I'm forced to bow down and walk for a few hours as the North Tonto courses around the head of Ninety-one Mile Creek beneath the daunting Redwall ramparts guarding the 7,012-foot high twin peaks of Isis Temple. As we continue bearing toward the mouth of Trinity

Creek, I make feeble attempts at running, because across the river a few miles distant, I can see myself flying along the South Tonto forty-five miles from Hermit Creek to South Bass on one of the best running days of my life. Today, however, I feel overcome with heat stress, mental fatigue, and swollen legs, and I stumble, jog, trot, and shuffle as hard and as fast as I can. When we reach the head of Trinity Creek, we fill up our bota bags. But the water has the foul brackish taste of Asbestos Creek water, and I gag and vomit when I force down enough water to finish running around the west side of Trinity Creek. When we reach the base of 6,092-foot Tower of Set, we make camp for the night.

My T-shirt soaked with sweat and encrusted with salt, I lay back on the cool, flat bed of Tapeats sandstone, rest my head on a damp leather bota bag, and trace out the ripples and trilobite trails that track across this soft brown stone toward the head of Trinity Creek. I continue tracing the arms of Trinity Creek as they split around the base of

Having run . . . 85 percent of the first four days . . . running now seems impractical for the extreme terrain we're crossing.

7,646-foot Shiva Temple, and wonder which fork Emery Kolb and John Ivens followed when they crossed the Colorado River in a small boat and climbed up to the base of Shiva Temple in 1909.

When geologist Clarence E. Dutton first viewed Shiva Temple from the North Rim in 1882, he wrote that it was "the grandest of all the buttes, and the most majestic . . . That summit looks down 6,000 feet into the dark depths of the inner abyss . . . It stands in the midst of a great throng of cloister-like buttes . . . with a plexus of awful chasms between them. In such a stupendous scene of wreck it seemed as if the fabled 'Destroyer' might find an abode."

Fifty-five years later scientists went searching for mythic creatures they believed might dwell atop such an abode. And, in 1937, the magnificent temple which soars over our tiny bivouac site became the center of one of the most preposterous, and perhaps deceitful, ascents in the history of climbing in the Grand Canyon.

The Grand Canyon theory of evolution at the time was based on the fact that the inner Canyon desert acted as both a physical and climatic barrier between the North and South Rims: thus, the gray-tailed Abert's squirrel, which lives atop the South Rim, evolved differently than its cousin, the white-tailed Kaibab squirrel, which roams the sub-alpine forests of the North Rim. Telescoping this theory onto the isolated, 275-acre micro-habitat of Shiva Temple, park rangers began wondering what kind of animals might still exist on a sky island that was

I feel overcome with heat stress, mental fatigue, and swollen legs, and I stumble, jog, trot, and shuffle as hard and as fast as I can.

cut off from the South Rim and, they believed, was isolated from the North Rim by 20,000 years of erosion. Perhaps creatures as fanciful as the hornless unicorns they'd hoped to track down in Havasupai country? No one knew for sure. Funded by the American Museum of Natural History, Dr. Harold E. Anthony and expeditionary forces that looked like they were ready to tackle a Himalayan giant were eager to find out. And the press was only too willing to cover the expedition to "The Lost World of Shiva Temple." But first expedition members had to scale what they viewed as a daunting summit below the rim. After considering the use of a gyrocopter, and one daredevil's offer to bail out of a slow moving plane *sans* parachute into a piñon pine so he could lower a rope down to the climbers, Walter A. Wood of the American Geographic Society was selected to lead climbers up Shiva Temple. And park superintendent Miner Tillotson was asked to cut a spur road out to the North Rim near 7,766-foot Tiyo Point, their jump off point for the ascent. Six Mormon lads from Kanab, Utah, were hired as sherpas to hump provisions and beds two-and-a-half miles down to Shiva Saddle, so that seven expedition members were comfortable enough to scramble the mile up to the summit of Shiva Temple, a mere 1,350 vertical feet and one ropelength of climbing above, on September 16.

But the circus was only beginning. Once base camp was established atop Shiva Temple, aviatrix Amy Andrews kept the expedition resupplied by bombing the summit regularly with 10-gallon milk cans of water, and other provisions dropped from her flashy red, single engine Stinson. However, after ten days of trapping and skinning defenseless pickle-sized rodents in the name of science, Dr. Anthony's expedition was a bust, and perhaps a fraud. In his 1937 *Natural History* account, "The Facts About Shiva—The Real Story of One of the Most Popular Scientific Adventures in Recent Years," Dr. Anthony wrote: "As this article goes to press [a] comparison has been made and reveals no noticeable difference between the animals [primarily leafy-eared mice] of Shiva and those of the rim." He also wrote: "We had no knowledge that a white man had ever climbed it."

Having climbed all the way up to the base of Shiva Temple from the Colorado River in 1909, Emery Kolb had recalled seeing a deer trail, probably an Anasazi route, he believed led to the summit. But Dr. Anthony rebuffed Kolb's offer to guide the expedition to the summit, no doubt because Dr. Anthony feared the press might get sidetracked reporting the latest exploits of a canyoneer and photographer who had become famous for boating the wild Colorado River all the way from Green River, Wyoming, to the Gulf

After ten days of trapping and skinning defenseless pickle-sized rodents in the name of science, Dr. Anthony's expedition was a bust, and perhaps a fraud.

of California in 1911. So Kolb quietly went about scrambling up Shiva Temple *twice* from the North Rim two weeks before the American

Museum claimed its "first ascent"; the second time Kolb climbed it, he climbed it with his daughter. It was during one of those ascents that Kolb carefully marked the corners of Shiva Temple with rock cairns, leaving irrefutable proof that he'd made the first recorded ascent before Dr. Anthony and naturalist Edwin McKee built a summit bonfire on September 16: "We could see the lights of El Tovar [Lodge] shining on the South Rim," wrote Dr. Anthony, "some nine miles distant; and we made a huge blaze of dry limbs on the south edge of Shiva which we felt sure would notify our friends that the expedition was finally on Shiva."

As darkness falls across our stony bivouac on the black rim of Trinity Creek, I wonder if the Anasazi or the Grand Canyon's other indigenous people made such fires to signal distant pueblos thoughout the inner Canyon, or from, say, temporary camps on Shiva Temple to the North Rim? The Anasazi were the first to climb, and perhaps dwell atop, Shiva Temple between A.D. 900 and 1100. And if the American Museum Expedition didn't admit to finding Emery Kolb's summit cairns, they did acknowledge discovering stone *yanta* ovens the Anasazi used for roasting mescal hearts, as well as projectile points for hunting deer that migrated between the North Rim and Shiva Temple, scrapers for tanning hides, and pottery used for cooking and storing food and water.

Staring into our small bivouac fire, rimmed by foot-high stones, it's easy to imagine the burning embers as small fires scattered throughout the depths of the Grand Canyon: one is blazing atop Saddle Mountain, another burns along the Butte Fault, still another is floating mid-stream on a log raft, and others light the treacherous course of the North Tonto all the way to Thunder River; carrying pine-pitch torches, Anasazi runners kick and chase a wooden ball, running night and day virtually nonstop over the 250-mile-long firelit course in three days. While there is no physical evidence, or oral tradition, that indicates ancient Canyon dwellers played such a game, what the Tarahumara call *rarajípari*, I wonder if they weren't capable of running the North Tonto as the Tarahumara once ran through the rugged barrancas of the Sierra Madre during 48-hour kickball races that cover 200 miles? Anthropologists surmised that: "Much of the traditional Tarahumara life ethnographically mirrors that of the Grand Canyon Anasazi. Groups moved seasonally from canyon to uplands, hunted deer and other animals, relied heavily upon Agave as a wild food source, and constructed masonry cliff dwellings for storage and habitation." But we'll never know for sure; because this area of the Grand Canyon, like much of the national park, is a cultural void, no longer populated by Native Americans we can still learn such lessons from. Saddened, yet held rapt by the burning embers of our fire, I

> I wonder if [the ancient Canyon dwellers] weren't capable of running the North Tonto as the Tarahumara still run through the rugged barrancas of the Sierra Madre during 48-hour kickball races that cover 200 miles?

recall the words of Edward Curtis, who foretold the demise of ancient Native America in 1909: "Alone with my campfire, I gaze on the completely circling hill-top crested with countless campfires around which are gathered the people of a dying race. The gloom of the approaching night wraps itself about me. I feel that life of these children of nature is like the dying day drawing to an end; only off in the west is the glorious light of the settng sun, telling us, perhaps, of light after darkness."

Curled up on raw stone, I shiver next to our fire throughout the night dreaming of torch-bearing Tarahumara running through the heart of the Grand Canyon. When I finally glimpse light after darkness the next morning, I'm struck by the thought I'm six days out from Saddle Mountain— and I never expected to get this far. But we are out of food and dangerously low on bad water. We consider backtracking to the head of Trinity Creek to replenish our water, but after gagging at the source and yesterday's turnaround we agree we can't afford to log any more 'dead miles'. So we douse the dying embers of our fire with coarse sand and gravel, and start running before the sun burns through our camp. Spring is turning to summer and with the wonderful display of wildflowers comes rashes, scabs, blotches, and water blisters that now cover my swollen legs as I continuing running across the North Tonto. The extremes of heat almost upon us, we're not sure whether we'll find water before we run out, and it becomes a test of will to save some of the vile Trinity Creek water in each of our bota bags as backup. Without water, we are at the mercy of this inner Canyon stretch of Sonoran Desert, locked in by the Redwall looming above us and rimrocked by the Granite Gorge gaping below.

It is dreary work, running through the morning heat toward Ninety-four Mile Creek, sometimes fighting, othertimes drifting through a mirage induced by dehydration and heat waves shimmering off the hard ground of the North Tonto; the dry heat seers my face, mouth, nostrils, and throat; salt burns my cracked lips; and sweat stings my eyes, making it difficult to focus on the Redwall escarpments swaying over us as we continue running through the glaring white light. But there's also a timeless beauty to the running, as if we're drifting in a cloud. And with each mile we float in and around the bays and amphitheaters below 6,075 Tower of Ra, stopping when ever we see a silver pool of water, my mind floats toward the horizonline.

By noon Crystal Creek is in sight, thirteen-hundred-feet below. Careful not to dislodge boulders, rocks, or scree on top of one another, the two of us climb down a dangerous break that cleaves the Tapeats formation beneath the steep North Tonto, leery of slender scorpions and Mojave rattlesnakes that may be poised on the dark shelves we use for hand- and footholds during our precarious hundred-foot descent to the talus below. We stumble down to the cool, trickling waters of Crystal Creek, our empty bota bags flapping at our sides in the hot canyon wind; we don't know where on the North Tonto to the west we'll find our next water hole. So we linger a long time in the hot sun, soaking our weary bodies in the cool creek water, while drinking like horses at a trough. We pay little attention to the Anasazi ruins nearby, or to Crystal Rapid, one of the most feared rapids in Norh America.

Formed in 1966 when fourteen inches of rain hammered the North

Rim over a thirty-six hour period, the flood that raged down Crystal Creek destroyed Anasazi ruins and erased evidence of all previous floods dating back to A.D. 1050; a torrent of mud, boulders, stones, and trees estimated to be twenty-feet deep and sixty-feet wide boiled into the mainstem of the Colorado River at Mile 98, creating overnight a deadly cataract that did not exist when Tíyo, James White, and Major Powell made their legendary river journeys so long ago. Yet, today, we see no river runners trying to elude the fangs of the treacherous Class 10 Big Drop that, a year hence, would flip and eat bus-sized motor rigs, kill tourists, and see entire river parties helivaced out of the Canyon when a maelstrom of white water roared down the Colorado River at 93,000 CFS.

> There's also a timeless beauty to the running, as if we're drifting in a cloud. And with each mile we float in and around the bays and amphitheaters below 6,075 Tower of Ra.

Hungry, but rehydrated, we struggle through the hot white sun across what seems like the most difficult mile-and-a-half on the entire journey, the craggy section between Crystal and Tuna creeks; the schist, gneiss, and quartz burns our hands and seers our legs to touch, but it is the only passage back up to the North Tonto and our way westward to the South Bass food drop tonight. When Bob Marley and Robert Cree backpacked along the river corridor from Diamond Creek to Lee's Ferry in 1980, they were faced with climbs of up to 800 vertical feet throughout their 55 day adventure to avoid precipitous drops along the Colorado River. By the time Dick and I have climbed eleven-hundred vertical feet from Tuna Creek to the North Tonto along the Crazy Jug Fault, the heat has hammered us, and by late afternoon we realize we will not reach the South Bass tonight.

Seen from the South Tonto, 5,832-foot Scorpion Ridge looks like a monumental stone arachnid crawling down from the North Rim to the river for a drink of water. By the time we contour around its west pincher of Redwall limestone, we decide to throw down camp when we see three aluminum canteens scattered across the ground and blackbrush scrub; the shiny, one-quart containers are melted to the cinders and shale like old church wax, disfigured from nearly four decades of blistering sun. They've been here since June 21, 1944, when three aviators parachuted out of a B-24 bomber that developed engine trouble while en route from Tonopah, Nevada, to Tucson, Arizona. Before managing to restart the engines, the B-24 captain ordered three of his airmen to make what was the first recorded night jump into the Grand Canyon. Facing violent prop wash and 75 mile an hour winds, Second Lieutenant Charles Goldblum, Flight Officer Maurice J. Cruickshank, and Corp. Roy W. Embanks jumped into the Canyon from 20,000 feet at 2:00 A.M., and began one of the most amazing rescue sagas in the history of the Grand Canyon. Early dispatches hammered out by the Associated Press reported, "The area the men are believed to have landed in is inhabited only by Indians." They were, in fact, floating down through the black abyss toward the no man's land of the North Tonto. And it was miraculous that they all survived the jump. Both Embanks and Cruickshank managed to land on the North Tonto, but Goldblum felt his chute snag on the edge of a cliff [probably the Tapeats sandstone]; he hung there motionless from his harness throughout the night when he realized he was dangling 1200 feet above

Carrying food, medical supplies, and two-way radios down from the South Rim, four mounted rangers led a string of seven pack animals over forty miles of trail in hopes of reaching the stranded airmen from the south side of the river.

the roaring Colorado River. At dawn, Goldblum climbed up the slippery shroud lines and, later, stumbled into the others who were wandering across the North Tonto toward Tuna Creek. That night, they holed up in what they called a "wildcat den in a cliff," and debated the merits of building a log raft to float across to the south side of the Colorado River.

At war in Europe and the Pacific, the nation's headlines beamed with reports of courage, bravery, and heroism on the front lines and at home: perhaps none was stranger than four-year-old Eddie Staeheli of Addy, Washington, who, the day the three airman jumped into the Grand Canyon, horrified his mother by twirling a live rattlesnake around his head; and none appeared to be more selfless than Coast Guard Lieutenant Stanley B. Kurta, who two days after the three airman found one another, dove into shark infested Carribean waters to wage "an incredible barehanded battle against a monster tiger shark in a vain attempt to save a shipmate." The lost aviators also caught the attention of the press, and when a parachute silk was sighted by searchers three days after they bailed out, a four-pronged rescue operation was launched to pluck them from the depths of the Grand Canyon, while they were resupplied by air with food, water, walkie talkies, flare guns, and boots.

Carrying food, medical supplies, and two-way radios down from the South Rim, four mounted rangers led a string of seven pack animals over forty miles of trail in hopes of reaching the stranded airmen from the south side of the river. They were followed a day later by a second party of rangers and U.S. Coast Guard boatswain mate Dan E. Clark, leading a pack string carrying a knock-down boat and a harpoon gun Clark planned to use to fire a cable across the four-hundred-foot wide river. Upon reaching the Colorado River, however, both parties turned back when they came face to face with "the roaring, swirling torrent, cutting through sheer rock walls." As a result, Col. Donald B. Phillips, commander of the Kingman Airfield, ordered a convoy of trucks out to 7,458-foot Point Sublime to begin searching for a route down to the airmen from that North Rim vantage; while across the bay ranger Ed Laws and canyoneer A.A. MacRae began descending a route below 7,763-foot Grama Point

Col. Phillips had reconned earlier from the air. Nineteen hours later, Laws and MacRae reached the bearded, sunburned aviators living high on K-rations they said tasted like turkey. When the trio finally reached the rim nine days after their adventure began, Cruickshank said: "I wanted to go back to that [wildcat] den on our fourth day. We were so hungry, and I hoped that cat had come back so we could eat it. I would have tackled it with my bare hands for food."

In spite of the air tour pilots Dick and I have occasionally heard flying over the inner Canyon since leaving Bright Angel Creek, aerial resupply was not an option for us. We are starved for food, and hungry enough to tackle anything that moves, but if there are caches of the airmen's K-rations still hidden amongst the boulders, we can't find them. In our search, however, we root out a large lizard called a

We are starved for food, and hungry enough to tackle anything that moves, but if there are caches of the airmen's K-rations still hidden amongst the boulders, we can't find them.

chuckwalla; it scurries into a crack and inflates itself. Anasazi and other Native peoples used pointed sticks to remove chuckwallas from such fissures, and we do the same, knocking it over a stone to finish the job. When its eyes glaze over, I use my knife to severe the abdomen, remove the bloody entrails, cut off its clawed feet and wedge-shaped head, and peel off its scaly, coal black skin. Disheartening, yes, but the sight of the molten canteens drives home the desperation of our situation. Not that a lone chuckwalla will save our lives, but it's a symbol that the survival process must be initiated before it's too late. We roast the lizard over the coals, Anasazi-style. Known to the Kaibab Paiute as *moywia*, and revered for its medicinal use, Dick calls the sweet, tender spit-roasted flesh "chuck steak."

The seventh day, and I tell myself we're supposed to rest. But unless we go on a chuckwalla roundup, we can't linger or we'll starve long before we reach the South Bass food drop. So we make another predawn start, running into the infinity of the west, contouring the endless unnamed drainages that stand between us and Monadnock Amphiteater toward Hotauta Canyon. Only two people I knew of had been across this no man's land before us: Ginny Taylor and her companion Chris Wuerhman in 1976; throughout their arduous five week trek below the North Rim, Ginny carried a 70 pound pack on her winsome frame, and it was Ginny's route description that provided us with the only guide through this frontier. The Anasazi who followed the precipitous tributary canyons down from the North Rim to the river no doubt crossed this stretch of the North Tonto, and perhaps, too, the Kaibab Paiute, but no one else that I knew of. Even Harvey Butchart suggested we go around this desolate stretch, when I consulted with him once by phone, and he advised me instead to follow the natural fault line of Tuna Creek and Flint Creek on the opposite side of 6,297-foot Sagitarrius Ridge. But if I wanted to avoid the North Tonto I wouldn't have ventured beyond Bright Angel Creek. I now wanted to

When its eyes glaze over, I use my knife to severe the abdomen, remove the bloody entrails, cut off its clawed feet and wedge-shaped head, and peel off its scaly, coal black skin.

embrace the white heat of this inner Canyon desert, feel the ice stinging my face from the North Rim, and come to grips with whatever else the canyon would throw at me in order to understand once and for all what ancient traders might have endured to cross the spiritual frontier between their inner Canyon cliff dwellings and rimtop pueblos.

Aye na-ya-ya-ya, aye na-ya-ya-ya, aye na-ya-ya-ya, aye na-ya-ya-ya
I have gone to the end of the earth.

I have gone to the end of the waters.

I have gone to the end of the sky.

I have gone to the end of the mountains.

I have found no one who was not my friend.

Aye na-ya-ya-ya, aye na-ya-ya-ya, aye na-ya-ya-ya, aye na-ya-ya-ya.

Somewhere on the crimson horizon to the west is Hotauta Canyon, and fortunately we've found enough seasonal water in the intervening tributary canyons to continue running toward the Hotauta Canyon descent route Ginny said links the North Tonto with the Colorado River across the river from the South Bass food drop. But she was trekking from the west, and we are running from the east. Staring fourteen-hundred-feet down into the perplexing geological maze of Hotauta Amphitheater, we must read the confusing terrain and translate her description in reverse: "Follow river along main trail to Hotauta, take easternmost of two ridges

The author explains to his support crew members—Tim Ganey, Craig Hudson, and a companion—the objective hazards of the final leg of the run, escape route alternatives, and the slim chance of their finding him if he makes a mistake.

down, furthest upcanyon. If you've started going up into Hotauta, you've missed it [the descent line]." Our throats are parched, our bota bags are empty, and our stomachs are crying for chuckwallas, when we finally reach the Colorado River late that morning.

We are half a day late, whatever that means in Canyon time, and when we're spotted by our resupply team across the river, bodies jump into action. Craig Hudson, the best swimmer in the crew, paddles across the river above Bass Rapid in a navy survival raft, towing a large air mattress behind him. He is not only our ferry back across the river but our caterer. He offers us a bagful of foil-wrapped bean burros, and we wolf through them before we utter word one.

We spend the rest of the afternoon racked out in the sand at the foot of the South Bass Trail, bringing Craig, Tim, and Chris Keith up to date; judging by the meager rations I'll be sent back across the river with the following morning, one of their companions evidently thought the responsibilities of a resupply member was to consume most of the food drop carried in to finish the journey. I look to Tim, to see what he reads

Thunder River. Author reconns the treacherous crossing of Thunder River on a tyrolean rope traverse the year before. (Annerino collection)

in my eyes, but he does not suggest I pack it in here; nor does he suggest anyone one else accompany me for the final push to Thunder River. And I nod off in the gray light of twilight to the soothing melody of Bass Rapid.

The next morning, I'm ferried back across the river and suddenly I feel abandoned. The support crew is hiking out the South Bass, where Tim and Craig will try pulling another rabbit out of their hat: climb seven miles and forty-five-hundred vertical feet out to the South Rim, drive 238 miles around the Grand Canyon to Monument Point on the North Rim, and trek another ten

> Our throats are parched, our bota bags are empty, and our stomachs are crying for chuckwallas.

miles down the blistering Thunder River Trail to rendezvous with me tomorrow afternoon: assuming I can overcome my fears long enough to finish this last daunting leg. I am alone, again, struggling on the north side of the river along a route that Francois Matthes's survey party took six days to cross from the South Rim to the North Rim in 1902. And being alone feels odd after running—and surviving—with Dick for two days, especially after he and the support crew provided me with an island of security in this inner Canyon frontier. It feels especially odd because, after eight days of struggling toward Thunder River, and eight nights of dreaming about it, I still can't see the "summit" of this inverted mountain range; if I hadn't drunk from Thunder River pouring through doorway-high fissures in the Muav limestone, if I hadn't failed near the foot of it trying to walk this same route years earlier, if I hadn't climbed into its subterranean aquifer with other boatmen and -women the summer before, if I hadn't reconned the treacherous crossing last fall, I would have doubted the very existence of that dreamy cataract.

Shinumo Creek takes its name from the Paiute word *shinumo*, "cliff dwellers," and Powell expedition member Frederick S. Dellenbaugh gave it that name in 1872; wrote Dellenbaugh: "We called it Shinumo Canyon because we found everywhere indications of the former presence of that tribe." After crossing the no man's land between Bright Angel Creek and Shinumo Creek, it is reassuring to know that people once lived in this isolated canyon wilderness, though the dwellings, granaries, and check dams they constructed here were used so long ago. I wonder, too, if it was more practical for these Anasazi to venture along the North Tonto to Bright Angel Creek, or climb up Shinumo Canyon to the North Rim, cross over the Kaibab Plateau, and descend Bright Angel Canyon—as Matthes's survey party had; or swim or raft the Colorado River in order to make use of the South Tonto to reach Bright Angel Creek if they journeyed to that settlement, or east to Clear Creek, to trade?

My route takes me along the east bank of Shinumo Creek, past the site of William Wallace Bass's old tent camp to a dead end. Shinumo Creek must be crossed, but it's too cold, too deep, and moving too fast to try wading across it at this point. So I inflate my life vest and run up and down the boulder-strewn banks looking for a way to cross it.

There's only one option and I decide to chance it, trying not to dwell on the likelihood of being bruised from the landing, or drowning if I'm knocked unconscious from a fall. So I don't hesitate. I hurl my pack twenty feet to the opposite shore. A cottonwood seedling is my bridge. I climb up it until it bends over an exposed boulder mid-creek, hoping it doesn't snap. It doesn't, but it's not quite long enough to reach the other side.

> Shinumo Creek must be crossed, but it's too cold, too deep, and moving too fast to try wading across it at this point.

I'm forced to drop from its willowy upper branches onto the moss-covered rock. I touch down and slip, hugging the rock with both hands to keep from being swept into the deadly torrent.

Gingerly I stand up and look at the jump I've got to make to get to the opposite side. There's no way; it's a good ten feet across. The best standing broad jump I did in high school was a little over seven feet. There's only one thing to do; I can't reverse my move, even if I wanted to. I try not to think what it will feel like. I just dive, head first, my arms outstretched, hoping I haven't misjudged the distance. Dust whirls, rocks fly. I take the brunt of the fall on my rib cage, slamming the air out of me and banging my right hand as I claw at rocks and willows for handholds. But I'm across.

Throughout the day, I'm seized with loneliness and fear as I struggle out of the inner Canyon desert up the incipient North Bass "trail," my ribs aching from the landing. Traces of the old trail are marked by elusive rock cairns, and they lead me through the dense brush and boulders of White Creek, into the depths of Muav Canyon, where I'm finally able to climb up to the ancient spring below Muav Saddle. Critical to the survival of several hundred Anasazi who inhabited the forested realm of 7,661-foot Powell Plateau between A.D. 1050 and 1150, I drink deep from the sacred waters until my stomach is swollen; I wash my sunburned face and cracked lips, wring out my salt encrusted bandannas, fill up my tattered bota bags with clear sweet water, then lurch toward the crest of 6,711-foot Muav Saddle a half-mile beyond.

> I just dive, head first . . . dust whirls, rocks fly. I take the brunt of the fall on my rib cage, slamming the air out of me . . . but I'm across.

As the sun begins to set, the temptation to quit nearly overcomes me. No more than two miles away is a fire road. All I've got to do is hike up to Swamp Point, and follow the road through the maze of fire roads that probe the rim of Tapeats Amphitheater between here and Thunder River trailhead. If I ran all night through the dark woods, and didn't get sidetracked, I could cover the thirty-five miles by dawn. It would be over, I'd be free of the Canyon's tenacious grip, and nobody would blame me. But the summit of my dreams, and the pathway leading to it, is finally within sight. So I have to push on and follow the rushing waters of Saddle Canyon and Tapeats Creek to the source of Thunder River; although I desperately fear the uncertainty of what awaits me in the Kaibab Paiute's ancestral canyon domain between here and that spectacular cataract.

The only known trail descending into the region of Tapeats Amphitheater was what Dutton described as being long, devious, and treacherous; Dutton wrote that it was used in 1876 by gold seekers chasing the rumor "that gold had been found in the sands of the river, and it gained credence enough to attract a number of people who tramp the deserts of the far west in pursuit of—they know not what."

Overcome with loneliness and impending darkness, I wonder if I was any different, running the ancient trails of the Grand Canyon—in search of what? Depressed at my commitment to venture back into the Canyon's grip when escape from it is so near, I look around forested Muav Saddle for a level place to bivouac; to my surprise, I discover an abandoned cabin that I would learn later was a snowshoe cabin built for rangers in 1926. It is rickety and weather beaten, and when I open the door and peer inside I see a wood stove, a rack of firewood, a steel bed frame, and a can of chili sitting on a cobweb covered shelf. I throw my pack inside, sit on the front porch, and watch sunset's last golden rays dance across the rim of Tapeats Amphitheater, as I cut open the can of chili with my steel knife. This is it, I tell myself, the time of reckoning.

When Julius Stone and Nathaniel Galloway rowed wooden boats through the Grand Canyon in 1909, trapping beaver and hunting bighorn sheep along the way to stay alive, Stone reached a point in his fabulous journey when he noted in his diary: "I have reached the land where dreams come true." After three years of chasing phantoms, spirits, dreams, and visions throughout this canyon odyssey, and after eight days of struggling against myself and the forces of the North Rim, when dawn's golden glow alights the treetops the next morning, I realize I, too, have finally reached "the land where dreams come true." I feel as though the Grand Canyon has finally unveiled its secrets for me. I'm now an insider, and the rest of my run will flow like the river, unimpeded by ego and self-doubt.

Named by Major Powell for the Paiute guide *tumpits*, "small rocks," who showed the one-armed canyoneer Tapeats Creek and claimed ownership of it, I bushwack down the densely wooded canyon at a trot, raked by thorns of New Mexico locust, and dropping from one cliff-cupped plunge pool of water to the next, as if I were put on this planet to do nothing but run. I feel strong, refurbished by the can of cold chili. Eating out of that rusty can with my knife on a starlit perch overlooking Tapeats Amphitheater

After eight days of struggling against myself and the forces of the North Rim, when dawn's golden glow alights the treetops the next morning, I realize I, too, have finally reached "the land where dreams come true."

was the best meal in my life. And this, I tell myself, will be the best running day in my life.

It is. The scrambling behind me, my movement is brisk and sure-foot-ed. I suck in cool, fresh morning air, I blow out hot moist breath: *Hih-huh, hih-huh, hih-huh, hih-huh, hih-huh.* My lungs heave in and out, my arms swing in rythmic unison to my breathing. My legs charge toward the run-ning power I've always hungered for, *galkeʔhoʔndi.* If the white coyote bounced out in front of me now, it would be mine—I'd grapple with it, as we rolled over the rimrock together. What a day to be alive and running! I'm gushing with joy and excitement. I can see the summit and the end of a five-year dream; the long journey will be over as soon as I cross Tapeats Creek.

I follow the right bank, running higher and higher, hoping to skirt Tapeats Narrows, but my path deadends before I reach Tapeats Falls. I backtrack, always running, sprinting, leaping, and bounding down through the rocks, cactus, willow, and brush. But there's only one option.

I blow up my yellow life vest again, and with my pack strapped to my back, I leap across the swollen channel. But I'm too carefree and I miss the small ledge, sliding ten feet down the bare rock and splashing into the torrent. Clear headed, I struggle. There will be no drowning today, I tell myself, no slime-green *paan?pic* dragging me under. I'm finally in control of my actions, no more dorphed-out mistakes like the Lava Canyon crossing. Using my feet in front of me to take the brunt of each boulder, I grab the limb of a tree fifty yards downstream and drag myself out. I stand up and, seeing that I'm unharmed, jump up and down, waving my hands over my head in triumph for no one by myself to see.

It's all coming together, I tell myself, running like the canyon winds that whirl down the throat of Tapeats Creek. I can finally imagine the sweet taste of success. But when I reach the confluence of Tapeats Creek and Thunder River, still dripping with water, I see there is no way to ford the two creeks below the confluence. Fear overcomes me again, but I try to rein it. I see clearly what will happen if I make a mistake: I will be swept to my death over the series of falls that surge through the narrows between this confluence and the Colorado River two miles below. To compound matters, if I managed to cross Tapeats Creek, I still have to cross Thunder River; spewing out of a 515 million year old wall of marine limestone, and plummeting 959 feet in a half-mile, the raging rainbow-hued cataracts of the shortest river in the world were worse.

I'm stuck.

I try wading across Tapeats Creek above the confluence, but once it gets chest-deep I back out.

Okay, I tell myself, burn your last bridge. I throw my pack across the rushing torrent and look for a proper vaulting pole; not that I've ever pole-vaulted before, but I won't let that stop me now.

The best thing I come up with is the semigreen stalk of an agave about ten feet long. I break the stalk off near its base, above the heart Anasazi used to roast and eat. I pull off some pointed husks, then trot back to what looks like a suitable launch pad atop a boulder. I plunge the stalk into the torrent, but the end of it is swept downstream before it touches bottom. If I can put enough body weight on it to gain purchase, maybe I can arc forward.

After being swept down Tapeats Creek and later pole vaulting it, Annerino crosses
Thunder River via a cottonwood tree.

The author ends his 250-mile North Rim run at Thunder River, cooled by the spray of its magnificent falls. He has batttled raging streams, precipitous terrain, loneliness, and fatigue.

There are no other options to consider. Gripping the top of the pole tightly with both hands, I plant the pole and dive for the other side. As soon as the pole jars against the bottom, I hear a crack then a snap. The pole breaks, hurling me against the opposite bank shoulder first. I grab desperately, repeatedly missing the exposed roots of a cottonwood tree as I'm swept hopelessly downstream toward the maelstrom of the confluence, swallowing water and gurgling foamy air. A thud jars my right hip, I cough up water and mucus, then clutch the large root that finally stops me.

I drag myself out, still hacking up water, and wonder how many more times this will happen. I look up, humbled by the roaring plumes of Thunder River cascading into Tapeats Creek at a forty-five degree angle. When I reconned Thunder River last fall, I was nearly swept to my death while setting up a treacherous tyrolean rope traverse I tested in the event I needed one to cross the falls now.

> I grab desperately, repeatedly missing the exposed roots of a cottonwood tree as I'm swept hopelessly downstream toward the maelstrom of the confluence, swallowing water and gurgling foamy air.

But fall runoff was relatively mild compared to this late spring rampage, so I know there's no way to cross it at this point without one. But I told Tim not to bother with the ropes and hardware, because I'd find a way to get around the falls without them—if I had to recross Tapeats Creek and follow it all the way to the river and double back. I start scrambling up the bank, to see if I first can't somehow traverse above the falls. But suddenly I see the door has swung open again. A large, moss-covered trunk of a cottonwood tree bridges this short awesome river. After five years, the dream has finally become a reality. I carefully step across the gnarled, slippery bark, and it's over.

When I see Tim and Chris near the foot of the great falls, the three of us are showered by cool sunbowed mists, and I scream the first words out of my mouth: "WE'RE OUTTA' HERE!!!"

But there were other words, far more reverent and beautiful, sung on the burnished rims of this ancient canyon long before I had the incredible fortune to emerge from the depths of it alive:

The author collapses on the trailhead sign of Thunder River, the exit point of his unprecedented 250-mile North Rim run.

. . . On the trail of the pollen of dawn

I am wandering.

Where the dark rain cloud

Hangs low before the door

I am wandering.

In the house of long life

I will wander.

In the house of happiness

I will wander.

With beauty behind me
I will wander.
With beauty above me
I will wander.
With beauty below me
I will wander.
In old age traveling
On the trail of beauty
I will wander.
It shall be finished in beauty.
It is finished in beauty.
Hozhoni.

EPILOGUE

If a person does not fear to look

into the Canyon and see distance

such as he has never seen else-

where, depth such as he has never

dreamt of . . . he will have feelings

that do not well go into words and

are perhaps more real on that

account.

Haniel Long,
A Letter to St. Augustine

FOR YEARS AFTER TIM, CRAIG, AND I WALKED AWAY FROM THE NORTH RIM, I would not—could not—go back to either rim of the Grand Canyon. While I continued to work seasonally as a Colorado River boatman, rowing and paddling the legendary river that surged through the Canyon's granite breach, I feared looking into the immense chasm from the rim world high above. I'd never crossed such distances before, through such daunting depths; nor had I such visions before or experienced the sensation of movement within the specter of time standing still. And the fact that I'd followed, and survived, pathways that bridged the threshold between ancient paths and the modern world, the river corridor and the distant rims, marked me in ways I was reluctant to try explaining in casual conversation. The pathways were dreamways, really, because after the tears, joy, and suffering the Grand Canyon of the Colorado River remained unmarked by my passage. As it well should.

What do remain are the lifelong kinship I feel toward the kind, selfless friends and others who helped me fulfill an impossible dream and perhaps some insight into the questions I sought to answer when I first stepped off the rim and ran through the heart of stone: Could ancient Canyon dwellers like the Anasazi, and perhaps later the Hopi or Kaibab Paiute, have run through the depths of the Grand Canyon?

While there's no oral tradition or written record to indicate that the Anasazi actually ran through the inner Canyon, they had the canyoneering skills to negotiate the Grand Canyon's most precipitous ledges and travel along its most treacherous corridors. And while the lifeway of the

Grand Canyon Anasazi has been compared to that of the Tarahumara, it can't be proved that the Anasazi came from the rich running tradition that enabled the Tarahumara to cover extraordinary distances through the Barranca del Cobre region of the Sierra Madre Occidental. Why did the Tarahumara run through rugged canyons that ranged from subtropical thorn forests to the lofty old-growth forests of the Continental Divide? Apart from their ultramarathon kickball races, which were ceremonial and socially cohesive events that united the widely dispersed Tarahumara who dwelled throughout a twenty-thousand square-mile ancestral region, it's long been believed that running was simply the most efficient means for the Tarahumara to travel throughout what has often been described as Mexico's Grand Canyon. Whether the same held true for the Anasazi may never be known, but I would be inclined to say it did. The ancient knowledge of running was passed on to the Grand Canyon's, the Painted Desert's, and the Mojave Desert's indigenous peoples by their ancestors, and in the case of the Grand Canyon there seems little reason to doubt that long-distance fleet-footed travel was passed on by the Anasazi, or perhaps even earlier by the people of the Desert Culture.

Pose the same question of the indigenous groups that inhabited the region encircling the Grand Canyon after it was abandoned by the Anasazi circa A.D. 1150, and there's little doubt that the Navajo, Hopi, Kaibab Paiute, Apache, Chemehuevi, and Mojave had the endurance to run through the heart of the Grand Canyon, but they had to have a reason and the canyoneering skills to do so. Based on my experiences, ethnographic reports of intertribal trade, and oral and ceremonial traditions of running and Canyon exploration, my initial reaction would be to narrow the field down to the Hopi and the Kaibab Paiute: the Hopi, because of their salt expeditions into the eastern Grand Canyon, their mines in Tanner Canyon and on Horseshoe Mesa, and the rim-top Hopi-Havasupai trade route; the Kaibab Paiute because of their presence in Nankoweap Canyon, along the Butte Fault, Little Colorado River Gorge, Tapeats Amphitheater, and their rimtop routes across the Kaibab Plateau.

While it's easy to imagine the great Hopi runner Charlie Talawepi running the Hopi-Havasupai trail in less than half the time I had—if the third-hand report was accurate that he maintained a sub-seven-minute-mile pace for 156 miles across the Painted Desert—it's not known whether other renowned Hopi runners had the canyoneering skills of the Anasazi, or Kaibab Paiute, to run through the inner Canyon if they used it as an alternate route to the rimtop Hopi-Havasupai trail. And Charlie Talawepi's extraordinary run posed another question for me. While I am the first who'd like to believe all the legendary running feats of Native Americans, many are based on historic secondhand and thirdhand reports rather than eyewitness accounts; therefore it's often been difficult to decide which ones I thought were based on fact and which ones I thought were based on myth. When fifty-five-year-old Tarahumara grandfather Victoriano Churro won the Leadville Trail 100 mile race in 1993 in twenty hours, two minutes, he wore a pair of huaraches to cross the high passes of the Taviwach Ute's lofty ancestral ground in the Colorado Rockies; a victory that inspired jealousy, praise, and contempt among non-Indian ultra-runners, Churro's glorious victory dispelled many doubts about the Tarahumara's legendary running prowess—as did twenty-five-year-old Tarahumara Juan Herrera when he crushed the Leadville 100 competition in 1994 with a course record of seventeen hours and thirty-five minutes.

When Major John Wesley Powell met with Chuarumpeak to discover the fate of William Dunn, Seneca, and O.G. Howland, he recalled seeing a Kaibab Paiute runner: "Early the next morning the Indians came to our camp. They had concluded to send out a young man after the Shi-wits [Paiute]. The runner fixed his moccasins, put some food in a sack, and some water in a little wicker-work jug lined with pitch, strapped them on his back, and started off at a good round pace." Powell didn't say how far the young Kaibab Paiute ran, but another passage attests to the Kaibab Paiute's intimate knowledge of canyoneering: "I have prided myself on being able to grasp and retain in my mind the topography of the country, but these Indians put me to shame. . . . They know every rock and ledge, every gulch and cañon."

That the Kaibab Paiute did. But did ancient Hopi runners, who dwelled in the Painted Desert east of the Grand Canyon, also "know every rock and ledge, every gulch and cañon" throughout the inner Canyon, and did they have the climbing skills of the Anasazi? After returning from his first salt expedition in 1912, twenty-one-year-old Hopi Don Talayesva of the Sun clan recalled his elders' fear before they descended over a crumbly ledge of Tapeats sandstone for salt near the confluence of the Colorado River and Little Colorado River Gorge: "I noticed that his hands and knees were trembling and asked if he were in danger. My father answered, 'We are getting old and may not be able to climb the ladder with our salt.' I saw his chin quiver as he talked and knew that he was afraid." Such fears are not uncommon for modern canyon climbers when they step backward over a cliff while rappelling. And the feelings Talayesva described may be contrary to the fearlessness Hopi men demonstrate each year when they descend over the rim of Canyon Diablo to gather golden eagles—a practice that disturbs neighboring Navajo traditionalists. But the precarious rim-to-river routes of the Grand Canyon Anasazi suggest they were fearless climbers. When modern canyoneers tried following the route of the Anasazi up from their ancient footbridge in the depths of Marble Canyon, it took several attempts to trace the frightening route through the Redwall limestone up to 4,484-foot Point Hansbrough. And when cavers and archaeologists descended into the Anasazi's ceremonial caves below the South Rim's 7,268-foot Yaki Point in 1954, it was disturbing to learn they removed split-twig figurines from what they described as shrines and a sacred human-hair bundle that hung from the ceiling. They wrote: "This cave, about sixty-five feet in depth, was very difficult to enter and required considerable mountaineering skill and equipment, including ropes and pitons." While the Anasazi were master canyoneers, as were the Kaibab Paiute, it's not known whether either ran the Butte Fault and the North Tonto to Thunder River; nor is it known whether the Hopi ran the South Tonto and the Apache Trail to Havasupai. In retrospect, though, I would be inclined to say the Anasazi ran through the heart of the Grand Canyon for the same reason the Tarahumara ran through the Barranca del Cobre region: it was the most efficient way to travel through the inner Canyon, whether for ceremony, trade, hunting, or even racing. If the Kaibab Paiute and Hopi did not run through the inner Canyon, I believe they were certainly capable of it. But these are mysteries still lost to modern knowledge, and the Grand Canyon may never unveil them.

What did not remain a mystery, at least to myself, was the burning desire to continue running wild down the path I first embarked on not long after I hobbled up that black pyramid of stone in the Arizona desert. The fall and the Grand Canyon odyssey had changed me forever. The Himalayan giants I once longed to climb were distant dreams, but the void that still ached in me after reaching Thunder River was not. Ambition, the quest for ancient knowledge, an inexplicable need to live in a time that no longer existed—I did not know what caused such a feeling. But there was only one way to try filling the void: up the ante and cross the 750 miles of desert, mountains, and canyons that stand between Old Mexico and the red-rock badlands of Utah, what early explorers called the "Last Frontier of Arizona." Follow the spirit tracks of the Apache, the ancient dreams of the Chiricahua, and run wild through . . .

In the aftermath of that monthlong odyssey, which crossed the heart of the Grand Canyon, I still feared to look into the great canyon and come to terms with what I experienced and survived earlier. While there had been fleeting moments—even hours—of clarity and reality throughout the Grand Canyon odyssey, so much of it took place in dreamtime that the reality of it had never quite settled in. I did not know why. I returned once to the Canyon for a wedding, often as a boatman, and several times as a tourist, but it wasn't until 1997 that I could stare into the depths of the Grand Canyon again.

I had gone to Desert View to trace out the route the Hopi and Navajo used to descend Tanner Canyon. I had long surmised both tribes used Tanner Canyon as the western approach to their salt mines when the Little Colorado River flooded the Salt Trail Canyon approach—as Craig Hudson and I discovered we had to do two days before using the Tanner Trail as our own alternate approach for the South Rim run. Nonetheless, as I stood with rim-bound tourists awestruck by the sight of the great chasm, I gave little thought to my journeys years earlier. When I returned to my wife and son, who were waiting in the woods on a park bench nearby, she said she had just seen a coyote. Of course, she told me it was white, but I did not believe her. She'd read an early draft of this work, and I suspected the image of a white coyote still lingered.

There was an older man talking to his wife on the park bench next to us. Evidently, he was disappointed by the hazy view, the result of the coal-burning Navajo power plant, or the elbow-to-elbow crowds that would total five million visitors this year. Nonetheless, he remarked to his wife, "Well, at least we saw a coyote."

"What color was it?" I asked him.

"Creamy white. It was beautiful," he said.

I looked at my wife then ran through the woods hoping to catch a glimpse of it. I did not. But knowing it was out there, running along the rim of the Grand Canyon, was a turning point for me. It was the path I followed years earlier, and directly or indirectly it had lead me to this point. Standing on the rim of the great abyss, I suddenly realized it was the path I needed to continue following until the day I died.

But I was not the first to try following the path of the coyote, and I hope I will not be the last. The great Navajo warrior and chief Barboncito was one of the first I knew of. Known to his people by his war name *Hashké yich`i´ dahilwo´*, "he is anxious to run at warriors," Barboncito performed the *M'ii Bizéé naast'á*, Put a Bead in Coyote's Mouth, ceremony that many Navajo believed was responsible for their freedom from their devastating forced internment at Bosque Redondo in 1868: "His people formed a big circle and started closing in. There was a coyote within the circle. Barboncito approached the coyote, a female, who was facing east. Barboncito caught the animal and put a white shell, tapered at both ends, with a hole in the center, into its mouth. As he let the coyote go free, she turned clockwise and walked . . . toward the west. Barboncito remarked: 'There it is, we will be set free.'"

I was no Barboncito. I never caught the white coyote, nor did I even glimpse it running along the Canyon rim. But running wild in its spirit tracks finally set me free.

Appendix

KEY TO ABBREVIATIONS USED IN APPENDIX

Area

AL	Ancestral Land
BLM	Bureau of Land Management
NM	National Monument
NP	National Park
NWR	National Wildlife Refuge
PA	Primitive Area
RA	Roadless Area
RES	Indian Reservation
USFS	U.S. Forest Service
WA	Wilderness Area

Life Zones

CA	Canadian
CD	Chihuahuan Desert
GBD	Great Basin Desert
LS	Lower Sonoran Desert
MD	Mojave Desert
MT	Mountain Transition
SA	Sub-Alpine
SD	Sonoran Desert
US	Upper Sonoran Desert

Conditions

BH	Boulder Hopping
BIV	Bivouac
BW	Bushwhacking
CL	Exposed Climbing
CN	Canyoneering
ST	Sandy Track
SW	Swimming
TR	Trail
TRNM	Non-maintained Trail
XC	Cross-country
2XWD	Two-wheel Drive Dirt Road
4XWD	Four-wheel Drive Dirt Road

Elevation Gain/Loss

EW	Each Way
OW	One Way

Distance

o&b	Out-and-back
p-p	Point-to-point

Appendix

Mileage Logged on Foot: 47,240 Miles

(Recorded from January 1, 1976, to May 31, 1997)

Approximately 90 percent of this mileage involved long-distance wilderness running and daily training on dirt roads and desert, mountain, and canyon trails. Approximately 10 percent entailed cross-country trekking or climbing, backpacking, and running on pavement when it couldn't be avoided.

The following running and training logs include the period after my fall through the completion of the North Rim run. I kept no yearly logs of my mileage before 1976 and have not included logs of non-running wilderness travel and exploration, such as climbing, river running, and trekking.

1976: 1,046 miles

Ran an average of six miles a day, five days a week, often at night, at 1,260 feet above sea level, on the level dirt roads and creosote flats of the Salt River Indian Reservation in the lower Sonoran Desert. Mixed in occasional ten-mile runs and many runs up and down 2,608-foot Squaw Peak, a rocky desert trail that climbs twelve hundred vertical feet in 1.1 miles.

1977: 1,428 miles

Moved to mile-high Prescott and spent much of the year acclimating myself to the increased altitude and mountain running in the ancestral lands of the Yavapai, on the trails and dirt roads of the 7,180-foot Sierra Prieta, the 7,626-foot Granite Mountain, the 7,693-foot Spruce Mountain, the 7,979-foot Bradshaw Mountains, and the mile-high grasslands of Coyote Springs. Mixed in more ten-mile runs, bouldered in Groom Creek, and frequently rock climbed at Granite Mountain. The profile of my normal training routes, which began this year and continued long after I returned from the North Rim, was as follows:

Route	Condition	Elev. Low Point/High Point	Elev. Gain/Loss	Mileage
Senator Rd.	2xWD Mtn.road	6,300ft./6,800ft.	+500ft./- 500ft.	10-12/o&b
Thumb Butte Rd.	2XWD Mtn.road	5,600ft./7,000ft.	+ 500ft./- 1,500ft.	10-12/o&b
Granite Mtn. Rd.	2XWD Mtn.road	5,500ft./6,000ft.	+1,000ft./-1,000ft.	10-13/o&b
S. Spruce Ridge	Mtn. trail	6,300ft./7,696ft.	+1,500ft./-1,500ft.	11/o&b
Coyote Springs	Mesa Trail	4,900-ft./5,600ft.	+ 200ft./- 200ftt.	10-12/o&b
Granite Creek Park	Dirt trail	5,6000ft.		10/laps
Prescott Jr. High	Track	5,600ft.		6-10/laps

1978: 1,480 miles

Much of the year was spent training on the same mountain trails and roads I'd run the previous year, the high point being our ascent of the Southwest Face of Zoroaster Temple. My formative introduction to canyon running took place during the early summer: I worked as a boatman on the Green and Yampa Rivers in Dinosaur National Monument on the Colorado-Utah border, and I took advantage of the river access to run the trails and tributaries of the Canyon of Lodore and Whirlpool Canyon, as well as trails in the High Uintah Primitive Area between river trips.

1979: 2,427 miles

Inspired by the previous year, I increased my daily mileage to tens, my weekend mileage, and my explorations further afield with wilderness running. Some notable highlights for me were as follows:

Date	Area	Life Zone	Conditions	Elev. Gain/Loss	Mileage
January 1	"White Coyote" Salt River Res	LS	2XWD road	None	16/laps
January 7	Granite Mtn. USFS WA/Yavapai AL	MT	TR & XC Icy w/snow	+1,600ft./-1,800ft.	12/p-p
January 13	Pine Mountain USFS WA/Apache AL	MT	TR, XC Many lion tracks	+1,800ft./-1,800-ft.	17/loop
January 20	Saguaro East NP WA/Sobaipuri AL	SD & MT	TR Snowdrifts	+5,000ft./-5,000ft.	28/o&b
January 27	Pusch Ridge USFS WA/Apache AL	MT & SD	TR	+2,300ft./-5,600ft	21/p-p
January 28	Wasson Peak NP WA/Papago AL	SD	TR	+2,000ft./-2,000ft.	11/o&b
February 3	Organ Pipe NM/SAND Pápago AL	LS	ST Smugglers Route	+150ft./-150ft.	24/p-p
February 10	Superstitions USFS WA/Yavapai AL	SD	TRNM, XC Flash floods	+1,700ft./-1,900ft.	31/loop
February 14	Sierra Prieta USFS/Yavapai AL (Whiskey Row Marathon course)	MT	2XWD Knee-deep snow	+1,500ft./-1,500ft.	17/loop
March 3	Castle Creek USFS WA/Yavapai AL	US & MT	TRNM, XC, 2XWD	+4,200ft./-4,200ft.	23/loop
March 10	Gailuro Mtns. USFS WA/Apache AL BIV	CD & MT	TRNM, BH, BW, XC	+3,200ft./-4,200ft.	48/p-p
April 7	Painted Desert NP WA/Navajo & Hopi AL	GBD	XC	+1,700ft./-1,700ft.	14/o&b
April 8	Rainbow Forest NP WA/Navajo & Hopi AL	GBD	XC	+ 400ft./-1,300ft.	12/p-p
April 15	Juniper Mesa USFS WA/Hualapai AL	MT	TRNM, BW Many deer	+2,200ft./-2,200ft.	12/p-p
April 28	WF Oak Creek/ Secret Mountain USFS WA/Yavapai AL	MT, CA	CN, XC, SW, CL	+2,400ft./-2,400ft.	30/p-p

May 12	Sierra Prieta	MT	2XWD	+2,400ft./-2,400ft.	46/o&b
	USFS/Yavapai AL				
	(Whiskey Row Marathon: run 10,000-meter, half-, and full marathon back-to-back)				
August 4	Mt. Union	MT, CA	2XWD	+1,600ft./-1,600ft.	16/o&b
	USFS/Yavapai AL				
August 11	Woodchute Mtn.	MT	TRNM	+1,000ft./-2,300ft.	16/p-p
	USFS WA/Yavapai AL		Heat Stress		
August 18	Mt. Baldy	CA, SA	TR, 2XWD	+2,700ft./-2,700ft.	18/loop
	USFS WA/Apache AL		Summit Hailstorm		
September 6	Arches	GBD	XC	+ 250ft./-250ft.	11/p-p
	NM WA/Paiute AL		Heat stress		
September 7	Kendrick Peak	CA, SA	TR	+2,500ft./-2,500ft.	10/o&b
	USFS WA/Havasupai AL				
September 15	San Francisco Peaks	CA, SA	4XWD, TRNM	+4,400ft./-4,400ft.	18 /o&b
	USFS WA/Havasupai-Yavapai AL		Summit ice storm		
September 30	Sycamore Canyon	MT, SD	BH, XC	+0ft./-3,000ft.	35/p-p
	USFS WA/Yavapai		BIV		
November 18	Grand Canyon NP	MT, SD	TR	+4,000ft./-3,900ft.	22/loop
	NP WA/Cohonina AL				

1980: 2,405 Miles

(Including inner Canyon run below South Rim)

Much of the three months leading up to my South Rim run was devoted to a weekly training regime of ten to-twelve-mile runs at Coyote Springs, Senator Road, Granite Mountain, and South Spruce Ridge and seventeen-mile weekend runs across the Sierra Prieta: two notable exceptions were a thirty-mile run on the Camino del Diablo and a fifty-mile run across the Bradshaw Mountains. Once I recovered from the South Rim run, I resumed training on these same courses, as well as exploring different wilderness and roadless areas.

Date	Area	Life Zone	Conditions	Elev. Gain/Loss	Mileage
January 20	El Camino	LS	ST	+150ft./-150ft.	30+/o&b

	NWR WA/Sand Pápago AL		Infamous border route		
January 26	Crook Trail	MT	TR	+0ft./-700ft.	18/p-p
	USFS/Apache AL		Historic Route		
February 2	Bradshaw Mtns.	MT	2XWD	+3,300ft./-3,800ft.	50/p-p
	USFS/Yavapai AL				
May 26	Paria Canyon	GBD	TRNM, XC, SW	+0ft./-2,500ft.	35/p-p
	BLM WA/Kaibab Paiute AL		BIV		
August 31	San Francisco Peaks	CA, SA	4XWD, TRNM	+4,700ft./-4,700ft.	24/p-p
	USFS WA/Havasupai & Yavapai AL				
September 1	Bill Williams Mtn.	MT, CA	TR	+2,100ft./-2,500ft.	9 /p-p
	USFS/Havasupai & Yavapai AL				

1981: 3,065 miles

(Including run of Hopi-Havasupai trade route)

During the four months leading up to running the Hopi-Havasupai trade route, I began streaking—running six to ten days in a row—ten to twelve miles a day and ran separate legs of the Mojave Trail. Once I returned from the Hopi-Havasupai run, I resumed my normal training runs. During the summer, I worked as a Grand Canyon boatman, and I took advantage of the river access to run many of the trails along the Colorado River and to explore many of its wonderful tributary canyons without a cumbersome pack or the pressure of survival, including: Badger Creek, Silver Grotto, Buckfarm Canyon, Nankoweap Canyon, Little Colorado River Gorge, Cardenas Creek, Grapevine Creek, Clear Creek, Bright Angel Creek, Blacktail Canyon, Shinumo Creek, the North Tonto east of Tapeats Creek, Thunder River, Deer Creek, Olo Canyon, Matkatamiba Canyon, Upper Elves Chasm, Havasu Canyon, Fern Glen, Tuckup Canyon, and the South Tonto near Separation Canyon. In the fall, I resumed serious training for the North Rim run.

Date	Area	Life Zone	Conditions	Elev.Gain/Loss	Mileage
March 16	Mojave Trail	MD	XC, ST	+0ft./-400ft.	15/p-p
March 17	Mojave Trail	MD	XC, ST	+1,300ft./0ft.	15 /p-p

March 18	Mojave Trail	MD	XC, ST	+0ft./-1,800ft.	21/p-p
March 19	Mojave Trail	MD	XC, ST	+0ft./-600ft.	9/p-p
	BLM/Mojave Chemehuevi AL				
April 5	Sierra Priera	MT	2XWD	+1,400ft./-3,000ft.	20/p-p
	USFS/Yavapai AL				
April 25	Bradshaw Mtns.	MT	2XWD	+2,500ft./-2,900ft.	28/p-p
	USFS/Yavapai AL				
Summer	Grand Canyon	SD	TR, XC, CL, SW	Variables	2-19/o&b
	NP WA/Anasazi, Cohonina, Kaibab Paiute, Havasupai & Hualapai AL				

1982: 3,417 miles

(Including inner Canyon run below North Rim)

During the three and a half months leading up to the North Rim run, I continued streaking many of my normal training runs, averaging eleven to thirteen miles a day. For the most part, though, I tried to eliminate many of my long weekend runs so I'd have more of a reserve to draw on once I departed Saddle Mountain.

CARTOGRAPHY

I. Inner Canyon Run Below South Rim of Grand Canyon

The following U.S. Geological Survey topographical maps of Arizona from the 15 Minute Series were used for the journey from east to west: Vishnu Temple (1962); Bright Angel (1962); Havasupai Point (1962); Supai (1962).

Other

Grand Canyon National Park and Vicinity (1962).

II. Mojave Trail

The following U.S. Geological Survey topographical maps of California from the 15 Minute series were used for the journey from west to east: Barstow (1956); Daggett (1956); Newberry (1955); Cady (1955); Cave (1948); Soda Lake (1956); Old Dad (1956); Kelso (1955); Mud Hills (1955); Lanfair Valley (1956); Homer Mountain (1956); Davis Dam (1950).

Other

The Mojave Road: And Other Early Wagon Roads of the Eastern Mojave Desert by Dennis Casebier, from *The Mojave Road*, Norco, CA: Tales of the Mojave Road Publishing, 1975.

III. Hopi-Havasupai Trade Route

The following U.S. Geological Survey topographical maps of Arizona from the 15 Minute series were used for the journey from east to west:

Oraibi (1966); Tovar Mesa (1966); SP Mountain (1962); Coconino Point (1962); Grandview Point (1962); Havasupai Point (1962); Supai (1962).

The following U.S. Geological Survey topographical maps of Arizona from the $7^1/_2$ Minute series were used for the journey from east to west: Garces Mesa NE (1967); Sand Springs (1967); Monument Point (1967); White Water Tank (1969); Standing Rocks (1969); Wupatki SE (1969); Wupatki NE (1969); Wupatki SW (1969); Gray Mountain (1969); Red Butte (1979); Red Butte SW (1980); Howard Hill (1979); Metzger Tank (1979); Box K Ranch (1979).

Historic

-Paso Por Tierra a la California. 1701. Eusebio Francisco Kino.

-*Report of an Expedition Down the Zuni and Colorado Rivers*. 1851. Lorenzo Sigreaves.

-*Rio Colorado of the West*. 1853. Explored by 1st Lieut. Joseph C. Ives, Topographical Engineer, drawn by F.W. V. Egloffstein, Topographer to the Expedition.

-*Explorations of the Colorado River of the West* . . . 1886. U.S. Geological Survey, Major John Wesley Powell. A.H. Thompson, Geographer in Charge, Triangulation by A.P. Davis and H.M. Wilson, Topography by E.M. Douglas.

IV. Inner Canyon Run Below North Rim of Grand Canyon

The following U.S. Geological Survey topographical maps of Arizona from the 15 Minute series were used for the journey from east to west: Emmett Wash (1954); Nankoweap (1954); Vishnu Temple (1962); Bright Angel (1962); Havasupai Point (1962); Powell Plateau (1962).

Historic

Bright Angel (1903). (15 Minute Series). Surveyed by Francois Emile Matthes in 1902.

Other

Grand Canyon National Park and Vicinity, AZ (1962), U.S.Geological Survey Shaded Relief Edition (1972), Geologic Map of Grand Canyon National Park, Arizona, Grand Canyon Natural History Association and Museum of Northern Arizona (1976).

BIBLIOGRAPHY

"After Commercial Aviation's Worst Disaster: A Perilous Searching Operation."
Life, 16 July 1956, 19–25; photoessay.

Anderson, Anne, ed., and Joe Anderson, trans. *Plains Cree Dictionary: In The "y"
Dialect*. Edmonton: Alberta Government, 1975.

Anell, Bengt. *Running Down and Driving of Game in North America*. Uppsala:
Institute Studia Ethnographica Upsaliensia, 1969.

Annerino, John. *Adventuring in Arizona*. San Francisco: Sierra Club Books, 1991;
rev. and exp. 1996.

———. *Canyons of the Southwest: A Tour of the Great Canyon Country from
Colorado to Northern Mexico*. San Francisco: Sierra Club Books, 1994; with
photographs by the author.

———. *High Risk Photography: The Adventure Behind the Image*. Helena, Mont.:
American and World Geographic Publishing, 1991; with photographs by the
author.

———. *Hiking the Grand Canyon*. San Francisco: Sierra Club Books, 1986; rev.
and exp., with trail map by author drawn by Hilda Chen, 1993.

———. *People of Legend: Native Americans of the Southwest*. San Francisco:
Sierra Club Books, 1996; with photographs by the author.

———. *The Wild Country of Mexico/La tierra salvaje de México*. San Francisco:
Sierra Club Books, 1994; with photographs by the author.

———. "Kaibab Deer Drive Is Called Off: Snowstorm Ends Plans of M'Cormick."
The Arizona Republican (Phoenix), 18 December 1924, 1 and 2.

Anthony, Harold E. "The Facts About Shiva Temple: The Real Story of One of the
Most Popular Scientific Adventures in Recent Years." *Natural History* 40, no.
5 (December 1937):709–721, 775–776.

Aubin, George F. *A Proto-Algonquian Dictionary*. National Museum of Man
Mercury Series, no.29. Ottawa: Canadian Ethnology Service, 1995.

Barnes, William C. *Arizona Place Names*. 1935; Revised by Byrd H. Granger. Tucson: University of Arizona Press, 1960.

Bartlett, Katharine. "How Don Pedro de Tovar Discovered the Hopi and Don García López de Cárdenas Saw the Grand Canyon, with Notes Upon Their Probable Route." *Plateau*, 12, no.3 (January 1940): 35–45.

Basso, Keith, ed. *Western Apache Raiding and Warfare: From the Notes of Grenville Goodwin*. Tucson: University of Arizona Press, 1971.

Baum, Dan. "Sacred Places." *Mother Jones*, 2 (March–April 1992), 32–28, 75.

Beer, Bill. "We Swam the Colorado." *Collier's*, 5 August 1955, 19–21.

Blofeld, John Eaton Calthorpe. *Mantras: Sacred Words of Power*. London: Allen and Unwin, 1977.

——— . *The Secret and Sublime: Taoist Mysteries and Magic*. London: Allen and Unwin, 1973.

Boardman, Peter. *Sacred Summits: A Climber's Year*. London: Hodder and Stoughton, 1982.

Boardman, Peter, and Joe Tasker. *The Shining Mountain: Two Men On Changabang's West Wall*. London: Hodder and Stoughton, 1978.

Bolton, Herbert Eugene, ed. *Coronado on the Turquoise Trail*. Albuquerque: University of New Mexico Press, 1949.

——— . *Spanish Exploration in the Southwest, 1542–1706*. New York: Charles Scribner's Sons, 1916.

Bourke, John G. "Notes on the Cosmogony and Theogony of the Mojave Indians of the Río Colorado, Arizona." *Journal of American Folklore* 11, no.6 (July–September 1889): 169–189.

"Boy, Four, Twirls Rattlesnake by Tail." *The Arizona Republic*, 22 June 1944, 4.

Brinkley-Rogers, Paul, and Richard Robertson. "The Curse of the Taalawtumsi: Stealing the Hopi Soul." *The Arizona Republic* (Phoenix), 14 March 1993, 1, 16–17.

Bryant, Harold Child. 1945. "First Climbers Scale Vishnu Temple, Grand Canyon Peak." *The Arizona Republic* (Phoenix), 9 August 1945, B–1.

——— . "Memorandum for the Files." Grand Canyon National Park, Superintendent's Office, 17 January 1944, 1.

Buhl, Hermann. *Nanga Parbat Pilgrimage*. Translated by Hugh Merrick. London: Hodder and Stoughton, 1956.

Butchart, J. Harvey. *Grand Canyon Treks: A Guide to Inner Canyon Routes*. Glendale, Calif.: La Siesta Press, 1976.

——— . "Summits below the Rim: Mountain Climbing in the Grand Canyon." *Journal of Arizona History*. 17, no.1 (spring 1976): 21–38.

Calloway, Donald G., Joel C. Janetski, and Omer C. Stewart. "Ute." In *Great Basin*, vol. 11 of *Handbook of North American Indians*. Washington, D.C.: Smithsonian Institution, 1986.

"Canyon Parachutists Radio Only Need Is Pair of Shoes." *The Arizona Republic* (Phoenix), 29 June 1944, Sec. 2, 1.

Carmony, Neil B., and David E. Brown, eds. *The Wilderness of the Southwest: Charles Sheldon's Quest for Desert Bighorn and Adventures with the Havasupai and Seri Indians*. Salt Lake City: University of Utah Press, 1994.

Casebier, Dennis G. *The Mojave Road*. Norco, Calif.: Tales of the Mojave Road Publishing, 1975.

Cassanova, Frank E. "Trails to Supai in Cataract Canyon." *Plateau* 39, no. 3 (winter 1967): 124–130.

Chatwin, Bruce. *The Songlines*. New York: Viking, 1987.

"Cheers & Jeers." *The Arizona Republic* (Phoenix), 5 May 1982, 6.

Child, Greg. "Seeking the Balance: The Great Survivor." *Climbing Magazine*, February 1989, 66–76; on Doug Scott.

"Chronology of Grand Canyon Trails." Unpublished manuscript. Grand Canyon National Park, n.d.

Coleman, Jay. "A New Pioneer Blazes Old Trail." *The Arizona Republic* (Phoenix), 24 March 1980, C1; with photo by Charles Krejcsi.

Colton, Harold Sellers. *Black Sand: Prehistory in Northern Arizona*. Albuquerque: University of New Mexico Press, 1960.

———. "A Brief Survey of the Early Expeditions into Northern Arizona." *Museum Notes of the Museum of Northern Arizona* 2, no. 9 (March 1930): 1–4.

———. "Prehistoric Trade in the Southwest." *Scientific Monthly* (April 1941), 308–319.

———. "Names at Wupatki." *Plateau* 29, no. 1 (July 1956): 22–24.

———. "Principal Hopi Trails." *Plateau* 36, no. 3 (winter 1964): 91–94.

Conner, Daniel Ellis. *Joseph Reddeford Walker and the Arizona Adventure*. Norman: University of Oklahoma Press, 1956.

Cooley. M.E., B.N. Aldridge, and R.C. Euler. *Effects of the Catastrophic Flood of December 1966, North Rim Area, Eastern Grand Canyon, Arizona*. Geological Survey Professional Paper 980. 1–43. Washington, D.C.: U.S. Government Printing Office, 1977.

Cory, Kate T. "Life and Its Living in Hopiland." *The Border* (Phoenix). Vol. 1 August 1909. 1–2.

Coues, Elliot, ed. and trans. *On the Trail of a Spanish Pioneer: The Diary and Itinerary of Francisco Garcés (Missionary Priest) in His Travels Through Sonora,*

Arizona, and California, 1775–1776; Translated from an Official Contemporaneous Copy of the Original Spanish Manuscript, and edited, with Copius Critical Notes by Elliot Coues. 2 vols. New York: Francis P. Harper, 1900.

Culin, Stewart. *Games of the North American Indians.* Twenty-fourth Annual Report of the Bureau of American Ethnology for the Years 1902–1903. Washington, D.C., 1907.

Curtis, Edward Sheriff. *The North American Indian: Being a Series of Volumes Picturing and Describing the Indians of the United States and Alaska,* vol.2,. edited by Frederick Webb Hodge. Norwood, Mass.: Plimpton Press, 1908; with photographs by the author.

Cushing, Frank Hamilton. "The Nation of Willows." *Atlantic Monthly,* September–October 1882, 362–374, 541–559.

David-Neel, Alexandra. *The Magic and Mystery in Tibet.* New York: Crown, 1932.

Davis, Dan E. "River to Rim Routes: Marble and Grand Canyon." Unpublished manuscript. Grand Canyon National Park, n.d.

———. "A Traverse of the Colorado River from Lee's Ferry to Lake Mead." Unpublished manuscript. Grand Canyon National Park, n.d.

———. "Voyages Down the Colorado." Unpublished manuscript. Grand Canyon National Park, 19 November 1957.

Dawson, Thomas F. "First Through the Grand Canyon." U.S. Senate 1st Sess., Senate Exec. Doc 42, no. 79, 4 June 1917.

Dellenbaugh, Frederick S. *A Canyon Voyage: The Narrative of the Second Powell Expedition down the Green-Colorado River From Wyoming, and the Explorations on Land, in the Years 1871 and 1872.* New Haven, Conn.: Yale University Press, 1926.

———. *The Romance of the Colorado River.* New York: G. P. Putnam's Sons, 1906.

DeSaussure, Raymond. "Remains of California Condors in Arizona Caves." *Plateau* 29, no. 2 (October 1956): 144–45.

Dobie, J. Frank. *The Voice of the Coyote.* Lincoln: University of Nebraska Press, 1947.

Dobyns, Henry F. *Havasupai Indians I: Prehistoric Indian Occupation Within the Eastern Area of the Yuma Complex,* vol. 2. New York: Garland Publishing, 1974.

Draeger, Don F., and Robert W. Smith. *Asian Fighting Arts.* New York: Berkeley Medallion Books, 1974.

Drago, Harry Sinclair. *Lost Bonanzas: Tales of the Legendary Lost Mines of the*

American West. New York: Bramhall House, 1966.

Dutton, Clarence Edward. *Tertiary History of the Grand Canyon District, with Atlas.* Department of Interior Monographs of the United States Geological Survey, vol. 2. Washington D.C.: U.S. Government Printing Office, 1882.

Effland, Richard W., Jr., A. Trinkle Jones, and Robert C. Euler. *The Archaeology of Powell Plateau: Regional Interaction at Grand Canyon.* Grand Canyon, Ariz.: Grand Canyon Natural History Association, 1981.

Eiseman, Fred B., Jr. "The Hopi Salt Trail." *Plateau* 32, no. 2 (October 1959): 25–32.

Euler, Robert C. "The People." In *The Moutain Lying Down: Views of the North Rim.* Grand Canyon, Ariz.: Grand Canyon Natural History Association, 1979.

Euler, Robert C., and Catherine S. Fowler. *Southern Paiute Ethnohistory.* Anthropological Papers, no. 78, and Glen Canyon Series, no.28. Salt Lake City: University of Utah press, 1966.

Farmer, Malcolm F. "The Mojave Trade Route." *The Masterkey* (Los Angeles) 9, no. 5 (September 1935): 154–157.

Farmer, Malcolm F., and Raymond DeSaussure. "Split-Twig Animal Figurines." *Plateau* 27, no.4 (April 1955): 13–23.

Fewkes, J. Walter. "The Snake Ceremonies at Walpi." *A Journal of American Ethnology and Archaeology,* vol. 4. Cambridge, Mass.: Riverside Press, 1984.

———. 1892. "The Wa-Wac-Ka-Tci-Na, a Tusayan Foot Race." *Bulletin of the Essex Institute,* 24, nos. 7, 8, 9 (1982): 113–133.

"Flares Indicate Trio Safe in Grand Canyon." *The Arizona Republic,* (Phoenix), 27 June 1944, 4.

Fletcher, Colin. *The Man Who Walked Through Time.* New York: Alfred A. Knopf, 1967.

Ganci, Dave. "Zoroaster Temple." Backcountry Rangers' Office file. Grand Canyon National Park, 18 September 1958.

———. 1959. "Zoroaster Temple." *Summit* (Big Bear Lake, CA), January 1959, 16–17.

Goodwin, Grenville. *The Social Organization of the Western Apache.* Chicago: University of Chicago Press, 1942.

Govinda, Lama Anagarika. *The Way of the White Clouds: A Buddhist Pilgrim in Tibet.* Boulder, Colo.: Shambala Publications, 1966.

Grant, Blanche Chloe. *Taos Indians.* Taos, N.M.: New Mexican Publishing Corp., 1925.

Grey, Herman. *Tales from the Mohaves.* Norman: University of Oklahoma Press, 1970.

Harwell, Henry O., and Marsha C. S. Kelly. "Maricopa." In *Southwest*, vol. 10 of *Handbook of North American Indians*. Washington, D.C.: Smithsonian Institution, 1983.

Hayden, Julian D. "Hohokam Petroglyphs of the Sierra Pinacate, Sonora and the Hohokam Shell Expeditions." *The Kiva* (Tucson) 37, no 2 (Winter 1972): 74–83.

Herzog, Maurice. *Annapurna: First Conquest of an 8,000 Meter Peak*. Translated from the French by Nea Morin and Janet Adam Smith. New York: E. P. Dutton, 1952.

Hughes, J. Donald. *The Story of Man at the Grand Canyon*. Grand Canyon, Ariz.: Grand Canyon Natural History Association, 1967.

Ives, Joseph Christmas. *Report Upon the Colorado River of the West: Explored in 1857 and 1858*. Washington D.C.: U.S. Government Printing Office, 1861.

James, George Wharton. *The Grand Canyon of Arizona: How to See It*. Boston: Little, Brown & Co., 1905.

————. *In and Around the Grand Canyon: The Grand Canyon of the Colorado River in Arizona*. Boston: Little, Brown & Co., 1900.

————. *The Indians of the Painted Desert Region: Hopis, Navahos, Wallapais, Havasupais*. Boston: Little, Brown & Co., 1900.

Johnson, Ann. "Finding 'Real World' in the Canyon." *The Phoenix Gazette*, 13 May 1982, D1, 2; with photos by Chris Keith.

————. "History Relived in Canyon Run." *The Phoenix Gazette*, 19 May 1981, D1, 2.

————. "The Journey: Wilderness Runner Retraces Indians' Historical Steps." *The Phoenix Gazette*, 20 May 1981, F1, 3.

Judd, Neil M. *Archaeological Observations North of the Río Colorado*. Smithsonian Institution, Bureau of American Ethnology Bulletin 82. Washington D.C.: U.S. Government Printing Office, 1926.

Kelly, Isabel Truesdell. *Southern Paiute Ethnography*. Anthropological Papers, no. 69, and Glen Canyon Series, no. 21. Salt Lake City: University of Utah Press, 1964.

————. *Southern Paiute Shamanism*. Anthropological Records, 2, no. 4. Berkeley: University of California Press, 1939.

Kelly, Isabel T., and Catherine S. Fowler. "Southern Paiute." In *Great Basin*, vol. II of *Handbook of North American Indians*. Washington, D.C.: Smithsonian Institution, 1986.

Kino, Eusebio Francisco. *Kino's Historical Memoir of Pimería Alta: A Contemporary Account of the Beginnings of California, Sonora, and Arizona, by Father Eusebio Francisco Kino, S.J., Pioneer Missionary Explorer, Cartogra-*

pher, and Ranchman, 1683-1711, Published for the First Time from the Original Manuscript in the Archives of Mexico. Edited and translated by Herbert E. Bolton. Berkeley: University of California Press, 1948.

Klah, Hasteen, recorded by Mary C. Wheelwright. *Navajo Creation Myth: The Story of Emergence.* Navajo Religion Series, vol. I. Sante Fe, N.M.: Museum of Navajo Ceremonial Art, 1942.

Kluckhorn, Clyde. *Navajo Witchcraft.* Papers of the Peabody Museum of American Archaeology and Ethnology, no. 2. Cambridge, Mass.: Harvard University Press, 1944.

Kolb, Ellsworth. 1914. *Through the Grand Canyon from Wyoming to Mexico.* New York: Macmillan, 1914.

Kolb, Ellsworth and Emery. photography and text. "Experiences in the Grand Canyon." *National Geographic.* Vol. XXVI, No. 2. (August 1914): 99-184.

Kroeber, Alfred L. *Handbook of the Indians of California.* Smithsonian Institution, Bureau of American Ethnology Bulletin 78. Washington D.C., 1925.

———. "The Route of James O. Pattie on the Colorado in 1826." *Arizona and the West* 6. (Summer 1964): 119–136.

Laird, Carobeth. *The Chemehuevis.* Banning, Calif.: Malki Museum Press, 1976.

Lamphere, Louise. "Southwestern Ceremonialism," In *Southwest,* vol. 10 of *Handbook of North American Indians.* Washington, D.C.: Smithsonian Institution, 1983.

Leonard, George. *The Ultimate Athlete: Re-Visioning Sports, Physical Education, and the Body.* New York: Avon Books, 1974.

Lingenfelter, Richard E. *First Through the Grand Canyon.* Los Angeles: Glen Dawson, 1958.

Link, Margaret Schevill. *The Pollen Path: A Collection of Navajo Myths.* Stanford, Calif.: Stanford University Press, 1956.

Lockwood, Frank C. "Captain John Hance: He Built Trails and Spun Yarns at Grand Canyon." *Desert Magazine,* July 1940, 15–18.

Long, Haniel. *A Letter to St. Augustine, after Re-reading His Confessions.* New York: Duell, Sloan, and Pearce, 1950.

Luckert, Karl W. 1979. *Coyote-Way: A Navajo Holyway Healing Ceremonial.* Translated by Johnny C. Cooke. Tucson: University of Arizona Press and Museum of Northern Arizona, 1979.

Lumholtz, Carl Sofus. "Among the Tarahumaris: The American Cave Dwellers." *Scribner's Magazine,* July 1894, 31–48.; with photographs by the author.

———. *Los Indios del Noroeste, 1890–1898.* México, D.F.: Ini-Fonopas, 1982; with photographs by the author.

————. "Tarahumari Life and Customs." *Scribner's Magazine*, September 1894 296–311.; with photographs by the author.

————. "Tarahumari Dances and Plant Worship." *Scribner's Magazine*, October 1894, 438–456.; with photographs by the author.

————. 1902. *Unknown Mexico: A Record of Five Years' Exploration Among the Tribes of the Western Sierra Madre; in the Tierra Caliente of Tepic and Jalisco; and Among the Tarascos of Michoacán*, vols. 1 and 2. New York: Charles Scribner's Sons, 1902; with photographs by the author.

Matthews, Washington. "The Mountain Chant: A Navajo Ceremony." *Fifth Annual Report of the Bureau of American Ethnology for the Years 1883–1884*. Washington, D.C.: U.S. Government Printing Office, 1887.

McNitt, Frank. *Navajo Wars: Military Campaigns, Slave Raids, and Reprisals*. Albuquerque: University of New Mexico Press, 1972.

Messner, Reinhold. *All 14 Eight-Thousanders*. Translated by Audrey Salkeld. Seattle, Wash.: Cloudcap Press, 1988.

————. *The Big Walls: History, Routes, Experience*. Translated by Audrey Salkeld. New York: Oxford University Press, 1978.

Morgan, William. "Human Wolves Among the Navaho." *Yale University Publications in Anthropology*, no. 11 (1936).

Murphy, Michael, and Rhea A. White. *The Psychic Side of Sports: Extraordinary Stories from the Spiritual Underground in Sports*. Reading, Mass.: Addison-Wesley, 1978.

Musashi, Miyamoto. *A Book of Five Rings. (Go Rin No Sho)*. Translated by Victor Harris. 1654. Reprint, New York: Overlook Press, 1978.

Nabokov, Peter. *Indian Running*. Santa Barbara, Calif.: Capra Press, 1981.

Newberry, John S. 1861. *Report Upon the Colorado River of the West, Explored in 1857–58 by Lt. Joseph C. Ives*. Washington, D.C.: U.S. Government Printing Office, 1861.

"Old Letter Casts Doubt on Deaths of 3 in 1869 Powell Expedition." *The Arizona Daily Star* (Tuscon), 12 December 1993, B5.

Opler, Morris Edward. *An Apache Life-way: The Economic, Social, and Religious Institutions of the Chiricahua Apache*. Chicago: University of Chicago Press, 1941.

Ortiz, Alfonso, ed. *Southwest*, vol. 9 of *Handbook of North American Indians*. Washington, D.C.: Smithsonian Institution, 1979.

————. *Southwest*, vol. 10 of *Handbook of North American Indians*. Washington, D.C.: Smithsonian Institution, 1983.

Page, Jake. *Hopi*. New York: Harry N. Abrams, 1982; with photographs by Susanne Page..

Pattie, James Ohio. *Pattie's Personal Narrative of a Voyage to the Pacific and in Mexico: June 20, 1824- August 30, 1830*. Edited by Timothy Flint. Cleveland, Ohio: Arthur H. Clark Co., 1905.

Peattie, Roderick, and Weldon Fairbanks Heald. *The Inverted Mountains: Canyons of the West*. New York: Vanguard Press, 1948.

Powell, John Wesley. *Explorations of the Colorado River of the West and its Tributaries: Explored in 1869, 1870, 1871, and 1872*. Washington, D.C.: U.S. Government Printing Office, 1875.

Powell, Walter Clement. "'Letters of Walter Clement Powell to the *Chicago Tribune* [March 21, 1872],' from the *Journal of W.C. Powell*, edited by Charles Kelly." *Utah Historical Quarterly* 16–17 (January, April, July, October 1948–1949): 257–478.

Rawicz, Slavomir. *The Long Walk: The True Story of a Trek to Freedom*. New York: Lyons and Burford, 1984

Reichard, Gladys A. *Navajo Religion: A Study of Symbolism*. 2 vols. Bollingen Series 18. New York: Pantheon Books, 1950.

Reif, Rita. "A Law, a Legacy, and Indian Art." *New York Times*. 6 November 1994, Sec. 2, 39.

Reisner, Marc. *Cadillac Desert: The American West and Its Disappearing Water*. New York: Penguin Books, 1986.

"Rescue Planned for Airmen Marooned in Grand Canyon." *The Arizona Republic* (Phoenix), 26 June 1944, 5.

Roessel, Robert A., Jr. "Navajo History, 1850–1923." In *Southwest*, vol. 10 of *Handbook of North American Indians*. Washington, D.C.: Smithsonian Institution, 1983.

Russell, Frank. *The Pima Indians*. Smithsonian Institution, Twenty-Sixth Annual Report of the Bureau of American Ethnology for the Years 1904–1905. Washington, D.C.: Government Printing Office, 1908.

Sapir, Edward. *The Southern Paiute Language*. Proceedings of the American Academy of Arts and Sciences, vol. 65, nos. 1–3 (June 1930–May 1931). Reprint, New York: AMS Press, 1990.

Schroeder, John. "Ancient Path: Runner Finishes 210-Mile Jog Retracing Route Along Canyon." *The Arizona Republic* (Phoenix) 12 May 1981, B1, 2;.with photos by Chris Keith.

———. "Canyon Wilderness Tests Runner's Skills." *The Arizona Republic* (Phoenix) 6 June 1982, B1, 2;.with photos by Chris Keith.

——— "Runner Ends 170-Mile Trip over Rugged Canyon Trails." *The Arizona Republic* (Phoenix) 2 May 1980, B1.

————. "Runner Will Relive History in Trip Along Canyon Route." *The Arizona Republic* (Phoenix) 30 April 1981, B1.

————. "Runner Will Trek Grand Canyon." *The Arizona Republic* (Phoenix) 25 April 1980, B3.

————. "Survival Expert Seeks to Retrace Old Hopi Havasupai Trade Route." *The Arizona Republic* (Phoenix) 5 May 1981, B2.

————. "Survival Teacher Performs Grand Feat: Runner Conquers Canyon to Test Hopi Travel Theory." *The Arizona Republic* (Phoenix) 4 May 1980, B1, 2.

Schwartz, Douglas W. "Archaeological Investigations in the Shinumo Area of Grand Canyon, Arizona." *Plateau* 32, no. 3 (January 1960): 61–67.

————. "An Archaeological Survey of Nankoweap Canyon, Grand Canyon National Park." *American Antiquity* 28, no. 3 (January 1965): 289–302.

————. "Nankoweap to Unkar: An Archaeological Survey of the Upper Grand Canyon." *American Antiquity* 30, no. 3. (January 1965): 278–296.

Schwartz, Douglas. W., Arthur L. Lange, and Raymond DeSaussure. "Split-Twig Figurines in the Grand Canyon." *American Antiquity* 23, no. 3 (January 1958): 264–273.

Schwartz, Douglas W., Richard C. Chapman, and Jane Kepp. *Archaeoloogy of The Grand Canyon: Unkar Delta.* Grand Canyon Archaeological Series 2. Sante Fe, N.M.:School of American Research Press, 1980.

————. *Archaeology of the Grand Canyon: The Walhalla Plateau.* Grand Canyon Archaeological Series 3. Sante Fe, N.M.:School of American Research Press, 1981.

Sitgreaves, Lorenzo. *Report of an Expedition Down the Zuni and Colorado Rivers.* 33rd Cong., 1st sess., 1851. S. Doc. 59.

Spier, Leslie. "Havasupai Ethnography." *Anthropological Papers of the American Museum of Natural History* 29, no. 3 (1928): 81–392.

————. *Yuman Tribes of the Gila River.* Chicago: University of Chicago Press, 1933.

Standing Bear, Luther. 1933. *Land of the Spotted Eagle.* New York: Houghton Mifflin Co., 1933.

Stanislawski, Micheal Barr. "Wupatki Pueblo: A Study in Cultural Fusion and Change in Sinagua and Hopi Prehistory." Ph.D. diss., University of Arizona at Tucson, 1964.

Stephen, Alexander M., and Elsie Clews Parsons, ed. *Hopi Journal of Alexander M. Stephen.* Columbia University Contributions to Anthropology, vol. 23, parts 1–2. New York, 1936.

Stevens, John. *The Marathon Monks of Mount Hiei.* Boston: Shambhala

Publications, 1988; with photographs by Tadashi Namba.

Stewart, Kenneth M. "Southern Pápago Salt Pilgrimages." *The Masterkey* 39, no. 3 (July–September 1965): 84–91.

Stoffle, Richard W., et al. *Piapaxa 'Uipi (Big River Canyon).* Bureau of Applied Research in Anthropology. Tucson; University of Arizona, 1994.

Stone, Julius. *Canyon Country: The Romance of a Drop of Water and a Grain of Sand.* New York: G. P. Putnam's Sons, 1932.

Suzuki, Daisetz Teitaro. *The Training of a Zen Buddhist Monk.* Berkeley, Calif.: Wingbow Press, 1974.

Talayesva, Don C. *Sun Chief: The Autobiography of a Hopi Indian.* Edited by Leo W. Simmons. New Haven, Conn.: Yale University Press, 1942.

Tasker, Joe. *Savage Arena.* New York: St. Martin's Press, 1982.

Thompson, Almon Harris. 1939. "Diary of Almon Harris Thompson, Geographer, Explorations of the Colorado River of the West and Its Tributaries." *Utah State Historical Society,* Vol. VII, Nos. 1, 2, & 3 (January, April, and July).

Thrapp, Dan L. *Al Sieber: Chief of Scouts.* Norman: University of Oklahoma Press, 1964.

"Three Chutists Climb Out of Canyon." *The Arizona Republic* (Phoenix), 1 July 1944, 3.

"Three Fliers Lost in Gorge for Days Before Realizing It Was Grand Canyon." *The Arizona Republic* (Phoenix), 2 July 1944, 1, 5.

"Three Stranded Fliers On Way Out of Canyon." *The Arizona Republic* (Phoenix), 30 June 1944, 7.

Tillotson, M. R., and Frank J. Taylor. *Grand Canyon Country.* Stanford, Calif.: Stanford University Press, 1935.

Titiev, Mischa. "Hopi Racing Customs at Oraibi, Arizona." Papers of the Michigan Academy of Science, Arts, and Letters, vol. 24, part 4: 33–42. Ann Arbor, 1939.

———. "A Hopi Salt Expedition." *American Anthropologist,* 39, no. 2 (April–June 1937): 244–258.

Tohei, Koichi. *Aikido in Daily Life.* Tokyo: Rikugei Publishing House, 1966.

Tower, Donald B. "The Use of Marine Mollusca and Their Value in Reconstructing Prehistoric Trade Routes in the American Southwest." *Papers of the Exacavator's Club* 2, no. 3 (1945): 1–54.

Turney, Omar A. *Prehistoric Irrigation.* Phoenix: Arizona State Historian, 1929.

Underhill, Ruth M. *The Navajos.* Norman: University of Oklahoma Press, 1956.

———. *Papago Indian Religion.* New York: Columbia University Press, 1946.

Underhill, Ruth M., Donald M. Bahr, Baptisto López, Jóse Pancho, and David López. *Rainhouse and Ocean: Speeches for the Pápago Year.* Flagstaff:

Museum of Northern Arizona Press, 1979.

Van Dyke, John C. *The Desert*. New York: Scribner's, 1901.

Van Valkenburgh, Richard F. *diné bikéyah (The Navaho's Country)*. Edited by Lucy Wilcox Adams and John McPhee. U.S. Department of Interior, Office of Indian Affairs, Navajo Service. Window Rock, Ariz., 1941.

Van Valkenburgh, Richard F., and Clyde Kluckhorn, ed. *Navajo Sacred Places*. New York: Garland Publishing, 1974.

Walsh, Patricia. "Fraught with Peril: Canyon Run Was Nearly Too Much." *Los Angeles Times*, 13 June 1982, Sec. 2, 4.

———. "Runner Begins Third Trek Through Grand Canyon." *The Phoenix Gazette*, 23 April 1982, C1.

———. "Runner Overcomes 250-Mile Canyon Obstacle Course." *The Arizona Republic* (Phoenix) 2 May 1982, B4.

———. "Situation: Rocky at Best." *The Phoenix Gazette*, 27 April 1982, 1; with photo by Chris Keith.

———. "Taking On a Flat Everest—The Grand Canyon." *San Jose Mercury*, 21 April 1982, 2; with photo by Chris Keith.

"Water Sources in Grand Canyon National Park." Unpublished manuscript. Grand Canyon National Park, 1967.

Whiting, Beatrice Blyth. *Paiute Sorcery*. Publications in Anthropology, no. 15. New York: Viking Fund, Inc., 1950.

Williams, Kitty. "Return of the Tarahumara." *Native Peoples Magazine* (spring 1994): 20–27.

Young, Mark C., ed. *The Guiness Book of Records 1995*. London: Guinness Publishing Ltd., 1994.

Zolbrod, Paul. *Dini Bahane: The Navajo Creation Story*. Albuquerque: University of New Mexico Press, 1984.